Assignment

The USA

A Conversation with Julia Child

I remember there were nine of us girls, as we were always called, and we started from Washington. We were going over to Southeast Asia. We got on an Army train with a whole lot of actual Army people and a whole lot of OSS people . . . we were all dressed in fatigues and a very bedraggled looking bunch . . . .

. . . It took us about a week to get over to the West Coast. We were not to say where we were going or anything. Suddenly, as we approached, there was a great big sign outside of this camp saying, "U.S. Debarkation for the Far East." Our cover was blown at once.

SPIES,
BLACK & TIES,
MANGO PIES

Stories and Recipes from
CIA Families all over the world

This book is dedicated to CIA families: the men, women,
and children who quietly serve wherever, whenever,
and however they are called upon.

Acknowledgments

A book of this sort is the result of the efforts of many people. The Family Advisory Board would like to thank everyone who submitted a story or a recipe, and all of those who provided encouragement, support, and suggestions along the way. Many thanks to the Family Liaison Office, the CIA50 Program Office, the volunteer typists and artists, cover spy character artist Ronny Leigh, the Editorial Committee, and to the members of FAB. Special thanks to dietitian Jean M. Luther, to food and travel writer Kay Shaw Nelson, and to Julia Child for their time, support, and indispensable advice.

A Note About the Organization of This Book

The book is arranged by geographic area based on the location of each story. A story may take place in one part of the world, but include a recipe from another region. A geographic listing of recipes is included in the back of the book for the convenience of the reader.

Some of the stories were originally written without a corresponding recipe, and some recipes were submitted without a story. The editors have fitted those recipes and stories together. All recipes have been tested by members of the Family Advisory Board's Book and Scholarship Project Committee, except Pizza the Hard Way Sausage, Chicken Moamba, Catch/Grab Soup, Scampi Flambés, Basic Fried Dumplings International, and those in Just For Fun.

The Family Advisory Board of the CIA is made up of Agency spouses committed to promoting effective communication between the Agency and its employees' families. The Board's goal is to assist families at home or overseas by advocating policies and practices which recognize the needs of employee families as well as the needs of the Agency in successfully accomplishing its mission. Board members are not CIA staff employees and participate voluntarily without remuneration.

CIA's Publications Review Board has reviewed the manuscript for this book to assist the authors in eliminating classified information, and poses no security objection to its publication. This review, however, should not be construed as an official release of information, confirmation of its accuracy, or an endorsement of the authors' views.

Spies, Black Ties, & Mango Pies
Stories and Recipes from CIA Families
  All Over the World
Collected by the Family Advisory Board
  of the CIA
Nutritional analyses by Jean M. Luther,
  R.D., CNSD, CS

Community Communications, Inc.
Publishers: Ronald P. Beers and
            James E. Turner

Production Staff for
Spies, Black Ties, & Mango Pies
Executive Editor: James E. Turner
Editor: F. Clifton Berry Jr.
Managing Editor: Lenita Gilreath
Design Director: Camille Leonard
Designer: Katie Bradshaw

Table Of Contents

List of Foreign Ingredients

Bean Paste—a condiment made from soybeans, plain or with chilies. It can be found in markets specializing in Asian foods.

Besan—chickpea flour. It can be found in markets specializing in Middle Eastern or Asian foods. If unavailable for use as a thickener, substitute 1 Tbs. cornstarch for 2 Tbs. flour.

Carne Seca—dried beef. It can be found in markets specializing in Latin American foods.

Chili Paste—a hot seasoning or condiment made from ground chilies. It is available in markets specializing in Asian foods. Chili bean paste and sambal oelek are types of chili pastes.

Coconut Milk—extracted from the white meat of coconuts. It is available in supermarkets. It can also be found in markets specializing in Asian foods.

Fish Sauce—a salty, liquid seasoning made from fermented anchovies. It can be found in large supermarkets, sometimes labeled as fish gravy or fermented fish sauce. It can also be found in markets specializing in Asian food. If unavailable, substitute light soy sauce and increase amount of salt in recipe. Do not serve fish sauce undiluted.

Garam Masala—a mixture of spices. It can be found in markets specializing in Middle Eastern or Asian foods. If unavailable, substitute 1 pinch each of ground cinnamon, cardamom, nutmeg, cloves, and black pepper.

Ghee—clarified butter. It can be found in some supermarkets and in markets specializing in Middle Eastern or Asian foods.

Lemon Grass—an herb. It can be found at large supermarkets and markets specializing in Asian foods. If unavailable, substitute equal amount of minced lemon zest, moistened with fresh lemon juice.

Manioc Meal—a coarse meal made from the tuberous root of the tropical cassava (or manioc, mandioc or yucca) plant. It can be found in markets specializing in Latin American foods.

Sambal Oelek (or ulek)—a condiment made from pureed red jalapeno with salt and sometimes tamarind or fish paste added. It can be found in markets specializing in Asian foods.

Shrimp Paste—a seasoning (with a pungent smell) made from salted shrimp. It can be found in markets specializing in Asian food. If unavailable, substitute anchovy paste.

Food Safety Notes

When considering any recipe calling for uncooked eggs, cooks should be aware that the USDA advises against eating foods containing raw eggs due to the risk of salmonella bacteria contamination, especially to people at high-risk for food-borne illnesses (including the very young and the elderly).

When following a recipe that calls for fish to be served uncooked, be sure to buy the fish from a reputable fish monger or grocer; prepare it on a freshly cleaned, dry surface; and thoroughly wash hands (preferably with antibacterial soap) before, and after, handling raw fish.

When preparing hot peppers for use in a recipe, avoid touching mouth or eyes; handle pepper seeds as little as possible; thoroughly wash hands and work surface after handling the peppers. If particularly sensitive to skin irritants, wear rubber or disposable gloves when working with peppers.

Introduction

Stars carved in marble solemnly stare down from a prominent wall in the foyer of the CIA Headquarters Building in Langley, Virginia. Each represents a "fallen star"—an intelligence officer who sacrificed his or her life for our country, but whose name must remain concealed in the interest of protecting others. Displayed nearby is the Book of Honor commemorating all Agency officers who have died in the line of duty.

The men and women of the CIA continue to serve in some of the most dangerous parts of the world, risking their lives every day. They work in the shadowed background, quietly performing their mission for our country, carrying out their endeavors with integrity and honor. They do so in the belief that their work is vital to the preservation of our country's security. They provide the President, the Secretaries of State and Defense, and other senior policy makers with critical information unobtainable by any other means. They help protect the lives of our soldiers during conflict, prevent terrorist acts before they occur, work to stem the flow of drugs into our country, and anticipate crises around the world. Most of their efforts and successes go unheralded in the print or network news. The dedication of CIA officers and their families goes hand-in-hand. Serving sometimes in remote and primitive corners of the globe, Agency families are called upon to make extraordinary contributions, freely volunteering their support and assistance. They make sacrifices and face challenges that could never be accurately described by even the most talented author of spy novels.

Spies, Black Ties, & Mango Pies gives the reader an understanding of how real CIA families face some of the more familiar challenges of raising children, running households, and entertaining guests. Food is a unifying factor in many of our life experiences. Agency families all over the world have shared with each other their joys and heartaches, often over a good meal. In this book, they share recipes and anecdotes which have nourished their bodies and souls. The authors of the stories include accomplished women who were part of the CIA family when their husbands served as Director, as well as members of the Agency's forerunner, the Office of Strategic Services. But, for the most part, the stories come from current and retired CIA employees and spouses. Their names will remain anonymous, and they will not receive public recognition or applause for their efforts—that, too, is part of belonging to an Agency family.

Good food, drink, and espionage seem to go hand in hand in imaginative minds. The reader will find here delicious declassified delicacies and real recipes for survival in the field and at home. So, eat, drink, and be careful. Someone is always trying to steal a great recipe.

—Stephanie Glakas-Tenet

Proceeds from sales will provide scholarship aid for Agency dependents.

How To Go From Spies To Pies

Operation Gastronomy

by Kay Shaw Nelson
Food and Travel Writer, Syndicated Columnist

In 1948 I had no idea that my recruitment to the CIA would incite my curiosity in food and, in turn, lead to unforgettable culinary quests and dining adventures; or that I was destined to be a writer of 15 cookbooks, hundreds of food and travel articles, and also a culinary historian.

My pleasures of educated eating around the world began in Washington, where, with a degree in Russian Studies and Journalism, I was an intelligence officer with the Directorate of Operations.

I was unprepared for a lonely CIA life. It was indeed strange. While I was proud to be serving my country and enjoyed the challenge of the work, the demands of life undercover, and an office where so much could not be openly discussed, sometimes got to me. By chance I discovered the world of food, which proved to be a welcome relief, an absorbing interest which provided an escape from the bizarre work of espionage. Conversation about foreign culinary specialties and where to eat was a delightful change of pace.

The diversion of dining was an innocent and entertaining topic in the office. Colleagues who traveled widely or served overseas liked to tell about cosmopolitan menus and famous restaurants they had enjoyed, or been horrified by, in other countries. Even seasoned officers, reluctant to speak seriously about anything except work, would indulge in mouth-watering talk about food, even cooking.

Soon a group of women from the office, myself included, began exploring some of Washington's restaurants after we left the "tempos" (the temporary buildings along the Capitol Mall which housed the early CIA). It began with tasting dishes of the countries that we researched as part of our work. I didn't know the term "gastronomique" or even "gourmet." Soon, however, I developed a gastronomical inquisitiveness. Thus Operation Gastronomy began.

By the early 1950s, following my marriage to an OSS veteran and CIA officer, I was in Istanbul with my husband. For the wives it was especially lonely, as the policy was for us to more or less stay at home and keep a low profile. Instead, I began exploring the exciting marketplaces. Some Americans, I found out, were reluctant to eat the marvelous Turkish food, and spent their time complaining because they didn't have familiar canned goods, condiments, and packaged cereals. I discovered eggplants that were new to me, shimmering fish fresh from the sea, marvelous fruits, all kinds of nuts, aromatic breads, and round tins of pastries, dripping with honey and sprinkled with chopped nuts. On weekends my husband and I sought out tiny lokantas (restaurants) and outdoor cafes serving authentic local fare, and I learned that Turkish cuisine evolved centuries ago.

I was hooked. Here was my opportunity to learn to cook, and with an

Armenian maid as my teacher! Soon I met Turks who gave me recipes and invited us to their homes for festive meals. Food again proved to be a safe topic of conversation, but this time with foreigners. Spies, of course, don't discuss their work, politics, or personal interests. But I could always manage to get a lively discussion going around food.

For more than 25 stimulating, and often perplexing, years as the wife of an intelligence officer, and occasionally working myself in several foreign posts, I had the unusual opportunity to traverse a good part of the world. My involvement with gastronomy not only led me to explore the countries in which we lived, but also allowed us to meet engaging people, making our assignments abroad more personally rewarding. As I often say, an interest in food introduces you to the agriculture of the country, to its history, and to its religions, but most importantly, food introduces you to the people.

I've often wondered what my life with the CIA would have been like without a passion for gastronomy. For food and cooking, along with my family, allowed me to cope with and even enjoy my strange world. In the cloak-and-dagger business it's necessary to have an individual lifeline. Fortunately, I found mine: gastronomy.

- - - - - - -

A Conversation with Julia Child

Julia Child served in the Office of Strategic Services (OSS), the forerunner of the CIA, during World War II. The Family Advisory Board interviewed her for this book, inviting Ms. Child to reflect on her experiences. Excerpts from that interview are placed throughout the book. The FAB and the editors express their appreciation to Julia Child for her participation. Ms. Child's participation in this interview should not be interpreted as a recommendation of any of the recipes presented here.

I should say that I began in General Donovan's office in Washington and that was a treat. He was rather small and rumpled; piercing blue eyes; and it was said that he could read a document just about by turning the pages, he was so fast at it. He gave you his complete attention and you were just fascinated by him. I was a lowly file clerk at the time, so we hardly spoke, just "Yes, sir" and "No, sir." But I was under his spell.

I was there about a year when they were opening up something we called the "fish squeezing unit," which was the emergency air/sea rescue equipment section. It was staffed by the OSS, housed in the Army Quartermaster building, and run by the Bureau of Ships in the Navy and the Coast Guard. It was a weird concoction of people, and very interesting. Shortly after that had started, they began recruiting people to go over to the Far East. I was just out of college and didn't have any real equipment or talent, except I could typewrite, and I was eager to serve. In those days women weren't trained to do much of anything. I had gotten a little bit out of the files in the fish squeezing unit, but the only available position overseas was in the files again, so I went . . . .

Was it the first time you had ever been away from the United States?

I had been to Tijuana. That was all. But I knew that I'd probably get to Europe sometime, so I'd better go to the Far East while I had the chance.

. . . [In Ceylon] it was a seven-day work week for everyone, including the file clerks. I had two other friends and we sort of invented our own filing system, and we also played a lot of jokes on people. But nobody—I mean, nobody—ever notices the file clerks walking around delivering things, do they? I remember once we delivered them wearing mustaches; nobody noticed . . . .

When China opened up, I offered to go and fix their files in the same way. And then, Paul Child was also going there . . . I was in their files, but I'm sure that anything that was really secret was probably put somewhere else. It's amazing to think that we had no computers; everything was done by hand on little 3x5 cards. All that paper . . . .

. . . I developed no cooking skills whatsoever. All that I developed was a certain method of how to manufacture a filing system. I knew nothing. I just enjoyed every time we went to a Chinese restaurant. All I did was eat. I had no culinary skills whatsoever.

So what was the main factor that motivated you to learn to cook?

It was after I got married. My Paul had grown up with very good food, and I found that I enjoyed it. Then we went over to France, to Paris, and that's when I took fire and that was it. But I'd never done any cooking at all until I got to France.

After the war, newly-wed Julia Child accompanied her husband to France on his first overseas assignment for the U.S. Information Agency.

It was worth the whole war just to meet him. I loved this fellow.

There, she began to cook and teach cooking, embarking on a career which has made her name synonymous with great cooking.

- - - - - - -

Office of the Director of Central Intelligence

NOW WHO AM I ?

by Cynthia Helms

Not long after I married, my husband and I were on an official visit south of the border. My first. We were late, so we were rushed from the airport to a hotel, ushered into a suite on an upper floor. I was told I was there under an assumed name and, as there was business to be done, I retired to a bedroom. Lunch was served to my husband; I could hear the rattling of china. I fell asleep to awaken to complete silence. Hungry, I searched the room for some sign of lunch for me, or at least a crust left from my husband. None. I picked up the telephone to order, realized I did not know the room number, opened the door only to look into the faces of two security men who spoke no English. There was no number on the door. Untrained, I was unable to master the art of ordering with no name, no number, and no language. I believe now I would be more resourceful. Instead, I dreamed my lunch: vichyssoise!

Later in the day my husband returned to nap before being picked up and taken by limousine to an official dinner. I was escorted there on foot.

As we were leaving the next day I was beginning to enjoy my alias when I glanced down at our suitcases in the foyer of the hotel and wondered if I should remove our real name tags!

Vichyssoise

(a lower carbohydrate version, with no potatoes, but cream allowed)

4 large leeks, white parts only, well washed, and thinly sliced
2 tablespoons unsalted butter
1 cup chicken broth

1 cup chopped cooked cauliflower
1 cup heavy cream
1 tablespoon minced chives
salt and pepper, to taste

Sauté leeks in heated butter in a large saucepan. Put leeks with chicken broth into blender. Blend on high speed, covered, 10 seconds. Add cauliflower, cream, salt and pepper. Blend 20 seconds or until well blended. Pour mixture into saucepan. Cook slowly 10 to 15 minutes. Serve hot or chilled. Garnish with chives.

Per serving (based on 4 servings per recipe): Calories 349 (71% from fat), Carbohydrates 20.9 g, Protein 5 g, Total Fat 28.6 g, Sodium 571 mg, Saturated Fat 17.4 g, Cholesterol 97 mg, Diabetic Exchanges: veg 4, fat 5.5

LA DOLCE VITA

by Barbara Colby

I am passing along a recipe for a favorite dessert which I took with us to far-flung outposts—places Irma Rombauer, author of *The Joy of Cooking*, may never have dreamed about, but where her "Mont Blanc" inspired my version and was a culinary pinnacle of success.

But first I can't resist sharing a rather spicy appetizer for the first course. It seems there was a certain "safe house" in a charming neighborhood in one of the world's oldest cities. And this hideaway needed to present the appearance of being occupied by regular people. So, guess who got the assignment of showing up there from time to time with keys to the front door and a picnic lunch? Yes, an ordinary couple from the American Embassy would spend tête-à-tête lunches in this cozy hideaway, and, as far as is known to this day, the secret that it was really a "safe house" was never discovered.

Following these interludes, we would resume our daily routines and our conservative lives, gathering with the family for dinner at home where Mont Blanc was always a special dessert treat.

Mont Blanc
(named for the snow-covered peak it resembles)

2 pounds chestnuts	1 cup heavy cream, chilled
1 quart milk	2 tablespoons powdered sugar
¼ teaspoon salt	1 teaspoon vanilla extract
1 cup granulated sugar	sweet chocolate, grated, for garnish
2 tablespoons brandy	(optional)
(or 1 teaspoon vanilla extract)	

In a large pot, boil chestnuts in water to cover for 10 minutes. Drain. While chestnuts are still warm, remove shells and skins. Place the chestnuts in the top of a double boiler; add milk. Cook over boiling water for 20 minutes; stir in salt, sugar, and brandy; continue cooking about 10 minutes more or until chestnuts are tender; drain. Put nuts through a ricer or food mill over a large round plate. Let pile on the plate into a mound. Try not to touch or move the mound to avoid packing it down. Chill.

When ready to serve, whip cream until stiff; fold in vanilla and powdered sugar. Spoon the cream mixture onto the top of the mound, allowing it to overflow down the sides. Garnish cream with grated chocolate, if desired.

Substitution: If whole chestnuts are unavailable, 3 cups canned unsweetened chestnut puree can be substituted. Pour spoonfuls of puree into ricer and continue as above.

Per serving (based on 8 servings per basic recipe): Calories 503 (32% from fat), Carbohydrates 78.1 g, Protein 6.5 g, Total Fat 18.3 g, Sodium 140 mg, Saturated Fat 10.7 g, Cholesterol 57 mg, Diabetic Exchanges: fruit 5, milk 0.5, fat 3.5

SOME CUCUMBERS ARE NOT VEGETABLES

by Barbara Bush

George served as Chief of the U.S. Liaison Office to the People's Republic of China, and we discovered, like all people serving overseas, that part of understanding the culture was eating the local food. The following excerpt from my memoirs reveals our first Chinese culinary experience.

"The cooks were excellent, although the one who knew how to cook Western food didn't do it very well, so George and I ate Chinese food and loved it. The first time we ate in our upstairs dining room, we had a beautiful meal. I think the cooks were trying to please us and show off. At one point we were served some delicacy that almost did us in: rubbery, gray-looking things about two inches long with spikes all over them. George and I debated what to do with them. Should we eat them so that we wouldn't hurt their feelings? Should we flush them down the toilet when the cook was out of the room? After much discussion, George said that we better just leave them on our plates so they wouldn't think we liked them and serve them again. We later learned they were sea slugs, or sea cucumbers, and the Chinese believe they are a great treat. Whenever we had Chinese guests, our chef insisted we serve them. To add insult to injury, sea slugs cost $25 a pound. When we were served them at banquets, we bit the bullet and ate them."

We were still living in Beijing when George received a "for eyes only" cable asking him to come home and head the CIA. The following recipe for Lettuce Packages was one of the adapted Chinese recipes I brought home with me. Luckily, it does not call for sea slugs!

Lettuce Packages

(serve as an appetizer, first course, or light meal)

1 large firm head iceberg or large leaf lettuce
½ cup fine diced bamboo shoots
12 to 16 water chestnuts, fresh or canned (if fresh, peel and run them under cold
  water before slicing)
6 to 8 dried black Chinese mushrooms (if unavailable, fresh mushrooms can
  be used)
¾ pound very lean pork, coarsely ground (use the tenderloin if available)
1 egg lightly beaten
1½ tablespoons dark soy sauce (any soy sauce can be used if necessary)
1 tablespoon plus 1 teaspoon cornstarch, corn flour, or arrowroot
2 large fresh garlic cloves, crushed (may use powdered garlic but fresh is better)
2 tablespoons dry or cocktail sherry, shao hsing wine, or sake
½ cup chicken broth (I use bouillon)
1½ teaspoons sugar
1¾ to 2 teaspoons salt (I use kosher salt but any will do)
5 tablespoons unrefined peanut oil (that smells like peanuts), or vegetable,
  or corn oil

1. Remove the outside leaf of the lettuce and cut head into 2 pieces with a knife.
   Save about 16 of the largest pieces, place on a serving dish and put into the
   refrigerator covered with a damp cloth.

2. Chop the bamboo shoots and water chestnuts into very fine dice. Soak the mushrooms in boiling water for 20 to 30 minutes. Drain, then squeeze them of as much water as possible. Cut off the stems and shred the mushrooms fine, then chop into fine dice.

3. Combine bamboo shoots, mushrooms and water chestnuts and set aside.

4. Mix the pork with the egg, soy sauce, 1 tablespoon of the cornstarch, and 2 large garlic cloves crushed. Set aside.

5. Mix the wine, half the chicken broth, sugar, and salt. Set aside (half the broth is ¼ cup or 4 tablespoons or soup spoons).

6. Blend the remaining teaspoon of cornstarch with the rest of the chicken broth and set aside (again ¼ cup or 4 tablespoons).

7. Heat 4 tablespoons oil in a wok or skillet, and when almost smoking add the pork mixture, stirring quickly and constantly to separate the bits of pork. When the pork is cooked (no longer pink), add the mushroom mixture and cook, stirring, about 2 minutes. Add the wine, broth, and sugar mixture and cook about 15 seconds, stirring, always on high. Stir the cornstarch mixture to make certain it is properly blended and stir into the pork. Cook, stirring rapidly, about 15 seconds.

8. Add the remaining 1½ tablespoons oil, stirring to distribute it. This will glaze the dish. (Adding this additional oil at the end of the recipe is optional.)

9. Turn the garnished dish out onto a heated serving platter and accompany the meat with the plate of lettuce leaves. To serve, let each guest help himself to a cold lettuce leaf, the cup of which is then filled with a spoonful of pork. It is wrapped between the fingers, then eaten while the pork is still hot. It is also good served with hoisin sauce and thinly sliced spring onions or scallions.

10. Thinking ahead: This is one of those rare Chinese dishes that can be prepared the day before and reheated in the microwave or in a covered dish in the oven. Microwave is best. I have also frozen it with success though it is best made fresh. Don't be afraid to adjust the seasonings to your personal taste.

Per serving (based on 30 servings per recipe): Calories 49 (60% from fat), Carbohydrates 1.7 g, Protein 3 g, Total Fat 3.3 g, Sodium 227 mg, Saturated Fat 0.7 g, Cholesterol 13 mg, Diabetic Exchanges: meat 0.5, fat 0.5

AN INFAMOUS DINNER PARTY

by Patricia Turner

This story is not on the funny side; life in the CIA was not all fun. In January of 1978, eighteen months before the Iranians captured our Teheran Embassy and held the hostages, my husband informed me that he had an important Iranian general to entertain. "Just a small dinner party; the General and his interpreter, the Iranian Ambassador, and my parents, who will be here for a few days."

A dinner for seven was no problem; I only needed to phone his parents and tell them to bring formal dinner clothing. Since the General was deemed "important," I made out my menu accordingly:

Tomato and Orange Soup
Filet Mignon topped with Broiled Mushroom Caps
Béarnaise Sauce
Potatoes "Anna"
Peas and baby boiled onions
Admiral Riley's Green Salad
Cheese tray with Assorted Cheeses
Water Biscuits and Melba Toast
Pinot Noir wine
Molded Chocolate Mousse
Demi-tasse coffee
Liqueurs

The evening of the dinner, my husband was late from the office, and dashed to change clothes and came down the stairs fixing his tie as the doorbell rang. I knew the Ambassador, and he kissed my hand in greeting, as did the General when he was introduced, as did the interpreter, whose name I never caught. The Ambassador was subdued, not his usual ebullient self, perhaps because of the General's importance. The General was a tough-looking man with a permanent five o'clock shadow, barrel-chested, his uniform bulging with rows of medals, the creases in his trousers sharp enough to draw blood. He never really smiled, just widened his straight lips a little, his eyes remaining dark and forbidding.

The dinner went well, though the conversation was awkward, with everything having to be translated from English to Farsi and back again. My father-in-law was delightful, filling the many gaps of silence with questions of world events.

Not long after the liqueurs had been served in the drawing room, the General rose to leave. It was as if he were paying an official call, and the amenities had been observed and it was over. The Ambassador escorted him to his car, then came rushing back inside.

"Dear lady, you could not have pleased the General more! In Iran, it is a great honor not only to be invited into your home for a dinner, but to be introduced to your parents is the greatest honor of all. It was a delightful dinner!"

When my in-laws had retired, I asked my husband, "Who was that General anyhow? He surely has a forbidding personality; even the Ambassador was intimidated."

"The General has a right to look forbidding. He is the head of the Iranian Secret Police, SAVAK," he answered.

"What? You mean I have entertained the butcher who is responsible for all those atrocities and torture in Iran in my own home?" I was furious and grabbed up the General's demitasse cup and brandy glass, took them to the kitchen myself, and scrubbed them with kitchen cleanser, before I calmed down.

I didn't sleep much that night, wanting to go downstairs and scrub everything the General had touched, to try to remove the impurity that I felt still lingered.

The next day a limousine from the Iranian Ambassador delivered five large tins of caviar and a magnum of champagne as his thank you, but I could never enjoy them.

When the Shah fell, the General was beheaded.

Recipes from that dinner party:

Tomato and Orange Soup

2 pounds (about 3 large)	4 cups chicken broth
ripe red tomatoes	3 tablespoons butter
1 medium onion, sliced	3 tablespoons all-purpose flour
1 carrot, chopped	½ cup fresh orange juice
1 strip lemon peel	1 teaspoon grated orange peel
1 bay leaf	granulated sugar, to taste
6 black peppercorns	½ cup light or heavy cream
salt, to taste	

Peel and seed tomatoes; cut in half. Combine with onion, carrot, lemon peel, bay leaf, peppercorns, salt, and broth in a large saucepan. Bring to boil; reduce heat. Simmer, covered, for about 30 minutes until tomatoes are pulpy. Remove from heat. Remove and discard bay leaf and peppercorns. Puree mixture in a food mill or processor, or by rubbing through a sieve. Set aside.

Melt butter in rinsed saucepan; stir in flour; cook, stirring, 1 minute. Stir in tomato puree; add orange juice and peel. Bring to a boil; reduce heat. Cook slowly, covered, about 7 minutes. Stir in sugar; add cream. Adjust seasonings. Serve at once. Serves 8.

Per serving: Calories 140 (64% from fat), Carbohydrates 11.5 g, Protein 2.3 g, Total Fat 9.4 g, Sodium 474 mg, Saturated Fat 3.9 g, Cholesterol 17 mg, Diabetic Exchanges: veg 2, fat 2

Admiral Riley's Green Salad

For the salad:

2 medium heads romaine lettuce	½ cup freshly grated Romano cheese
2 tablespoons virgin olive oil	½ pound bacon slices, cooked, drained
pinch of salt	and crumbled
1 clove garlic, halved	10 flat anchovies, drained
¼ cup finely chopped green onion	1 cup croutons

For the dressing:

3 ounces olive oil	¼ teaspoon chopped fresh mint
juice of 2 lemons	¼ teaspoon oregano
½ teaspoon freshly ground pepper	1 coddled egg

Wash romaine; separate leaves; break into bite-size pieces; dry thoroughly; refrigerate.

When ready to serve, pour olive oil into a large wooden salad bowl; sprinkle with salt. Rub cut garlic halves over inside of salad bowl. Remove and discard garlic.

Put romaine pieces in salad bowl. Add green onion, cheese, and bacon. Top with anchovies; toss lightly.

Combine salad dressing ingredients in a jar or measuring cup. Pour over salad; toss. Add croutons; toss again. Serve at once.

Serves 4 to 6.

Per serving (based on 6 servings per recipe): Calories 295 (80% from fat), Carbohydrates 7g, Protein 8.3 g, Total Fat 26.4 g, Sodium 634 mg, Saturated Fat 5.2 g, Cholesterol 19 mg, Diabetic Exchanges: meat 1, fat 4.5

Molded Chocolate Mousse

(Á la Chief Steward Gerardo)

1 pound sweet butter	4 squares unsweetened chocolate, melted
2 cups granulated sugar	1 tablespoon vanilla extract
1 dozen eggs, separated	1 cup chopped pecans
4 dozen coconut macaroons	2 or 3 packages Ladyfingers, split
1 cup bourbon	½ cup heavy cream, whipped

1. Cream butter and sugar together until light and fluffy. Beat egg yolks until light, then beat into creamed butter and sugar mixture.
2. Soak macaroons in bourbon.
3. Beat melted chocolate into the butter mixture. Add the vanilla and chopped pecans. Beat egg whites until stiff but not dry; fold into the chocolate mixture.
4. Line a 10-inch spring-form pan around the edges and bottom with split Ladyfingers. Alternate layers of soaked macaroons and chocolate mixture in the lined pan. Chill overnight. Remove sides of the pan. Decorate sides and top with whipped cream.

Makes 16 to 20 servings.

Per serving (based on 20 servings per recipe): Calories 773 (48% from fat), Carbohydrates 88.7 g, Protein 9.1 g, Total Fat 42.5 g, Sodium 433 mg, Saturated Fat 23.5 g, Cholesterol 173 mg, Diabetic Exchanges: starch 2, meat 0.5, fruit 3.5, fat 7.5

CIA CAKE

by Lynda Webster

I made the following recipe for Bill Webster on one of our first dates. He was FBI Director at the time, and, as it was the first time I cooked a meal for him, I looked for something special for the occasion. This recipe is adapted from one in *Maida Heatter's Book of Great Chocolate Desserts*. The author explained in her book that her recipe was called FBI Cake because it had been served to J. Edgar Hoover by the author's mother. Hoover liked it so much that he threatened an FBI investigation if he didn't get the recipe! Bill Webster must have liked it, too—he eventually married me! Ha!

We will call this version CIA cake!

CIA Cake

For the cake:

1¾ cups sifted flour
½ cups unsweetened cocoa powder
1 teaspoon baking powder
½ teaspoon baking soda
½ cup salted butter

1 teaspoon vanilla extract
1¾ cups granulated sugar
4 eggs, separated
1¼ cups 1% milk

For the frosting:

2 cups whipping cream, whipped
1 teaspoon vanilla extract

¼ cup sifted powdered sugar
1 cup slivered almonds, toasted

Preheat oven to 325° F. Generously grease and flour two 9-inch cake pans.

Sift together flour, cocoa, baking powder, and soda into a medium bowl; set aside.

Cream butter in a large mixing bowl. Add vanilla and sugar and mix well; add egg yolks. Add dry ingredients and milk, alternating a little at a time.

In a small bowl, beat egg whites until they hold shape, but are not yet stiff and dry. Fold about ½ of the egg whites into chocolate mixture only until blended, then fold and blend in the remaining egg whites. Bake in preheated oven for 35 to 45 minutes or until cake shrinks away from side of pans.

Remove from oven; run knife around edges of cake to loosen from pans. Cool on wire rack for 10 minutes. Remove cake from pans by inverting onto wire racks. Allow both layers to cool completely before frosting.

To prepare frosting

Spoon whipped cream into a large bowl. Slowly add vanilla and sugar; mix gently. Fold in almonds. Place one cooled cake layer upside-down on a cake plate or serving platter; the flat, even bottom is now the top of this layer. Spread about ⅓ cup of frosting over top of layer. Place remaining layer, right-side up on top of first layer; frost top and sides of cake. Refrigerate several hours.

Serve to an appreciative Director—or family or friend!

Makes 12 servings.

Per serving: Calories 382 (44% from fat), Carbohydrates 48.5 g, Protein 7.2 g, Total Fat 19.4 g, Sodium 173 mg, Saturated Fat 8.4 g, Cholesterol 101 mg, Diabetic Exchanges: starch 1, meat 0.5, fruit 2, fat 3.5

ONCE IN A LIFETIME
by Becky Gates

Although we never lived overseas, I had the opportunity to accompany my husband on two overseas trips in 1987 and 1988. These "once-in-a-lifetime" trips, where I visited sights I had only dreamed I would ever see, became "once-in-a-lifetime" opportunities to meet wonderful hostesses at each stop. They welcomed me so warmly, provided such genuine hospitality, and arranged for and accompanied me on my itinerary. It truly pleased me whenever a hostess mentioned that my visit had given her an opportunity to do or see something she might not have otherwise been able to; that was small payment for the efforts which had been made on my behalf. And, as those who have served in some particular posts will understand, a special thank you for blue plates and hugging Arab "mud men."

Chicken Crepes
A wonderful entree which can be prepared and refrigerated a day ahead or frozen several weeks ahead. Crepes may take a little time to prepare, but when you make a large recipe you are able to serve family or guests today or tomorrow AND AGAIN in a few weeks. The limited number of ingredients makes this a simple entree to prepare, and it seems to delight everyone.
(Allow 2 to 3 crepes per person)

Batter for 20 to 24 crepes:

1½ cups milk	1½ cups all-purpose flour
2 tablespoons vegetable oil	⅛ teaspoon salt
3 eggs	additional vegetable oil for coating pan

Put all ingredients in blender in order listed, cover, and process on high until smooth—OR—for double recipes or if using an electric mixer, beat eggs on medium, gradually add dry ingredients alternately with milk and oil, beat until smooth.

Batter may be used immediately or stored covered in the refrigerator for up to three days, stir well before using.

To cook crepes:

Use an automatic crepe maker with controlled heat (instructions for use should come with the appliance) or use a 7- or 8-inch nonstick omelet or crepe pan. Heat pan on medium-high, remove pan from heat, drop in ½ teaspoon of vegetable oil, and wipe pan lightly with paper towel to coat bottom and about ½ inch up side of pan.

The first crepe is an "experiment" to determine temperature and amount of batter needed. The crepe should be lightly browned and fairly thin, but not easily torn. Start with between ⅛ to ¼ cup of batter on medium-high. Lift pan and gently rotate to cover all the bottom (some batter will come up on the side of the pan). Watch for small bubbles in the crepe (like a pancake) and use a plastic spatula to lift the side to check for browning. When lightly browned, flip the crepe to cook and brown the other side. Adjust temperature and amount of batter based on this test crepe.

Prepared crepes may be stacked, tightly wrapped, and stored in the refrigerator for up to a week. To freeze, stack between layers of waxed paper and store in freezer bags or wrap.

Chicken filling for 8 crepes:

1 can (10¾ oz.) condensed
   cream of chicken soup
2 cups cubed cooked chicken
1 can (8 oz.) water chestnuts,
   drained and sliced

¼ cup dry white wine
¼ teaspoon Worcestershire sauce
salt and white pepper, to taste

Preheat oven to 325° F.

Combine all ingredients in medium saucepan and heat through, stirring to blend well.

To fill crepes, spoon a heaping ⅓ cup filling along center of each crepe. Fold the two sides over the filling. Place filled crepes, in a lightly greased 8x8-inch or 9x13-inch baking dish. Bake in preheated oven 10 to 15 minutes, or until bubbly hot. A longer baking time may be needed if crepes have been refrigerated or frozen and thawed, and are still cool when filled.

Per serving (based on 22 crepes per recipe): Calories 115 (39% from fat), Carbohydrates 9.9 g, Protein 6.9 g, Total Fat 4.9 g, Sodium 220 mg, Saturated Fat 1.5 g, Cholesterol 42 mg, Diabetic Exchanges: starch 0.5, meat 1, fat 1

QUICK AND EASY

by Suzanne Woolsey

The following recipes are favorites of mine, as I often find that quick and healthful meals need to be put together semi-spontaneously. They have come in handy when impromptu "intelligence community" meetings at the house have run longer than predicted and some sustenance was required, or when the long days at the Agency turned into long nights and meant that the exact moment for dinner was anybody's guess.

Grilled Fresh Tomatoes with Angel Hair Pasta

3 cups sliced yellow onions
½ cup olive oil, divided
¼ teaspoon black pepper
2 cloves garlic, slivered
2 cups cherry tomatoes

2 cups sliced or diced large tomatoes
pinch nutmeg
salt and pepper, to taste
4 tablespoons coarsely chopped parsley
8 ounces angel hair pasta

Preheat broiler. Line a cookie sheet with aluminum foil; spread onions on sheet and sprinkle with ¼ cup olive oil, and ¼ teaspoon black pepper. Place under preheated broiler; broil until slightly brown, 6 to 8 minutes. Add cherry tomatoes;

broil, stirring occasionally, 2 to 3 minutes until skin splits. Remove from broiler; set aside.

While onions are broiling, heat remaining ¼ cup olive oil in saucepan on stove over low heat; add garlic; sauté 2 minutes. Add sliced tomatoes, nutmeg, salt, and pepper; sauté one minute more to warm tomatoes thoroughly but not cook them. Remove from heat; stir in parsley. Reserve, keeping warm.

In a large pot bring 4 quarts water to boil. Add pasta; cook to al dente, about 2 to 3 minutes. Drain. To serve, transfer pasta to individual bowls; top first with sliced tomato sauce, and then with onions and cherry tomatoes.
Makes 6 servings.

Per serving: Calories 355 (48% from fat), Carbohydrates 40.5 g, Protein 6.8 g, Total Fat 19.2 g, Sodium 192 mg, Saturated Fat 2.6 g, Cholesterol 0 mg, Diabetic Exchanges: starch 2, veg 2, fat 3.5

JET LAG
by Pat Deutch

As a fourth generation Washingtonian who has never lived abroad, my seven trips with the DCI posed gastronomic challenges. Jet lag for me meant never being hungry at mealtimes, but eating hotel bananas in the middle of the night. It meant pushing ostrich, bird's nest soup, or baby goat around on my plate, and then indulging in cookies and tea in between meals. There have been epiphanies like being suddenly ravenous after a week or so of picking, when the best spouse/cook in East Africa served hot chicken pot pie and freshly baked bread.

I also became aware that the DCI's security staff is careful to eat only what the medic eats. If I were staying in a country more than a couple of days, I know I would eat most everything.

Homecoming meant eating the one dish I missed most overseas: a big salad with lettuce and tomato.

This main-dish salad from Suzanne Woolsey would also be a great homecoming treat.

Chicken and Ham Salad Veronique

4 whole chicken breasts, boned	1 cup mayonnaise
1 medium onion, peeled and sliced	½ cup sour cream
1 teaspoon salt	½ cup chutney, finely chopped
½ teaspoon poultry seasoning	1 tablespoon lemon juice
1 tablespoon curry powder	3 cups diced, cooked ham
6 whole black peppercorns	1 pound seedless grapes
	1 head Boston lettuce, chicory, or both

Place chicken, onion, and seasonings in large pot. Bring to boil water to cover; lower heat; simmer, covered, for 30 minutes or until tender. Remove chicken from broth and refrigerate until well chilled. Cut chilled chicken into bite-size pieces. (Use broth as you wish—it makes good soup by itself.) In a large bowl,

combine mayonnaise, sour cream, chutney, and lemon juice. Fold in ham, grapes, and chicken. In salad bowl, tear lettuce or chicory into pieces; spoon chicken-ham mixture over greens.
Makes 8 servings.

Per serving: Calories 474 (60% from fat), Carbohydrates 20.7 g, Protein 27.1 g, Total Fat 32.2 g, Sodium 1256 mg, Saturated Fat 7.3 g, Cholesterol 89 mg, Diabetic Exchanges: starch 1, meat 3, fruit 0.5, fat 3

YIA-YIA TO THE RESCUE

by Stephanie Glakas-Tenet

My first official trip overseas with my husband took me to the Middle East. Traveling through Biblical lands was historically and spiritually moving.

From the cobblestone streets, through the abundant museums, to the ancient ruins, our senses and palates were enticed by marvelous Middle Eastern food. Unfortunately, by the end of the trip I was besieged by a "bug" which tormented my digestive system for several weeks.

In such circumstances one turns to old familiar recipes which nourish and settle us down. In this case the prescription proved to be a recipe for chicken soup passed down from my grandmother, who grew up in a small mountain village near Sparta in Greece.

So the next time you overdo it, or simply want to return to basics, try my Yia-Yia's Chicken Soup.

Yia-Yia's Chicken Soup

10 cups water
1 whole chicken, with skin
1½ cups converted
  long grain rice
4 large eggs, separated

¼ cup fresh lemon juice
1 teaspoon cornstarch
salt to taste

In a large stockpot, bring water to boil; add chicken; return to boil. Cover and simmer about one hour until chicken is tender. Remove chicken; chop into bite-size pieces; set aside. Strain broth; add rice; return to boil. Reduce heat and simmer until rice is tender, about 20 minutes. Remove from heat.

In a large mixing bowl, beat egg whites until frothy; mix in yolks. Gradually stir in lemon juice. Add cornstarch and 8 cups of chicken broth; mix well.

Slowly add egg and lemon juice mixture to pot of broth and rice, stirring constantly. Add pieces of chopped chicken. Add salt to taste. Serve immediately. Allow any leftover soup to cool completely before covering to avoid curdling of egg whites.

Per serving (based on 8 servings per recipe): Calories 341 (35% from fat), Carbohydrates 29.0 g, Protein 26.3 g, Total Fat 13.3 g, Sodium 365 mg, Saturated Fat 3.8 g, Cholesterol 172 mg, Diabetic Exchanges: starch 1, lean meat 3, fat 1

- - - - - - -

A Conversation with Julia Child

We were very, very fortunate in our career being sent to the places we were, which I very much appreciated. If we'd stayed in longer in the service, we would have been in deepest Africa . . . that must be very difficult.

Were you looking for a career when the opportunity to write a book was presented?

No. I wasn't at all. I was just there to educate myself, and then it turned out that it was a career.

- - - - - - -

LIONIZED DINNER

What could feel more perfect—a day in the African bush, wonderful game sighting, good friends, and family around you? It was a perfect combination of ingredients to create that settled, complete-and-whole feeling that comes to me, every now and then. We had settled down around the campfire, at the water's edge. The only sounds were the night sounds of Africa: the hippos' snorts, the occasional lion's roar or jackal's laugh in the distance. From the round, thatch-roofed, mud kitchen we could hear the melodic voices of Zulu, the cook, and his wife, singing in harmony as they prepared our modest dinner with gentle pride.

It is amazing how hungry you get on a day's trek over the African plains. With anticipation, we awaited the tasty concoction of simple foods that Zulu doctored-up with pele-pele, the hottest African pepper you've ever tasted this side of the Zambezi! The chill of the night settled in on us, just as soon as the winter sun sank over the horizon at six o'clock sharp every evening.

The winter months of June, July, and August cast a spell over the African bush in the Southern Hemisphere. The days are bright and sunny, but a cool breeze reminds you that at sundown a crispness invades the night, with a coolness that a foreigner never quite expects to find on that continent.

As we finished an evening beer and relaxed, yet attentive for the call to the dining hut, we were jolted out of our reverie by the loudest, most raucous crash you can imagine— given, that is, the quiet of the nights in Africa...Zulu, carrying the entire dinner on his head, stepped out of the kitchen, prepared to port the meal to the dining hut. In his path, however, was a huge female lion, who, seeking the warmth of the cooking fire, had stretched out for an evening snooze right across Zulu's path to our table! Zulu, making his way in the dark by rote, tripped over the lion, sending him and the dinner head-over-lion into the small gulch which separated the kitchen from our dining hut! Zulu screamed and howled, the lion leaped and roared, we jumped and ran to see what had happened! Zulu, without hesitation said, "Do not worry, Bwana; I have too much elephant pudding for dessert!" So "Elephant Pudding" it was that we ate that night for dinner. I don't know if it is a truly delicious pudding, or if we were just so hungry that night that it really didn't matter what we ate. Whatever the case, we loved it then, and still do. I think you will, too, if you just remember the story that goes along with it when you eat it!!!

Elephant Pudding

3 to 5 cups diced, crushed
   or ground bread (stale is best)
3 cups warm milk
1 cup fruit juice
¼ teaspoon salt
3 eggs
⅓ to ½ cup sugar

vanilla extract (I like brandy, myself,
   or both), to taste
½ teaspoon nutmeg
½ teaspoon cinnamon
handful of raisins, diced apricots, crushed
   pineapple, even dried cranberries
orange marmalade (for frosting)

Soak bread in milk and juice. Add remaining ingredients, except marmalade, and let it soak for hours—overnight, if you want.

Pour pudding into a baking dish or large oven-proof mixing bowl (one that preferably looks like an elephant dropping). Set baking dish in pan of hot water. Place pan with baking dish and water in a preheated 350° F. oven. Bake for 1 hour or until knife inserted in center comes out clean. Be sure pudding is baked through. If crispy crust is desired, continue to bake, up to 1 hour more until top is crispy. Serve warm, or let cool, then spread marmalade over top.

If you soak your dried fruit in brandy before using, you'll have a tastier result!

Variation: For a different flavor, use dark or light rum, or both, in place of the vanilla.

Per serving (based on 16 servings per recipe): Calories 239 (16% from fat), Carbohydrates 43.8 g, Protein 6.8 g, Total Fat 4.2 g, Sodium 344 mg, Saturated Fat 1.7 g, Cholesterol 46 mg, Diabetic Exchanges: starch 1.5, fruit 1.5, fat 0.5

CREPES DOUBLE NOSTALGIA

After 25 years of traveling and living in a dozen different countries, it was tough to settle down in one place upon my husband's recent retirement. I shall never be cured of my nostalgia for the foreign service life we lived. I suffer double nostalgia for some countries—those to which I cannot return even for a short visit, because they have been drastically changed by civil war or other calamities. But happy memories last a lifetime!

One such memory is dining at Oscar's in Africa. Oscar's: an old-fashioned restaurant located in a former private residence, half hidden by palm trees near the water's edge; a roomy but gloomy locale with its red plush furniture and matching deep red wall coverings, where giant cockroaches would occasionally entertain the waiting dinner guests with acrobatic dances across expansive tabletops.

One evening we dined with intrepid British friends who, lacking fear of calories, challenged us to try the house specialty dessert. We finally agreed, with reluctance and foreboding once we heard that Crepes Suzette was the specialty dessert, to be digested along with the already consumed mountains of spicy, hot curry and pints of icy beer.

The crepe master arrived—an old Liberian who must have been around eighty, but was still performing his duties with more zest and energy than colleagues half his age. He was elegantly attired in tails, and wheeling in front of him a cart filled with crepe-making paraphernalia and a collection of brandy and liqueur bottles. Having parked the cart near our table, he proceeded with a flourish to heat the crepe pan over a flame, measure batter into it, and toss crepes, one after another, like the Galloping Gourmet.

When he had a neat stack of twelve, he melted butter in the pan, and added sugar and freshly squeezed orange juice until he had a bubbly liquid. He then poured a double shot of cognac into the sauce, followed by one more shot the same size before he reached for the Grand Marnier bottle. Two more double shots into the sauce! He was equally generous with the next ingredient: Cointreau. The sauce had turned into soup by now, but, undaunted, he added a couple more shots for good measure (I'm not even sure which bottle those came from). He folded the crepes like blankets and arranged three in each of four soup dishes. Then he poured the sauce/soup over them along with some extra cognac on top, ignited them, and presented them like four flaming volcanoes swimming in medieval moats of liquor. The alcohol fumes must have been too much even for the roaches—we saw none while ingesting our voluminous desserts. Next time at Oscar's we ordered dessert only—no curried meal, and no beer necessary.

I have not seen nor tasted a crepe since without remembering Oscar's sauce. The following is my own crepe recipe with a scaled-down imitation of his sauce.

Crepes Double Nostalgia

Crepes:

3 eggs or ¾ cup liquid egg substitute
2 cups 2% milk or whole milk
1 cup sifted all-purpose flour

pinch of salt
2 tablespoons melted butter

Beat eggs in a large bowl. Add milk, flour and salt, mix until smooth. Add butter, beat until smooth.

To cook crepes, mix batter again. Heat a lightly greased 6- or 7-inch crepe pan. Pour in 2 tablespoons batter. Lift and tilt pan at once to spread batter evenly. Fry until golden on underside; turn over with a spatula and cook on other side. Remove to a plate. Repeat with remaining batter, greasing pan as necessary. Makes 20 to 30 crepes.

Sauce:

2 tablespoons butter
2 tablespoons sugar
juice of 2 freshly
   squeezed oranges

2 tablespoons Grand Marnier
2 tablespoons Cointreau
2 tablespoons brandy

Heat butter in small saucepan. Stir in sugar and orange juice. Add Grand Marnier, Cointreau, and brandy; stir.

Assembly and service:

Fold each crepe in half and then half again, arrange on a large serving dish, and pour sauce over them. Sprinkle surface with a little brandy, light with a match, and serve flaming.

Per serving (based on 25 crepes with sauce per recipe, using eggs and 2% milk):
Calories 207 (40% from fat, 26% from alcohol), Carbohydrates 15.6 g, Protein 2.2, Total Fat 9.36 g, Sodium 111 mg, Saturated Fat 5.6 g, Cholesterol 49 mg, Diabetic Exchanges: fruit 1, fat 3 (calories from alcohol are counted as fat in the diabetic exchange system)

EXOTIC FARE

As part of a field trip to Central African nations, my husband as a senior CIA official brought an entourage of talented CIA personnel, as well as his wife, me. Our plane was scheduled to arrive shortly before noon at our next stop. Unfortunately for us, a three-day gathering of the leaders of African nations had just ended, and the airport refused to permit us to land until the leaders of the African nations' planes departed. We were supposed to be inconspicuous, so we flew in large circles around the airport, observing the hot, dry, mostly treeless, landscape again and again. After a good hour of "looping" we were allowed to land and directed to park in the farthest region available from the terminal amid repair hangars and sheds, "for security reasons," we were told. No doubt our host President had no intentions of letting his fellow African national leaders know he was also entertaining representatives of the American CIA.

We were met with many official cars and local government officials as well as locally assigned U.S. officials, and were told we were to join the President for luncheon immediately. It was to be my first luncheon with an African president, and I envisioned a grand setting in an air-cooled palace, perhaps. But not so. We were driven to a quite informal hall where a long, L-shaped table was covered with many dishes of food, arranged as a buffet. The rest of the room was dominated by a long table with perhaps 20 chairs, and at the fringes of the room were smaller tables for four or six people. There was no sign of the President.

"Please to take a plate and serve yourselves," we were instructed. As the only woman in our group I was pushed to start, my husband right behind me, and followed by all the other members of his official entourage. The only difficulty was that I had no idea what the food was that I was encouraged to begin taking. There must have been well over 50 different dishes and only a few of them looked at all familiar.

I recognized sliced cucumbers in sour cream, and a few salads, one of unusual lettuces, others of cut-up fruits, and others of cold marinated or curried vegetables and small broiled fish. I judiciously took small helpings, passing by many dishes of darkly sauced unknown ingredients. There was one huge bowl of what appeared to be mashed potatoes, but which I recognized as mashed manioc root, and avoided. I had tasted it before, and disliked the starchy, glutinous texture, and preferred it in another form, as tiny rice-like grains in tapioca pudding, none of which was on this buffet, however.

At the end of the table, there were suddenly 10 or more very European dishes: fried chicken drumsticks, cubed carrots and peas, slices of broiled squash, bowls of limp spinach with bits of ham or bacon on it, and a large basket of readily recognizable dinner rolls. We were saved!

I was ushered to sit at the right hand of the chair at the end of the table, where the President would soon sit, a seat of honor. When we were told to "Please eat," we did. Halfway through our meal, the President joined us. He was introduced to us, and seemed pleasant enough, and he spoke English.

The President was obviously hungry, and quickly ate whatever was brought to him, making no conversation with us at all. Then a waiter brought him a large bowl of some sort of stew. As he held it for the President to serve himself, I observed that it had vegetables in it and something that looked like an unusual pasta, five-inch-long sections of glistening white corkscrews. I was curious, and I asked him, "What is the name of that dish?"

"It is my favorite, Goat Entrails Stew," he obliged, and returned to it with slurpy relish.

My stomach clenched wildly at the thought of "goat entrails"! I quickly riveted my eyes onto my own plate, hoping to discourage any further discussion about his "favorite dish." Thankfully, the President did not offer me a serving of it. That glorious omission MADE my day!

I did not discuss any recipes with the African president, but here is one I like to use when I am hosting dinner guests:

Curried Fruit Bake

1 (29 oz.) can apricot halves
1 (29 oz.) can peach halves
1 (29 oz.) can pear halves
1 (20 oz.) can pineapple
  slices or chunks

6 Maraschino cherries with stems
¼ pound butter or margarine
1 cup light brown sugar, packed
3 teaspoons curry powder

Preheat oven to 350° F.

Drain fruit well (if not well drained, liquid will overflow the dishes and you will have to drain them—tough job, so beware). Lightly grease shallow casserole dish (or two pie pans); arrange fruit in attractive pattern in dish. Set aside.

Melt butter or margarine in a large skillet; add brown sugar and stir until mixture bubbles. Add curry powder; stir to mix. Carefully pour mixture over arranged fruit. Bake in preheated oven for 1 hour.

This can be prepared one day ahead and rewarmed in a 350° F. oven until heated through. Serve with ham, turkey, or roast beef.

Serves 8 to 10

Per serving (based on 10 servings per recipe): Calories 485 (11% from fat), Carbohydrates 109 g, Protein 2.9 g, Total Fat 6.1 g, Sodium 78 mg, Saturated Fat 2.9 g, Cholesterol 12 mg, Diabetic Exchanges: fruit 7, fat 1

THE DRINKING GOURDS

Roads in this parched African land were almost nonexistent, but one could follow general pathways etched by trucks and caravans to various parts of the country. We were making our way inland by car, when we became aware of a lone figure racing towards us. He was carrying on his shoulder a long staff which had been threaded with empty, dried gourds. Frantically, he waved at us to stop, which we immediately did. Then he pointed to the clouds overhead and to the merest speckles of water on our windshield; we had just passed through a light sprinkle a short distance back. We determined from his gestures that he wanted to know how much earlier we had been in rain. My husband guessed at the kilometers and the lone figure immediately resumed running down the road at breakneck pace in the direction we had come. We surmised that he was hoping to capture some of the blessed liquid for his drinking gourds.

We never again took water for granted, and whenever we celebrated our own good fortune, we remembered that lone figure racing toward the rain.

Celebration Punches
Citrus Punch

¼ cup water
1 cup lemon juice
1¼ cups granulated sugar
1⅓ cups grapefruit juice
peel of 1 lemon, cut into strips

3 cups orange juice
⅔ cup lime juice
2 (12 oz.) bottles ginger ale
lemon, lime, and orange slices

Combine water, lemon juice and sugar in large saucepan; bring to boil and heat for 2 minutes; add lemon peel. Remove from heat and let stand 2 minutes. Remove peel. Allow syrup to cool.

Add remaining ingredients to cooled syrup. Mix together and pour into punch bowl over ice. Garnish with slices of lemon, lime and orange.

Per serving (based on 30 servings per recipe): Calories 60 (1% from fat), Carbohydrates 15.5 g, Protein 0.3 g, Total Fat 0.1 g, Sodium 3.1 mg, Saturated Fat 0 g, Cholesterol 0 mg, Diabetic Exchanges: fruit 1

Lemon Champagne Punch

2 tablespoons lemon juice
3 tablespoons granulated sugar
peel of one lemon, cut in
   1 or 2 spiral strips

2 (25.4 oz.) bottles Moselle wine,
   well chilled
1 (25.4 oz.) bottle dry champagne,
   well chilled

Chill a glass punch bowl. Pour lemon juice into punch bowl; add sugar and dissolve in lemon juice. Rub lemon peel around sides of bowl and leave peel in bowl. Add wine; let stand in refrigerator 15 to 20 minutes. Add the bottle of champagne. Stir, and serve in punch cups with 1 small ice cube.

Per serving (based on 20 servings per recipe): Calories 90 (80% from alcohol), Carbohydrates 4.2 g, Protein 0.2 g, Total Fat 0 g, Sodium 6 mg, Saturated Fat 0 g, Cholesterol 0 mg, Diabetic Exchanges: fat 2 (calories from alcohol are counted as fat in the diabetic exchange system)

Peach Champagne Punch

2 (16 oz.) cans sliced peaches,
   drained
vodka

2 (25.4 oz.) bottles white wine, well
   chilled
1 (25.4 oz.) bottle champagne, well
   chilled

Several hours before serving soak peaches, in a shallow pan or bowl, in enough vodka to barely cover, and refrigerate until ready to serve.

Chill glass punch bowl. Pour peaches and vodka into punch bowl. Add white wine and champagne. Stir, and serve with at least one slice of peach in each punch cup.

Per serving (based on 20 servings per recipe): Calories 127 (78 % from alcohol), Carbohydrates 6.5 g, Protein 0.4 g, Total Fat 0 g, Sodium 7.3 mg, Saturated Fat 0 g, Cholesterol 0 mg, Diabetic Exchanges: fruit 0.5, fat 2.5 (calories from alcohol are counted as fat in the diabetic exchange system)

IN THE MOUTH OF THE BEHOLDER

I remember the wake up call. It was a loud explosion followed by bursts of automatic rifle fire. The time was around 4:00 A.M. In the darkness I found my way out of the bedroom and onto the balcony of our second floor apartment. In the distance the lights of the Presidential Palace were surrounded by smoke from the explosives—the automatic gunfire continued. At that moment, a voice came over the "lunch pail"—the station's two-way radio system. I was still half asleep, but there was work to be done.

This was my first overseas assignment, and up to that moment, I had been enjoying a quiet, but politically eventful, post in West Africa. It was considered a hardship assignment, but in reality it was quite pleasant in spite of the lack of "western" creature comforts. It was a great first posting, and had actually been fun.

Now I found myself in the early stages of a violent coup. I was assigned to work at the relay facility transmitter site, which was located several miles outside the limits of the capital city. The day before the coup began, I had packed the trunk of my car with about 10 cases of U.S. Army "C" rations. The station kept a quantity of these rations on site as emergency food supplies in case the staff had to take up temporary residence in a safe haven. If you ever had to partake of these rations, you can easily understand why we only used them as emergency supplies. You have to be very hungry to resort to their use. Moreover, as consumables, they carried an expiration date. The rations sitting in the trunk of my car were replacements for the stock that had expired at the transmittal facility.

My mind began to clear as I finally stumbled over to answer the radio call. I was told to get to the transmitter site as soon as I could, and then lock myself inside until further notice. With no American presence on site at this facility, in times of turmoil it was vulnerable to sacking by looters. I dressed quickly, ran to my car, and headed out to work. I could still hear gunfire and explosions coming from the Palace. The streets were deserted; I had the road to myself. After traveling a few miles, I quickly realized why. Near the entrance to the transmitter site, a tank was parked in the center of the road, blocking any traffic from passing. The barrel of the tank's cannon was pointing down at car windshield level. Behind the tank, stretching for what looked like miles, was a long line of buses, trucks, cars and motorcycles, and a lot of people on foot. The tank crew was squatting around a fire off to the side of the road. As I slowed to a stop, the tank commander came forward with his hand raised. He walked up to me and said I could not pass. I showed him my identification and, pointing to the building just behind the tank, I explained that I was an American and had to get to work there. He shook his head sternly and said he had been ordered to let no one pass. I tried to dissuade him, but he was adamant. As I started to turn my car around, he came up and asked if I had anything to eat. I was about to say "no" when I remembered the cargo I was carrying in the trunk. "Yes, I do have food with me," I replied. I got out of the car and opened the trunk to reveal the goodies that lay inside. "What is this?" he asked. I explained to him that this was an example of some of the best food that comes from the United States. It was so good, I added, that our army issued it to American soldiers when they were in the field. The tank commander looked at the contents carefully and finally nodded in apparent approval. He asked if I would give him a few boxes for himself and his crew. I put on my best bargaining face, and told him that I had been ordered not to lose any of it. "I'll tell you what, " I said. "If you allow me to pass so that I can get to work, I will give you two cases of these rations." The commander thought this over and finally agreed. I handed over the two cases, and he removed a barricade from the side of the road. I drove through and quickly made it into the transmitter facility.

I remained at the site for the next 12 hours. Two or three times during the day, I ventured outside the building and saw that the tank had not moved, nor had any traffic been allowed to pass. I had no news about the status of the coup taking place in the capital.

That evening I was replaced by a technician who lived in the apartment next door to me. As he entered the building, he asked me what I had done to the tank crew on the road. I related the story about the "C" rations incident that morning. My neighbor then told me that the tank crew commander had given him no trouble and had even been very friendly. In fact, the commander could not stop complimenting the fine food that the "other American man" had given him. In appreciation, he presented my replacement with two crates of oranges that he had "confiscated" from a truck on the road.

As the days went by, the coup ended and the regime was overthrown. The tank on the road near the transmitter facility departed, and we never saw it or its crew again. The city returned to relative peace. And, in renewed appreciation for the value of "C" rations, my next-door neighbor and I drank "screwdrivers" for what seemed to be weeks.

Canned Supper

1 (10¾ oz.) can condensed vegetarian vegetable soup
1 (10¾ oz.) can condensed cheese with broccoli soup, or cream of
    onion or cream of celery soup
2½ cups water
1 (12 oz.) can tuna, drained and flaked
chopped parsley, to taste
salt and pepper, to taste

In a large saucepan, combine soups and water; mix until blended. Stir in tuna, parsley, salt, and pepper. Cook over medium-high heat until heated through, stirring occasionally. Serve in individual soup bowls. Good accompanied by peanut butter sandwiches.
Makes 6 servings.

Variation: Reduce amount of water to 1-1/4 cups and add 1-1/4 cups milk. Do not boil when heating, and stir constantly.

Per serving of basic recipe (using tuna packed in water): Calories 132 (24% from fat), Carbohydrates 8.6 g, Protein 16 g, Total Fat 3.5 g, Sodium 920 mg, Saturated Fat 0.8 g, Cholesterol 23 mg, Diabetic Exchanges: starch 0.5, lean meat 2

Glazed Oranges

6 large navel oranges
5 cups water, divided

2 cups granulated sugar
2 tablespoons orange-flavored liqueur (optional)

Using a vegetable peeler, remove only the orange colored part of the rind from each orange. With kitchen shears or knife, cut rinds into thin strips. Bring 4 cups of water to boil; add strips of rind. Boil for 4 minutes. Drain rinds; set aside.

With a sharp knife, remove white skin and center core from each orange. Place oranges in a bowl or deep dish with a bottom just large enough for the oranges to fit (or, section oranges and arrange the sections in a large dessert bowl).

In a medium saucepan, stir sugar into remaining 1 cup water. Cook over medium heat, stirring constantly, until sugar is dissolved. Continue cooking, without stirring, about 10 minutes until mixture thickens. Add orange rinds; cook about 5 to 7 minutes until rinds become translucent. Remove from heat; add orange liqueur, if desired.

Pour syrup with rinds over oranges in bowl. Let cool; chill at least 2 hours or overnight in refrigerator. Serve each glazed orange on an individual dessert plate. Makes 6 servings.

Per serving: Calories 345 (1% from fat), Carbohydrates 88.4 g, Protein 1.7 g, Total Fat 0.2 g, Sodium 7 mg, Saturated Fat 0 g, Cholesterol 0 mg, Diabetic Exchanges: fruit 6

NOT AS EASY AS PIE

During my husband's career I accumulated many memories. Each country in which we lived gave us different situations, problems, and pleasures. However, I think that perhaps our tour in a capital city in central Africa was the ultimate experience in the unusual and challenging. When we landed in the city in October 1964, the country was still in a state of chaos following independence, activities of rebellion, etc. The grocery stores had shelves which were either empty or stocked with candles or vinegar. The candles and vinegar were produced in the country, thus the ample stocks of those items. Staples, personal supplies such as drug and laundry items, were ordered in bulk from Europe, which necessitated a certain level of awareness of usage needs and foresightedness. However, we survived and, in fact, thrived, and it turned out to be an assignment which forced me into a period of personal growth. Entertaining was vital to survival and all learned to be creative.

One of my more successful "creations" was a Pineapple/Apple Pie. We were expecting important visitors from headquarters, and my husband asked me to fix lunch for them. The dilemma of an entree was solved, but then came the question of dessert. I had one can of apple pie filling (a small can!) but I knew that would not adequately serve the number of guests we expected. After a brief period of panic I spied a can of crushed pineapple on the shelf—and I added that to the apple pie filling—bit more sweetener and spices—topped it with a crumb topping and baked it. It was the hit of the luncheon, particularly for one of the guests! Whenever my husband encountered him in the succeeding years, he would mention that pie, saying that it was the best pie he had ever eaten, and that he frequently mentioned it to his wife and so on.

Another effort, which my family has always loved, is my "made-from-scratch" pizza, and I remember a "pizza party" which we had while in Africa. Sounds easy—BUT—we had to impose on our next-door neighbor (who worked for Pan American World Airways) to order the mozzarella cheese from Johannesburg through their channels. Then I had to make the sausage several days ahead of time. A merchant from India had opened a butcher shop near our home, so I would purchase the ground pork, add spices, and let it "ripen" before I could make the pizza.

Pizza the Hard Way Sausage

2½ pounds ground pork
dash salt
1 teaspoon black pepper
dash cayenne pepper (more if
    you want it real peppy)

dash ground nutmeg
1 teaspoon thyme or 1 teaspoon
    basil or both

Mix well and let ripen in the refrigerator for at least one day. Enjoy!

Per 2-ounce serving (based on 12 servings per recipe): Calories 177 (64% from fat), Carbohydrates 0.3 g, Protein 15.2 g, Total Fat 12.3 g, Sodium 2365.5 mg, Saturated Fat 4.6 g, Cholesterol 56 mg, Diabetic Exchanges: meat 2

HOW NOT TO COOK A CHICKEN

Some thirty years ago as a new bride of five months, I accompanied my husband on assignment to a small African country. I had never cooked before and was really looking forward to being the woman of the house. Almost immediately upon arrival at the post, there was a coup in a neighboring country resulting in the evacuation of American dependents. Several evacuees stayed with us for a couple days until they could be moved on to safer quarters. To welcome my guests, I decided to roast a chicken, something that I had never done before.

Imagine my surprise when I carved the chicken and found that it had never been cleaned. Since the locals would use the internal parts, it was their custom not to clean chickens, but to just pluck the feathers. My guests, who up until dinner, were quite tense, having spent the previous night ducking gunfire, just roared with laughter; what an ice breaker!! We had a canned ham for dinner that night. Over the years my cooking has improved, but I have taken a lot of good-natured ribbing regarding my chicken recipes. Those in the know always request that I not cook chicken for dinner. The story of my roast chicken dinner has been the topic of conversation on many occasions.

There is also an anecdote, the origins of which are unknown, of a famous chicken in the freezer episode. In a steamy Southeast Asian country, an American wife instructed her cook to store in the freezer, as soon as possible, any fresh meat bought in the local market. Later that day, the wife went to the freezer to see what was available for dinner. She opened it—and discovered a barely alive chicken in advanced states of hypothermia.

For those who also find chicken a problem, a colleague suggests the following recipe.

Company Pork Chops

2 tablespoons butter, divided
4 loin pork chops, 1½ inches thick
salt and pepper, to taste
1 tablespoon minced shallots
1 tablespoon flour

1 cup chicken broth
2 tablespoons brown sauce or canned
  gravy
2 teaspoons Dijon mustard
2 tablespoons chopped sour gherkins or
  sweet pickles

Melt 1 tablespoon butter in a skillet; fry chops on both sides over high heat. Sprinkle chops with salt and pepper. Reduce heat and continue cooking over very low heat until chops are well cooked and tender, turning occasionally, using tongs. Transfer chops to platter; keep warm.

Pour off all but 1 tablespoon fat from skillet and add shallots. Sauté, stirring, until shallots are wilted. Sprinkle with flour and stir. Slowly add broth and brown sauce or gravy; whisk until blended. Return chops to sauce and cook another 5 minutes. Remove chops and return to platter.

Add mustard and gherkins or pickles and remaining 1 tablespoon butter to sauce. Swirl sauce until heated through, but do not boil. Spoon sauce over chops and serve.

Per serving (based on 4 servings per recipe): Calories 220 (50% from fat), Carbohydrates 4.8 g, Protein 22.6 g, Total Fat 12 g, Sodium 764 mg, Saturated Fat 5.8 g, Cholesterol 75 mg, Diabetic Exchanges: meat 3, veg 0.5

CHICKEN WITH A VIEW

My first overseas assignment to a tiny African country always will have a special place in my heart. First, it was one of those authentic African places where no tourists ventured. Outside the capital city, life had a rhythm undisturbed by the passage of centuries and the colonial experience. I lived in a beautiful old villa set among palm, avocado, and mango trees. The villa sat on a hill overlooking the capital and had a breathtaking view of a lake and mountains receding into the horizon. The view was so spectacular that it became part of a ritual. Before each meal, I stopped to take in the changing view and to listen for the sound of drums in the distance.

I was lucky to have a great cook, Bernard. Here is Bernard's specialty, Chicken Moamba.

Chicken Moamba

1. Three days before preparing the recipe, send your houseman up a palm tree to bring down palm nuts.
2. Extract the palm oil from the nuts in a sturdy, stone mortar.
3. The day before, slaughter a chicken from your chicken coop and pluck it.
4. Marinate the chicken in the palm oil.
5. The day you prepare the recipe, cut some manioc leaves from manioc plants in your vegetable garden and chop them coarsely.
6. Sauté the chicken in the palm oil until tender.
7. Steam the manioc leaves in a colander.
8. Prepare white rice in your favorite way.
9. Take Alka Seltzer after eating the meal.
10. Do not have Chicken Moamba two days in a row.

Dietitian's note: Because ingredient proportions are indefinite, nutritional values have not been determined.

SOME LIKE IT HOT, SOME DON'T!

A friend who had previously lived in Ethiopia asked if we liked spicy food. The cook who had worked for his family there had come to visit them and would be preparing a traditional Ethiopian dinner. We love different foods and were delighted to be included on his guest list. This, though, was probably not the best of evenings for another couple who attended. Apparently, a staple of Ethiopian cuisine is a hot powdered spice which the cook used with gusto. The other couple seemed to find the meal too hot for their taste, but made an honest effort to eat a small portion. However, as the wife ate, she began to perspire. Unbeknownst to her, a large dark-red blotch began creeping up her chest from beneath the front of her spaghetti-strapped sundress. As she gamely continued to eat small mouthsful, the rest of us watched with fascination as the blotch rose like a thermometer up her neckline and over the lower portion of her face. Our host, concerned, asked several times whether the food was too hot for her, but she had politely assured him that it was "fine." He finally suggested that perhaps she shouldn't eat any more. I have never seen such a look of relief on anyone's face!

The following recipe is a favorite of mine for entertaining because it is prepared in advance.

Spicy Moroccan Carrot Salad

1½ pounds carrots, peeled and cut diagonally into ¼-inch ovals
3 tablespoons freshly squeezed lemon juice
2 tablespoons granulated sugar
1 teaspoon olive oil
1 clove garlic, pressed
¼ teaspoon ground cumin (some may find this a bit much)
¼ teaspoon ground cinnamon
¼ teaspoon ground ginger

⅛ teaspoon salt
generous dash ground red (cayenne) pepper (think about your guests' taste preferences)
½ cup raisins

In a 4-quart saucepan, bring 2 quarts water to a boil. Add carrots and let return
to a boil. Cook about 2 minutes, until tender-crisp. Drain well and let cool slightly.

In a large bowl, whisk together juice, sugar, oil, garlic, cumin, cinnamon,
ginger, salt and red pepper; add carrots and raisins; toss. Refrigerate about 3 hours
until chilled.

When ready to serve adjust spices to suit the guests. Leftovers can be served
the following day.
Serves 6.

Substitutions: Chopped apples or orange segments can be substituted for the raisins.

Per serving: Calories 116 (8% from fat), Carbohydrates 27.6 g, Protein 1.7 g, Total Fat 1.1 g, Sodium 86.2 mg,
Saturated Fat 0.2 g, Cholesterol 0 mg, Diabetic Exchanges: fruit 1.5, veg 1

GOOD-BYE DOLLY!

One of my most remembered experiences in eating foreign cuisine was experienced
during my family's assignment to Northeast Africa.

The local national dish was unique and not often liked by Americans. But my family
did try it several times. It consists of a highly seasoned meat sauce made from mutton, beef,
or chicken, spiced with the local hot pepper. The sauce is served with a type of bread
resembling a spongy, aerated flat pancake with the feel of sponge rubber. It is a rather
unappetizing grey color. The meat sauce is ladled onto the flat bread, which is then
wrapped up and eaten with the hand.

The mutton version is the favored dish for the big festival at the end of September. This
holiday commemorates the finding of the "True Cross," believed by local custom to have
occurred in the fourteenth century.

Our household help had been feeding and raising a small lamb since spring in
anticipation of the holiday feast. Our youngest daughter also helped feed "Dolly" every day.
She became quite attached to the lamb.

On the day of the festival, our servant Tegga and her husband invited us to dinner at
their quarters. My husband and I and the three children all went down. After traditional
drinks of a golden beverage made of fermented honey and of a barley-based ale, the main
dish was brought in with much ceremony.

Our little daughter took one look at the lamb meat in it and suddenly proclaimed a
terrible stomach ache and wanted to go home! It was just too much for her to face "eating
little Dolly"! It took some finesse to give an explanation to our hosts and take her home
without eating.

The following recipe is for another regional dish—a vegetarian one!

Vegetables with Garlic

6 small boiling potatoes
½ pound string beans, cut into 2-inch long pieces
3 large carrots, cut into 2-inch long pieces
¼ cup vegetable oil
1 large green pepper, cut into 2-inch long strips
2 medium onions, cut into 1/2-inch pieces
2 whole hot chilies, washed, stems removed
1½ tablespoons minced garlic
2 teaspoons minced ginger root
½ teaspoon salt
½ teaspoon white pepper
6 large scallions, with some tops, sliced into 2-inch long pieces

Place potatoes in a large kettle of boiling water to cover; add carrots and string beans; boil for about 5 minutes; drain potatoes and vegetables in a colander; rinse in cold water; set aside.

Heat oil in the kettle or in a Dutch oven over moderate heat. Add onions, green pepper and chilies; cook, uncovered, stirring frequently, for 5 to 7 minutes, until vegetables are softened but not browned. Stir in garlic, ginger, salt and pepper; continue cooking for another 2 minutes. Return potato-vegetable mixture to pot; add scallions; stir until all vegetables are coated with oil. Reduce heat to low; cook, partially covered, for about 10 minutes until all vegetables are tender-crisp. Do not let vegetables get soggy. To serve, remove from oil with a slotted spoon, and place in warmed serving bowl.
Makes 6 servings.

Per serving: Calories 204 (39% from fat), Carbohydrates 28.9 g, Protein 3.6 g, Total Fat 9.3 g, Sodium 212 mg, Saturated Fat 1.3 g, Cholesterol 0 mg, Diabetic Exchanges: starch 1, veg 2, fat 2

AFRICAN CORDON BLEU

Our assignment in Africa from 1971 to 1976 was filled with many rich and varied experiences for our growing young family. During these years we did much entertaining, and I even enrolled in a Cordon Bleu cooking school headed by a British expatriate named Bunty O. and held in the industrial section of town. Spurred on by my newfound interest in the culinary arts, my husband and I had many a dinner party and made many new friends. Very often recipes would be discussed on these occasions, and promises to exchange particularly good ones offered. The following recipe was included in a "Thank you" letter I received from some British friends whom we had entertained. Like ourselves and so many of our acquaintances around the world, they have moved on, but have left behind fond memories. Those memories are revived whenever I see their note, which I keep tucked away in my Bunty O. Cordon Bleu cookbook. The note's faded edges and occasional tomato sauce stains attest to how often I have enjoyed using this recipe. The recipe is given as it was originally written, in our friends' style, and without specific ingredient amounts. Suggested proportions have been added—however, as our friends instructed us, "you'll have to judge amounts, but you can't go too wrong."

Moussaka

3 medium eggplants, peeled and cut into ¼ inch thick round slices
½ to ⅔ cup olive oil
2 cups white sauce**
1 cup finely chopped onions
3 to 4 cloves
1 bay leaf
2 tablespoons chopped parsley
1 clove garlic, minced

pinch of marjoram
2 pounds minced (ground) lean lamb or beef
1 cup dry white wine
1 cup tomato sauce
salt and pepper to taste
1 cup grated Parmesan cheese
2 eggs

Preheat oven to 350° F.

"Fry eggplant slices in olive oil until golden; prepare a white sauce with plenty butter, and a meat sauce as follows. Fry finely chopped onions, a few cloves, bay leaf, parsley, a bit of garlic and marjoram in olive oil or butter. As soon as golden brown, add lots of minced meat, and let this fry until brown. Then add a glass of dry white wine, fresh tomato sauce* (when that is not available, remember that tomato juice is the best substitute), salt and pepper, and let it simmer gently. You then alternate in an oven dish a layer of eggplants, meat sauce, grated Parmesan, eggplants, etc. until the dish is half full. Mix two whole eggs into white sauce and pour on top. Sprinkle with more cheese and bake until golden brown.

*I find tinned tomato puree and a little tomato paste is just fine.

"Hope you like it."

The editors suggest simmering the meat sauce about 30 minutes, and baking the casserole about 45 minutes until top is golden brown. After removing casserole from oven, let stand 20 minutes. To serve, cut into squares. Makes 8 to 10 servings.

**Editors' note: A white sauce can be made from ¼ cup each of butter and flour, blended over low heat. Slowly add 2 cups liquid (milk, cream, or stock). Simmer, stirring constantly, until sauce thickens. Yields 2 cups.

Per serving (based on 10 servings per recipe, using 1 cup 1% milk for white sauce): Calories 443 (60% from fat), Carbohydrates 17.7 g, Protein 23.6 g, Total Fat 29.9 g, Sodium 545 mg, Saturated Fat 10.3 g, Cholesterol 112 mg, Diabetic Exchanges: lean meat 3, veg 3, fat 4

PASSOVER IN AFRICA

Our first post was in Africa. We arrived in February 1983, and because Passover began in late March that year, we put all our Passover kitchenware in our air freight.

I explained to our cook Simon how on this week we did not eat any bread (among other foods), and that all food must be cooked and served using the special dishes and pots.

The kitchen was carefully cleaned, refrigerator shelves lined, and kitchen counters covered the day before Passover began. So you can imagine my horror when I found Simon dunking his morning baguette in coffee in my Passover pot!

I screamed so loudly you could have heard me in Kenya. He realized immediately what he had done, jumped up and started scrubbing the pot furiously, as if that would fix his faux-pas. By the end of our three-year stay, Simon was a pro at kashering the kitchen and all the necessary preparations for the holiday. I remember one Sunday we went to the pool and came back to find the entire kitchen kosher l'pesach. What a joy!

Simon made a mean charoses, matzo ball soup, and matzo kugel. I grew up with apple matzo kugel, but we couldn't get apples in sub-Saharan Africa in April, so we substituted mangoes.

By the way, Simon also learned to make bagels during the rest of the year. As a service to the bagel-deprived American community, we sold them by the dozen—plain, poppy, and sesame. Our bagels became famous all over Africa as word spread about "Barry's Bagel Bakery" (named after our oldest son). I once heard that they had been shipped to Chad on a military support flight and that the Ambassador's wife served them at a brunch.

Mango Matzo Kugel

8 matzos, broken into small pieces	2 teaspoons ground cinnamon
6 eggs, well beaten	1 cup chopped walnuts
1 teaspoon salt	2 mangoes, peeled and cut into pieces
1 cup sugar	1 cup raisins
½ cup vegetable oil	

Preheat oven to 350° F.

Soak matzos in water until soft. Drain in colander but do not squeeze dry. Beat eggs with salt, sugar, oil, and cinnamon. Add to matzo mixture in large bowl. Stir in nuts, mangoes, and raisins. Pour into well-greased 13x9-inch pan. Bake in preheated oven for 45 minutes or until lightly browned. Cool slightly. Cut into squares for serving. Freezes and reheats beautifully.

Per serving (based on 12 servings per recipe): Calories 375 (41% from fat), Carbohydrates 49.7 g, Protein 7.8 g, Total Fat 17.6 g, Sodium 208 mg, Saturated Fat 2.4 g, Cholesterol 94 mg, Diabetic Exchanges: starch 1, meat 1, fruit 2, fat 2

A CIA FAMILY CONFRONTATION WITH TERRORISTS

Once upon a time in the early 1960s, there were three brief wars in one of the provinces of a newly independent central African state. The mineral-rich region seceded from the rest of the country, which was in a state of chaos and anarchy, and set itself up as a sovereign nation prepared to defend itself militarily against efforts by the central government and foreigners to force its reintegration into the rest of the country. The central government was then incapable of doing this by itself.

The United Nations sent troops from other African countries and several European armies to assist the central government regain the secessionist province. The United States supported the central government and the UN. Two shooting wars resulted in practical victories for the province as it maintained its independence. The third war ended the secession. In addition to a fair number of troops trained by former colonial rulers, the province had at its disposal a force of European mercenaries and an organization of plain-clothes terrorists.

During periods of active fighting the CIA chief left his wife and two children plus a female station assistant "safe" at his home in the outskirts of the provincial capital, along with the dependents of other American families, including the family of the post's Principal Officer, while the men were at the office. On one occasion a band of terrorist killers combed the area around that home seeking victims to kill. Several persons from homes on both sides of the American sanctuary were summarily executed.

The terrorists forced their way into the back garden of the house where the American women and children were gathered. While the Principal Officer's wife went into the house seeking a gun, the CIA chief's wife tried negotiating with the terrorists. Meanwhile the CIA assistant quickly led the rather large group of children away from the terrorists and out of the potential line of fire.

Eventually the terrorists agreed to leave, did so, and continued their killing elsewhere. Quick, calm thinking and an ability to negotiate effectively in French while assuming command of the situation saved the day and protected our dependent community from harm.

Asia
& The South Pacific

A Conversation with Julia Child

We got onto a cruise ship that had been turned into a troop ship, and we were taken through the Panama Canal . . . and then several days to get to Australia, where we stopped and saw kangaroos . . . and then out to India. I can remember sitting on that troop ship out on the deck, and there was India with all her mystery. I remember thinking, "Oh, what am I doing here?" It was fascinating from the point of view that it was so strange.

. . . Then we all took the train across India to Madras. At one point we went through the jungle, and a whole town of monkeys chattered wildly. Then we got to Madras . . . there were unpaved roads and there was a beautiful long beach with a sign saying, "Beware of sharks." We took another train down to Colombo, which was beautiful, I must say, very sort of untouched; you just felt it was the way it had been for years and years. Then another train up to Kandy, Ceylon . . . They had commandeered a tea planter's property, including his bungalow, and our people had built some palm thatch "bashas," which were the offices. There was a main house with a big dining room, and there were some bashas where the men stayed. The women were brought [to work] every day from the Queens Hotel by a truck. And there were elephants everywhere. Sinhalese workmen used elephants as pack animals. The elephants would come and pick up logs and slowly move them to wherever they were working. Then in the afternoons, when the elephants had worked enough, they'd all go down to the Mahaweli Ganga, a wide river, and they'd lie in the river, and the mahouts, their trainers, would lie on the elephants. Then the mahouts would tap them, and the elephants would turn over on the other side, and they'd take their trunks and spray everyone with water. It was very nice.

You didn't have to do any cooking in those days?

Oh, no. There were Sinhalese people who did all the cooking, and they did beautiful arrangements in the dining room; they put petals in beautiful designs all over the tables, and it was very pretty.

Were they cooking Western food for you or local food?

It was sort of Sinhalese-Western. It was a kind of a mixture; it was very nice, though. And we had people like Dillon Ripley, anthropologists and so forth, who would bring in exotic food. One day we went into the dining shed and it had the most terrible smell. It turned out that Dillon Ripley had collected durian fruit . . . after about a week the novelty wore off and the terrible smell—camembert cheese, strawberries, and a very dead something—disappeared from our dining shed.

How did you go from Ceylon to China?

We flew over the "Hump." In Kunming, we had the English and the French and so forth, and each had a national compound. I remember at one point the Chinese woke everybody up at 2:00 in the morning and said, "We're having a little revolution and we don't want anyone to leave." Here were all these secret intelligence groups, and not one of them knew that anything was going on . . . I don't know, did anyone speak any Chinese? Of course, there were some people who did, who were old Chinese hands. But things were much more serious than I make out, definitely, but I only saw just my end of things . . . I remember more the food and drink than anything else.

Did you have any favorite Chinese dishes?

Oh, yes. I loved them all. I just loved the Chinese food; it was absolutely delicious.

Do you ever cook Chinese food?

A little bit, I'm so concerned with French that I haven't, but I love it. It's my second favorite . . .we particularly liked the northern Chinese, which I think was much closer to the French. Shanghai cooking is much more mixed up in sweet and sour and so forth. We had delicious, delicious Chinese food both in Chunking and in Kunming.

- - - - - - -

CURRY IN THE RAIN

Living in Asia was a memorable experience for our entire family. My husband enjoyed his work, I enjoyed my friends and activities, the children loved the International School. We had a lovely house and excellent household help.

Our house was on a street that was built over a canal. Unfortunately, the water in the canal had an unpleasant way of refusing to stay under the street. When we had heavy downpours during the rainy season, the water rose and it looked like we were living *in* the canal. Most houses were raised up above ground level because of the flooding problems, but sometimes the water rose so fast that it came right up inside the house. Our kitchen was a separate building and not raised up, so often our cook was making meals on the gas stove standing in water up to her knees. Our electric refrigerator was set up on cement blocks for safety.

The floodwaters were not a pretty sight; they often contained snakes as well as unidentified debris. Many times the children waited on the corner for the school bus with their pants rolled up and their shoes slung over their shoulders to be put on after they boarded the bus. We kept our typhoid shots up to date!

One night we were having a party, and an hour before time to begin, the rains came. If the residents there let rain spoil their plans, they would stay at home a lot. But this was a Big Rain, and we thought some of our guests would not be able to come.

Our cook was making her curry, a favorite dish with everyone. It is delicious left over, so we didn't mind that we would have a big pot of food and·no guests to enjoy it. However, that night everyone showed up—with their shoes in hand, skirts held high, pants rolled up. We had our curry party.

I have shared this recipe with many friends from several Asian countries and the U.S. Everyone loves it. One of our men friends has become famous in his circle for his "Ladda's Curry."

Ladda's Recipe for Yellow Curry

2 to 2½ pounds boneless, skinless chicken breasts (or thighs with skin and
    bones removed)
1 large onion, thinly sliced
⅓ cup peanut oil
1 heaping tablespoon yellow curry paste*, mixed with ¼ cup water
dash fish sauce (optional)
1 (14 to 16 oz.) can coconut milk
2 medium potatoes, peeled and cubed

Cut chicken parts into desired size or leave whole. Rinse well, and pat dry with paper towel. Set aside.

Heat oil in large, deep skillet or pot; sauté onion in hot oil, stirring constantly, until soft and translucent (not browned). Stir in curry paste; continue to cook 2 to 3 minutes until very fragrant; add dash of fish sauce, if using. Add chicken to pot, stirring constantly until chicken turns white and all ingredients are thoroughly mixed together. Add half of coconut milk, stir until milk boils, then cover and lower heat; simmer for 15 minutes.

Add cubed potatoes and the rest of the coconut milk; continue to simmer another 20 minutes or until potatoes are done. Curry can rest on the stove for about an hour. It's delicious reheated—some say even better!

Serve with rice and condiments. We prefer nuts, cucumbers, yogurt, eggs, and chutney, also bananas, all in separate bowls. Anything you like is fine.

Serves 4.

Variations: Red, green and Masaman curry are all made this same way, but instead of potatoes, red curry needs sliced carrots or tomatoes (something reddish, even pumpkin or squash will do); green curry needs blanched string beans, basil leaves, peas, etc.; and Masaman needs apples. Ladda says that these curries don't use condiments.

*Yellow curry paste is preferred for this recipe; be sure to check the label. It is available at markets specializing in Asian foods.

Per serving of basic recipe: Calories 483 (55% from fat), Carbohydrates 18 g, Protein 37 g, Total Fat 30 g, Sodium 97 mg, Saturated Fat 21.2 g, Cholesterol 95 mg, Diabetic Exchanges: starch 0.5, meat 4, veg 0.5, fat 4

A TALE OF TWO TAXIS, OR IS IT ONE?

The noon-day swelter embraced me as I stood on the steps of the elegant hotel. Embassy dress code and the formality of a Rotary lunch meant suit and tie, which I now carried over my arm. This Asian capital at noon was a little like entering a steam bath with your clothes on; beads of perspiration were already forming on my forehead, and my shirt was beginning to stick to my back.

The task was not to find a taxi, but to find one that was air-conditioned. Not likely this time of day. The only air-conditioned cars belonged to the hotel, and they had already been taken by the more experienced Rotarians, who slipped out early for that very reason.

That left me with the ever-present, milling mass of rusting '57 Datsuns that constantly struggled past the hotel belching soot-black exhaust into the steamy air. These poor machines had completed their life expectancy on the pot-holed roads of Tokyo and were headed for the junkyard and meltdown when some bright entrepreneur decided to divert them here to this country and a new cycle of tax depreciation.

The fact that these cars were still being used in the mid-seventies was a constant reminder that the local population has an uncanny ability to keep even the most obsolete machinery running, with or without the benefit of spare parts. The taxis had been manufactured for Japan's domestic market, were exceptionally small, and constructed of thin gauged steel. Each carried faded evidence of their original blue and yellow paint that had once made them the pride of the Ginza. The cab drivers here had continued to use the same colors to conceal huge areas of rust and corrosion as the tropical climate gradually consumed them.

I waved one of these museum pieces to the curb and climbed into the back seat.

"American Embassy, please," I shouted and we were off, with one of the finest Le Mans starts I have ever witnessed.

Traveling at top speed in a cloud of dust and smoke, mostly in the cab, the noise prevented any intelligible conversation with the driver, even though the back of his head was just a few inches in front of my nose. The car's tiny enclosure forced a body position that placed my knees somewhere near my earlobes. However, my full concentration was devoted to dispersing my body weight so that the seat of my trousers, that had split under similar circumstances the week before, would not again be tested. While I continued to search for better ways to brace myself against the vehicle's cocktail-shaker movements, the driver threw all caution to the winds and stomped firmly on the accelerator. We sped over the bumpy asphalt road as though we were being chased by a fire engine. Just as I managed to get firmly braced and somewhat comfortable, it happened . . . there was an enormous scraping and a thunderous crash that actually could be heard over the roar of the engine . . . suddenly, the driver's head, which had been only inches from my nose, vanished. In fact, not only the driver, but the entire front end of the car had disappeared. I was the front end, speeding down the street in my back seat, without so much as a steering wheel or a windshield.

The view was like being on a tilt-a-whirl at the carnival. The air was fresh. The smoke and engine noise were gone. Most pleasant. The kind of scenery one expects in exotic Asia. The green vegetation of the park . . . and then meditative silence. The back seat and the rear of the taxi had finally come to rest. I stepped out, with my briefcase, through the front of my chariot where the driver's seat had been, not bothering to open the side doors. I began to look around for the driver and the front-end of the car. At that moment, the driver appeared. Breathlessly, he described what had happened.

The automobile had hit a large bump and had broken into two pieces. The rusted body and weakened drive shaft had separated precisely at the back of the driver's seat, leaving each half to go its own way. My half, the back seat and rear wheels, had ended up on a grassy area near the curb. The driver and the front of the car, including the front two wheels, steering wheel, and engine, had come to a stop further down the street.

Miraculously, no one was injured in the slightest. It was truly one for the record book. "Car breaks in half, front and back, while traveling on crowded, bustling streets. Driver with steering wheel goes in one direction while passenger goes in another." I always thought those Laurel and Hardy routines were a bit far-fetched—not anymore.

The driver refused to accept payment for his fare because he had not taken me to the American Embassy as agreed. Instead, he hailed another blue and yellow bucket of rust, bargained a favorable fare, and sent me on my way to the office.

Most unusual. I didn't even split the seat of my pants.

Bourbon Slush
(cool and refreshing after a long, hot day!)

2 tea bags
½ cup bourbon
1 cup boiling water
3½ cups water
1 (6 oz.) can (or ⅔ cup) frozen
  orange juice

1 cup granulated sugar
½ of (6 oz.) can undiluted
  frozen lemonade, thawed
mint leaves, for garnish

Mix all ingredients. Pour into ice cube trays and place in freezer until completely frozen. Remove from trays and place in plastic food storage bags; seal and store in freezer.

To serve, scrape (or crush) cubes and put shavings into glasses, garnish with mint. Serve with a straw.

Per 4-fluid ounce serving (based on 4 servings per recipe): Calories 364 (17% from alcohol), Carbohydrates 76.3 g, Protein 1.1 g, Total Fat 0.1 g, Sodium 5 mg, Saturated Fat 0 g, Cholesterol 0 mg, Diabetic exchanges: fruit 5, fat 1 (calories from alcohol are counted as fat in the diabetic exchange system)

Papaya-Mango Smoothie

1 medium papaya
1 medium mango
2 to 3 tablespoons honey
1 (8 oz.) container plain yogurt
2 tablespoons lime juice

¼ teaspoon almond extract
½ cup ice cubes
1 lime, sliced (for garnish)
1 cup cold milk

Peel papaya and mango; remove and discard papaya seeds and mango pit. Coarsely chop fruit. In a blender, combine fruit, honey, yogurt, lime juice, almond extract. While blending, gradually add ice cubes through lid. Puree until smooth. If mixture is too thick, blend in additional ice until thinned to desired consistency. Serve in chilled glasses garnished with lime slices. Makes 4 servings.

Per Serving (using 1% milk and lowfat yogurt): Calories 170 (9% from fat), Carbohydrates 35.1 g, Protein 6.0 g, Total Fat 1.9 g, Sodium 79 mg, Saturated Fat 1.1 g, Cholesterol 6 mg, Diabetic Exchanges: fruit 2, milk 0.5

NOT ALL RICE IS NICE

In 1970, as a young married couple on our first overseas assignment, we were anxious to experience as many aspects of this new Asian culture as possible. Always interested in new tastes and good nutrition, we found the local diet delicious and healthful. The freshness of all the ingredients was always a pleasure, and the variety of fruits piled high in baskets in open markets was a visual delight.

The many spicy, exotically flavored curries served over fragrant jasmine rice were a special treat. They were often composed of such a complex blend of flavors, I was certain I could never learn to duplicate them. I was, therefore, especially pleased when we were served a simple rice and grilled fish meal at the home of new friends. The rice was rather like a wild rice, but red and ruddy brown with a nutty, sweet flavor. We asked how to find some and our host gave us the local name to give to our maid so she could purchase some for us. Therein lies the tale. Our maid politely resisted several requests for this special rice. Finally, with a certain restrained poise and no small amount of indignation, our maid revealed the reason she would not purchase this rice: Red rice, as it was translated, was prisoner's food, and no respectable cook would purchase it—no matter how healthful this unrefined rice was!

Happily, there were other, most delicious rice varieties readily available. Here is a recipe for glutinous (sticky) rice prepared to eat with fresh mangoes and lightly dressed with coconut cream. It is a wonderful dessert (also seen at the breakfast table in my home!)

Sweet Rice with Mango

2 cups sticky rice (glutinous rice) soaked overnight in water to cover
2 mangoes
1 teaspoon sesame seeds

For Sauce One:
1 cup of coconut cream   pinch of salt
½ cup sugar

For Sauce Two:
1 cup coconut cream   ½ cup sugar

Drain rice and place an even layer in a cheesecloth-lined steamer. Steam the rice on high for 15 minutes. While the rice is steaming, combine the ingredients for Sauce One in a small bowl. Remove the rice to a large bowl; mix in Sauce One while the rice is still hot. Carefully peel the mangoes; slice them in half to remove the pit; then cut each half into 1/2-inch slices. Arrange the sticky rice and mango slices on a platter. Garnish with sesame seeds.

Combine the ingredients for Sauce Two in a gravy or sauce bowl; serve separately. Makes eight ¾ cup servings.

Per serving: Calories 448 (41% from fat), Carbohydrates 63.3 g, Protein 5 g, Total Fat 21.4 g, Sodium 63 mg, Saturated Fat 18.6 g, Cholesterol 0 mg, Diabetic Exchanges: starch 2, fruit 2, fat 4

Dietitian's note: Adding Sauce Two increases the levels of calories, carbohydrate, and fat.

WHERE'S THE BEEF? BEAR WITH US

We were having a small dinner at our home in Southeast Asia with a few local and American friends, including a visiting colleague of such ursine proportions and temperament that he was known as, well, The Bear. The main course was a Vietnamese sort of fondue known as "thit bo nuong xa"—lemon grass beef—which involves each diner cooking his own thinly-sliced beef on a grill or hibachi in the center of the table. In this case we used an electric grill, which was connected by a flimsy extension cord to a transformer under The Bear's chair. After a while the transformer became overloaded and slowly caught fire—unbeknownst to The Bear hulking above it. The rest of us sat as if transfixed while—as The Unsuspecting Bear continued to talk in his lumbering way—first wisps, then billows of smoke and flame rose from under him, presenting an almost holy effect. The effect was heightened, so to speak, as The Bear's large corpus suddenly levitated when he finally felt the heat. The small fire was quickly extinguished and we all had a good—if nervous—laugh. Our sons, then 10 and 9, have indelible memories of "The Burning Bear."

Here is the recipe for thit bo nuong xa. Bear meat can be added to taste.

Thit Bo Nuong Xa (Lemon Grass Beef)

2 pounds filet, flank steak, or tip sirloin
2 teaspoons finely minced, moist lemon grass (remove tough outer layer before mincing)
4 spring onions, whites and tops, minced
2 cloves garlic, minced
3 teaspoons soy sauce
3 teaspoons vegetable oil
½ teaspoon granulated sugar
1 head of lettuce, washed, dried and torn into bite-size pieces
fresh mint and basil leaves, to taste
1 pound rice noodles, cooked
1 pound medium size rice paper

For the diluted dipping fish sauce:

2 tablespoons fish sauce
2 tablespoons white vinegar
2 tablespoons granulated sugar
2 tablespoons water
½ tablespoon minced garlic, or to taste
1 small chili pepper, minced, or to taste

Cut the meat into long, thin slices; trim fat. In a large bowl, thoroughly mix next 6 ingredients. Marinate meat in mixture 1 hour at room temperature or overnight in refrigerator.

In a bowl mix all ingredients for diluted fish sauce.

Prepare rice paper by sprinkling water over each paper. Let stand 5 minutes before serving.

To serve, each diner grills his/her own meat at a grill or hibachi on the table.

When grilled to taste, wrap small portions of meat, lettuce, mint, basil, and noodles in a piece of prepared rice paper, "hot dog" style. Dip in sauce.

Or, serve meat over lettuce, mint, basil, and noodles (a combination known as "bun bo") and diluted fish sauce in individual large bowls (do not serve fish sauce undiluted).

Serves 4.

Per serving: Calories 789 (40% from fat), Carbohydrates 64.1 g, Protein 51.1 g, Total Fat 34.8 g, Sodium 367 mg, Saturated Fat 13.4 g, Cholesterol 151 mg, Diabetic Exchanges: starch 3, meat 6, veg 1.5, fat 1

THE CHRISTMAS DINNER THAT FOUGHT BACK

In parts of Southeast Asia, geese are the best way to keep snakes away from the house. We had a flock, led by an exceptionally large and aggressive drake we called "Herman." Christmas time was approaching, and he was beginning to remind me of the lovely goose Scrooge had given Bob Cratchit in "A Christmas Carol."

One morning I was in a rush and backed the car out of the garage without warning, only to feel a sickening bump as the it rolled over something. I had run over Herman!

My wife scooped him up, hailed a taxi and was off to join the long line of people seeking treatment at the hospital emergency room. The sudden arrival of a tall, blond, foreign woman in tears, carrying a huge goose in her arms was enough to command the attention of even the most seriously injured. A large crowd had gathered by the time Herman's turn came to be examined. At first the doctor had difficulty understanding that it was the goose who needed attention—not my wife. Meanwhile, the onlookers decided that the solution was obvious; Herman should be served for dinner.

The doctor discovered Herman's leg was broken, but was not sure about complications; after all, the goose had been run over by an automobile. To be sure, Herman had to be X-rayed. The nurse mumbled something about medical insurance as she put the lead apron around my wife who held the hapless Herman motionless while the X-ray was taken. Herman tried to attack anyone else who came near.

The X-ray confirmed a fracture without other injuries. However, the physician could go no further; he was not qualified to treat geese—birds' bones are hollow. The crowd continued to press for putting Herman in the pot. Their cries were beginning to disrupt the hospital's emergency room operations. Herman looked worried.

Just as there appeared to be no alternative to Herman's involuntary participation as the main course in a good dinner, a small voice from the back of the room offered a suggestion, "Put him in the canal."

The crowd parted to reveal a round-shouldered old man with the sun-baked face of a gardener, who softly repeated his suggestion, "Put goose in water until he walk. Feed him with hand and make him stay in water until OK."

"It just might work," said the doctor. "The bird's weight will be off his leg. It will have time to heal."

"We have a pond in our yard," shouted my wife, and off she went with Herman under her arm. The goose was placed in our pond, where my wife fed him cooked rice for more than a month.

One bright morning, as I walked by, Herman slowly arose from the pond, and with a gait that resembled a wind-up Donald Duck, charged me! Herman was back in business and I was under attack—a goose has a long memory, especially around Christmas time.

Herb-Roasted Rabbit

1 fresh or frozen rabbit, cut into serving pieces	1 large clove of garlic, minced
2 tablespoons olive oil	⅔ cup dry white wine
	½ teaspoon dried rosemary

salt and pepper, to taste   2 tablespoons chopped fresh parsley
1 medium onion, cut lengthwise into thin slices

Preheat oven to 350° F.

Heat oil in a heavy skillet over medium-high heat. Fry rabbit pieces in heated oil about 6 minutes on each side until golden. Sprinkle with salt and pepper. With tongs remove browned rabbit to a shallow baking dish; set aside.

Add onion and garlic to the drippings in the skillet; sauté until tender. Pour in wine; bring to a boil, scraping up the browned bits at the bottom of the skillet; cook briskly 1 to 2 minutes. Reduce heat; add rosemary; simmer for 2 minutes. Pour sauce over the rabbit pieces. Bake, covered, in preheated oven for 45 minutes until meat is tender.

To serve, arrange rabbit pieces on individual plates or a platter topped with sauce. Garnish with chopped parsley. Serve immediately.

Makes 4 servings.

Per serving: Calories 571 (44% from fat), Carbohydrates 3 g, Protein 76.7 g, Total Fat 28 g, Sodium 660 mg, Saturated Fat 7.2 g, Cholesterol 215 mg, Diabetic Exchanges: meat 10, veg 0.5

FILL IN THE BLANKS

It sometimes seems that unusual or emergency situations take a spouse away just when it is time to move, leaving the other spouse to deal with all the details alone. The stories are endless because as any couple knows, when one spouse is gone for whatever reason, anything bad that can happen, will happen. For instance, I remember one particular move to a small city in Southeast Asia. Before moving in, we had requested that the house in our new location be painted. Since we were bringing our own furniture, we also asked that the furniture already in the house be removed. Upon our arrival, we discovered that the house had indeed been painted as requested; however, imagine my dismay to find that instead of first removing the furniture, the painters had simply painted around each piece. They could not understand why that would be a problem for me. Never mind that my furniture didn't quite fit in the right spaces!

Beef with Oyster Sauce

1½ pounds beef flank steak
4½ tablespoons vegetable oil
¾ teaspoon MSG
   (monosodium glutamate)
1½ teaspoons granulated sugar
1½ cups boiling water
2 cubes chicken bouillon
1 (10 oz.) package frozen
   snow peas, thawed and well drained
1 small, very hot red "bird's-eye" pepper, chopped (optional)

6 tablespoons oyster sauce
⅜ teaspoon black pepper
1½ tablespoons cornstarch
3 tablespoons cold water
2½ tablespoons vegetable oil
4 cloves garlic, minced

Slice the steak thinly at an angle across the grain; arrange slices in large bowl or deep dish. In a small bowl or measuring cup, combine the next three ingredients; pour over sliced steak. Marinate steak for 30 minutes.

Place bouillon cubes in a medium bowl; pour boiling water over cubes; stir to dissolve. Stir in oyster sauce and black pepper; set aside. In a small bowl or cup, stir cornstarch into 3 tablespoons cold water until well blended; set aside.

Heat 2½ tablespoons of oil in a wok over high heat; add garlic and sauté until lightly browned. Add meat with marinade (most of marinade will be absorbed into meat by this time). Stir fry until meat is browned. Push meat aside and add snow peas; stir fry 2 to 3 minutes. Add chicken bouillon, oyster sauce-pepper mixture, and red pepper, if desired; continue cooking an additional 2 or 3 minutes. Stir in cornstarch-water blend; continue to cook until sauce is heated through and thickens. Serve immediately over unsalted rice.

Makes 4 to 6 servings.

Per serving (based on 6 servings per recipe): Calories 385 (59% from fat), Carbohydrates 11.7 g, Protein 27.5 g, Total Fat 25 g, Sodium 1311 mg, Saturated Fat 5.6 g, Cholesterol 59 mg, Diabetic Exchanges: lean meat 3.5, veg 2, fat 3

FLIP ME ANOTHER DESSERT PLEASE, MR. SAMRANG

In the early 1970s while serving in an Asian capital, I made a quick visit back to the United States for consultations. Prior to returning, I visited a fast food chain for lunch and noticed that the chain was featuring a promotional deal offering a half dozen colorful plastic "Frisbee" flying disks for only $5.00 or a beach volleyball for $6.00. Thinking that my family and friends would be impressed with this bit of Americana, I selected six disks in different colors and stuck them in my suitcase.

Weeks later, after returning to post and stacking the Frisbees in my storeroom to await a gift-giving opportunity or a trip to the beach, I forgot about them until they suddenly appeared during a small dinner that my wife and I were giving for the representative of a not-so-friendly Middle Eastern country. Although participant beach games were not on that night's program, the Frisbees did end up playing an ice breaker role. After my wife carefully explained, in her best impression of the local language, that our guests were important people and that he should use our best china and not the usual stuff, Mr. Samrang, our cook, nodded affirmatively as usual and evidently decided that she must be referring to our newest and brightest "made in America" plastic dessert plates, complete with American fast food logo. And so, with much proud bowing and grinning, dessert was served to all in individual Frisbees.

While my wife and I fought to control our laughter watching our rather proper guests attempt to spear the dessert as the laden Frisbees slowly rotated on the polished table, I kept thinking that for only a dollar more, I could have had a volleyball as a table centerpiece.

Four Layer Pie

½ cup (1 stick) butter or
   margarine
1 cup all-purpose flour
1½ cup chopped walnuts
   or pecans
1 (8 oz.) package cream cheese,
   softened

2 (3.9 oz.) packages chocolate instant
   pudding/pie filling
2¾ cups milk
large container of whipped topping, divided

Preheat oven to 350° F.

1st layer:
Blend butter with flour and 1 cup nuts; press into bottom of 13x9-inch baking pan. Bake in preheated oven for 15 minutes. Remove from oven and cool on wire rack.

2nd layer:
Blend softened cream cheese with 1 cup whipped topping; spread over cooled crust.

3rd layer:
Whip chocolate pudding mixes with milk; spread on top of 2nd layer.

4th layer:
Spread remaining topping over 3rd layer; sprinkle with chopped nuts. CHILL OVERNIGHT.

Serves 12 to 15 people; dessert plates preferred!

Per serving (based on 15 servings per recipe): Calories 373 (65% from fat), Carbohydrates 28.8 g, Protein 5.3 g, Total Fat 27.7 g, Sodium 175 mg, Saturated Fat 15.1 g, Cholesterol 37 mg, Diabetic Exchanges: starch 1, fruit 1, fat 4

BISCUITS FOR LADY BLAZE

We were posted to the Far East, and could get just about everything from the market and the "van man" (portable grocery store), except dog biscuits without bugs. I looked in every cookbook I had, called neighbors, the Embassy's Community Liaison Officer, everyone—but nobody had any recipe suitable for dog biscuits. Finally, I called my sister-in-law in Wisconsin; she is a teacher's aide, and she put out the request via the teacher grapevine. In about two days, she had this recipe, based on one which someone had clipped from a magazine. Lady Blaze loves the biscuits—they give the house a nice aroma, too.

Dog Biscuits

1 envelope active dry yeast
¼ cup warm water
   (110° F.)
3½ cups unbleached
   all-purpose flour
2 cups whole wheat flour
1 cup rye flour

2 cups bulgar (cracked wheat)
1 cup cornmeal
½ cup instant nonfat dry milk powder
3 cups beef or chicken broth
1 egg, beaten slightly with 1 teaspoon milk

Preheat oven to 300° F.

Dissolve yeast in warm water. Combine dry ingredients in a large bowl. Add dissolved yeast; mix. Add chicken broth; mix by hand until dough forms and pulls away from sides of bowl. Roll out dough to ¼ inch thick. Cut out biscuits in bone shape, using a butter knife, or cut into other shapes with floured biscuit or cookie cutter. Place on greased cookie sheets. Brush tops with beaten egg.

Bake biscuits in preheated oven for 45 minutes. Turn oven off and do not open the door for about 8 hours or overnight, to allow the biscuits to harden. Store in freezer or fridge.

Makes 30 large biscuits.

Per serving: Calories 152 (6% from fat), Carbohydrates 30.9 g, Protein 5.9 g, Total Fat 1 g, Sodium 89.9 mg, Saturated Fat 0.2 g, Cholesterol 7 mg, Diabetic Exchanges: starch 2

MRS. PRETTYMAN'S DESSERT

When we were not overseas but stationed in the Washington area, I would sometimes be asked to substitute in my mother-in-law's bridge club. These ladies met twice each month, and the hostess had to design an original recipe, usually dessert. My favorite was a delicious creation by Mrs. Prettyman, wife of Federal Judge E. Barrett Prettyman. Mrs. P. is long gone, but her recipe lives on in all the places where we were stationed abroad.

I can still remember "stewing" over the menu for a small but rather important dinner party to be held that night in our flat in Southeast Asia. The hors d'oeuvres and main course were all set, but we still needed a small but elegant finish for the meal. Our cook came out of "his" kitchen and said, "Missy-Sir, how 'bout we make Mrs. Prettyman's dessert?" So, here it is!

Mrs. Prettyman's Dessert (Apricot-Almond Crumble)

2 cups crushed zwieback
  (yes, the biscuits our babies
  chewed when teething)
1 cup chopped pecans
2 large eggs, beaten
½ cup (1 stick) butter, softened
½ cup granulated sugar

½ cup brown sugar
1 (10 to 12 oz.) jar apricot jam
8 to 10 almond macaroons or cookies,
  crumbled
¼ cup sherry
unsweetened whipping cream
  (whipped at serving time)

Preheat oven to 350° F. Lightly butter and flour an 8x8x2-inch baking pan.

In a large mixing bowl, combine zwieback, pecans, beaten eggs, butter, and both sugars. Mix to blend well. Spread evenly in prepared baking pan. Bake in preheated oven for 20 minutes, or until a wooden pick inserted in center comes out clean. Remove from oven and place on wire rack to cool about 10 minutes. Carefully remove from pan and cool completely. Spread apricot jam over top. Stir the crumbled macaroons into sherry until moist. Sprinkle on top of apricot jam.

Cut into 9 squares. To serve, add dollop of whipped cream. This is very rich, hence the small-sized servings.

Per serving (9 servings): Calories 564 (56% from fat), Carbohydrates 55.2 g, Protein 7.1 g, Total Fat 36.5 g, Sodium 197 mg, Saturated Fat 10.3 g, Cholesterol 84 mg, Diabetic Exchanges: meat 1, fruit 3.5, fat 6.5

BARE NECESSITIES

One of the most interesting sights I saw in Southeast Asia was a Soviet driver changing from his swimming suit to his clothes using only a towel to protect his modesty. What made it almost unbearable (I wanted to laugh, but couldn't) was that this was during a good-bye ceremony at a pool party for another diplomat, and the speaker had reached the most tearful part of the good-bye. For the life of me, I still don't know how Europeans perform this public clothes-changing feat. I have heard from many people that this is common all over Europe. Such skills must be learned from childhood, I imagine!

The following recipe for sate, or kabob, with its accompanying peanut sauce is a great family favorite for grilling outdoors.

Sate Manis

1½ tablespoons brown sugar
3 tablespoons soy sauce
3 tablespoons water
2 teaspoons lemon juice
2 garlic cloves, crushed

2 red or green chilies, seeded and chopped
salt and pepper, to taste
1½ pounds rump steak (or pork),
  cut into thin strips
1 tablespoon peanut oil

Combine brown sugar, soy sauce, water, and lemon juice in a large, shallow dish. Stir in the garlic, chilies, and salt and pepper. Arrange the meat strips in the marinade and baste well. Set aside at room temperature for 4 hours, or refrigerate overnight, turning occasionally. Remove the meat from the marinade; pat dry with paper towels. Discard the marinade. Thread the meat strips onto skewers. Grill over hot coals, basting occasionally with the tablespoon of peanut oil, for 15 to 20 minutes until cooked through and tender. Or, grill under a hot broiler, turning 2 or 3 times.

Serve with peanut sauce. Serves 4 to 6.

Peanut Sauce

1 tablespoon peanut oil	½ teaspoon brown sugar
2 garlic cloves, crushed	5 tablespoons peanut butter
1½ teaspoons dried	1½ cups coconut milk
chilies or sambal oelek	2 tablespoons fresh lemon juice
1 teaspoon shrimp paste (optional)	

Heat oil in a small skillet; add garlic and chilies or sambal oelek; stir fry for 1 minute. Stir in shrimp paste, if using, (it adds an authentic flavor, but is an acquired taste, and is not essential) and brown sugar, until the sugar has dissolved. Add peanut butter and cook slowly, stirring, until smooth. Gradually add coconut milk and bring to a boil, stirring constantly. Remove from the heat and keep warm. Stir in lemon juice.

Sauce should be of a thick pouring consistency; it may be thinned with more coconut milk.

Per serving (based on 4 servings of sates with peanut sauce per recipe): Calories 681 (67% from fat), Carbohydrates 7.6 g, Protein 40.7 g, Total Fat 51.9 g, Sodium 2325 mg, Saturated Fat 25.5 g, Cholesterol 108 mg, Diabetic Exchanges: meat 5, fruit 0.5, veg 1, fat 6

FISH FOR BREAKFAST?

Foreign tours are not just a collection of different sights and sounds; they are also our memories of the people we meet along the way. The following dish always reminds me of one particular post and one special lady—my housekeeper, Samidah.

Samidah was a devout Muslim. She would refuse to wash the dishes or even enter the kitchen on any day we decided to have pork. She was faithful in her daily prayers, but did enjoy spending time gossiping with me about local personalities. She was an extremely honest person with a cheerful attitude, and I liked her for that.

Samidah's recipe for spicy fish played an unexpected role during a visit by my husband's boss from Washington. The boss was staying with us overnight, and for the evening meal I prepared the spicy fish recipe I had learned from Samidah. I was a little concerned about how the visitor might take to the local food, so I made sure that a full American-style breakfast awaited him the following morning. To my great surprise and equal delight, however, the visitor asked for reheated leftovers of my spicy fish for breakfast, and ended up finishing the plate. Later that day, before the noon hour call to prayers from the neighborhood mosque, Samidah washed the dishes and beamed with pride in the success of her recipe.

I have never been asked to prepare spicy fish for breakfast again, but the dish remains a popular serving at our dinner parties. Every time I cook this dish, I remember Samidah, who taught me how to prepare it, and the tearful day we said good-bye when I left her homeland for our next assignment.

Spicy Fish

4 tablespoons all-purpose flour
salt and pepper to taste
1½ pounds fillet of firm white fish (such as red snapper or cod),
    cut into 2-inch squares
6 tablespoons vegetable oil, separated as per recipe
2 cups chicken broth or bouillon
1 bunch green onions, cut into 2-inch lengths, including some green tops
2 green peppers, seeded, cut crosswise into round ⅓ inch slices
2 onions, cut crosswise into round ¼ inch slices
1½ inch piece of fresh ginger root, peeled, thinly sliced, then cut into
    tiny strips
1 to 2 green chilies, seeded, finely chopped
5 tablespoons Kecap Manis, a sweet soy sauce (or substitute according
    to recipe below)

Combine flour, salt, and pepper in a plastic food storage bag. Add fish pieces and shake to coat them with seasoned flour. Heat 4 tablespoons oil in a large, deep skillet or wide-bottomed pot; add fish pieces; fry about 1 to 3 minutes on each side until golden brown and fish flakes easily with a fork. Remove fish; set aside; discard oil.

Heat remaining 2 tablespoons oil in same skillet; stir fry ginger, green chili, and green onion, stirring frequently and quickly, about 1 minute. Add onions; stir fry about 3 to 4 minutes. Add chicken broth, Kecap Manis, fish, and green peppers. Cover and cook 4 to 5 minutes until vegetables are tender.

Substitution: Use skinned, boneless chicken instead of fish.

Per serving (based on 4 servings per basic recipe): Calories 455 (45% from fat), Carbohydrates 21.9 g, Protein 40.6 g, Total Fat 22.7 g, Sodium 1766 mg, Saturated Fat 3.25 g, Cholesterol 81 mg, Diabetic Exchanges: starch 0.5, meat 5, veg 2.5

Homemade Kecap Manis Substitute

1 cup dark brown sugar   7 tablespoons dark molasses
1 cup water   ½ teaspoon ground coriander
1 cup Japanese soy sauce   1 teaspoon grated ginger

In a saucepan over medium heat, combine sugar and water; bring to a boil, stirring until sugar dissolves. Increase heat to high; cook uncovered for 5 minutes. Reduce heat to low; stir in soy sauce, molasses, coriander, and ginger; simmer, uncovered, for 3 minutes. Remove from heat; cool. Store tightly covered. Will keep for 2 to 3 months with refrigeration.

Per 2-tablespoon serving: Calories 90 (<1% from fat), Carbohydrates 22 g, Protein 1.3 g, Total Fat 0 g, Sodium 1380 mg, Saturated Fat 0 g, Cholesterol 0 mg, Diabetic Exchanges: fruit 1.5

A SNACK ON THE TONLE SAP

There were three of them, two Sino-Khmer businessmen and a government official, my guests for a Sunday outing on a bamboo houseboat held in check against the strong brown pull of the Tonle Sap River by a few frayed ropes tied to trees on shore. We were a few kilometers south of the Cambodian capital Phnom Penh, just far enough away to avoid the malevolent scrutiny of Sihanouk's secret police. It was late morning, a time when local stomachs turned to thoughts of food. Any kind of food.

We had already consumed dried strips of water buffalo meat spiced with chili peppers and lemon juice, meat that would have made a hyena's jaws ache with pain. It went down in hard gulps, helped along by long draughts of the local beer, warm beer that reminded me of the currents that raced past our houseboat.

My guests weren't satisfied. "Are you hungry?" they asked. I knew that the question had less to do with my well-being than with their appetites. "I'm all right," I replied. "More meat?" I suggested, gesturing toward the pile of buffalo jerky, which resembled long, thin strips of gray bark. A futile gambit; a nearby sampan had heard their call and was on its way, commanded by a woman in black PJs and a conical hat, knees bent like a surfer as she moved her sweep oar back and forth across the swift waters in easy strokes. She could have been doing her living room rug with a Hoover vacuum cleaner, such was the ease with which she approached us. She steadied her craft against ours, her hands like grappling hooks, giving us a smile that resembled cracked corn.

Was I sure I wasn't hungry, I was asked. Have something, they suggested. Since my guests were recruitment prospects of interest to the station, I gave them my warmest smile. "Of course!" I responded and reached for my beer.

Too late. As I watched in amazement, the woman lifted a wicker cage of doves out of the sampan and plunged it into the river. She held it underwater for a few seconds and then jerked the feathery remains out of the current. The contents were dumped into a wok set above a small charcoal fire in a clay pot. The doves, most of their feathers singed to the flesh by the wok's hot oil, were passed to us. I reached for my beer again.

The flesh had hardly been cooked, and I tried nibbling on a wing but ended up with a mouth full of pin feathers. "You're not eating," one of my guests remarked. "No," I agreed. "I guess I'm not that hungry."

Obviously, a smaller snack was called for. Another order went out to the cook. This time, to my great horror, she raised a cage of small, red-breasted rice birds in the air and grinned, and they, too, were thrust into the Tonle Sap. At a speed worthy of any stateside fast food restaurant, the birds were served up to us. I was handed a tiny, pinkish lump of bone, flesh, and feather and told what a delicacy awaited me. As I watched with a deeper appreciation of the different world about me, my guests held the birds by the beak and swallowed the remainder.

I walked over to the railing of the houseboat and looked out over Cambodia. It would be another hot day. My guests would want to take a nap. I drank to that, and as I did, I quietly dropped my snack into the knowing waters of the Tonle Sap.

This recipe is a bit more familiar.

Poulet Nicoise (Chicken in Herbed Wine Sauce)

2 large chicken breasts	1 teaspoon dried basil or oregano
3 tablespoons olive oil	pinch of saffron
8 to 10 tiny whole white onions	2 tablespoons tomato paste
1 green pepper, diced	¾ cup red wine or stock
3 to 4 large garlic cloves, crushed	15 to 20 pitted ripe olives
1 pound tomatoes, peeled and chopped	2 to 4 anchovy fillets, finely sliced (optional)

Preheat oven to 350° F.

Remove and discard skin from chicken breasts; cut breasts in half. Heat oil in an oven-proof casserole; brown chicken quickly with whole onions in the hot oil. Remove chicken and onions; set aside. Add pepper slices and garlic to the hot oil; cook until soft but not browned. Return chicken and onions to pan; add tomatoes, herbs, saffron, tomato paste and wine; stir to mix. Taste, adjust seasonings.

Bake, covered, about 55 minutes in preheated oven, or on top of stove, over low heat for 40 to 45 minutes, or until chicken is tender. Halfway through cooking time, turn chicken pieces and stir pan contents. Chicken should be simmering in a light sauce, not stewed; however, if sauce is too abundant or too thin, cook uncovered for the remainder of cooking time.

About 10 minutes before chicken is done, add olives and anchovies, if using. Serve with rice and green salad.

Per serving (based on 4 servings per recipe): Calories 396 (46 % from fat), Carbohydrates 14.7 g, Protein 32.5 g, Total Fat 20.4 g, Sodium 485 mg, Saturated Fat 3.9 g, Cholesterol 85 mg, Diabetic Exchanges: lean meat 4, veg 2, fat 3

DO IT AGAIN!

The not-so-secret "Secret War" in Laos was a big part of our family's life for a number of years, and as such had a major impact on our lives. We have lots of war stories, but this one involves our then seven-year-old son and a smoke grenade.

Kip spent enough time in Laos during those years to become, as little boys often do, completely infatuated with weapons. He knew about grenades, of course, and one day his father brought home two smoke grenades and set one off for his benefit in our front yard. The billows of hot-pink smoke that filled our front yard were pretty impressive, and Kip naturally wanted to "do it again!" But Dad thought better of it and said we would save the second one for our last day there.

Well, time went by and our last day in Laos finally arrived. We were seated for the last time on the plane that regularly had ferried us in and out of the country. As we taxied down the runway, Kip's Dad suddenly jumped up from his seat next to me, sat a baby on my lap, leaned over to Kip's seat, and then rushed up the aisle to the cockpit. The next thing I knew, the plane was turning around and heading back toward the hangar. The door opened and Dad handed out a smoke grenade to a waiting officer. Dad had remembered his promise, and realized that Kip probably remembered it too. Sure enough, Kip had brought the grenade onto the plane. I have always wondered what would have happened if Dad had not thought of that promise made months before!

Yam Nua (Thai Steak Salad)

1 to 1½ pounds flank steak	1 head lettuce, washed, dried,
Thai Seasoning*	and torn into bite-size pieces
juice of 1 lime or lemon	1 medium onion, sliced
2 tablespoons fish sauce	2 tomatoes, chopped
½ teaspoon cayenne pepper	1 medium cucumber, sliced
1 tablespoon garlic chili sauce	fresh mint leaves, to taste
3 teaspoons granulated sugar	fresh coriander leaves, to taste

Coat steak liberally with Thai Seasoning, if available, or use garlic salt and black pepper (see note below). Grill steak over hot coals (or cook under broiler) until done to medium. Slice thinly at a severe angle; set aside.

Prepare dressing by combining lime or lemon juice, fish sauce, cayenne pepper, garlic chili sauce, and sugar in a small bowl or cup.

Combine vegetables in large salad bowl. Top with sliced steak, mint and coriander. Pour dressing over salad and toss to mix well. Serve as an appetizer, or as a main dish with rice.

Serves 6 to 8.

*Thai Seasoning can be found in some grocery stores and Asian specialty markets. If unavailable, substitute garlic salt and black pepper, using 1/4 teaspoon pepper for each 1 teaspoon of garlic salt.

Per serving (based on 6 servings per recipe): Calories 19 (36% from fat), Carbohydrates 9.3 g, Protein 21.2 g, Total Fat 7.7 g, Sodium 778 mg, Saturated Fat 3.3 g, Cholesterol 49 mg, Diabetic Exchanges: lean meat 3, veg 1

DON'T WORRY

When I heard the radio announcement that morning some thirty years ago that the American Embassy had been bombed, my first thought was why would the embassy here be bombed, and my second thought was why hadn't I heard it. Having been evacuated to this city from Vietnam a few weeks earlier with three children under five, the embassy in Saigon, and my husband still there, should have been my first thoughts. There was a sinking sensation and feeling of nervousness as the realization that it was Saigon the announcer was talking about began to take hold, and with it, the terrible significance that the news story had for us. There had been little contact with the station since our evacuation, but we "Saigon wives" were in touch with each other and eventually one of us received a call arranging a meeting that night to discuss the situation.

"Don't worry; no one was hurt." Nothing was learned that evening, and in the days that followed we continued to hear the refrain "don't worry . . . ."

There was no way for us to contact anyone, but the office would keep us informed, so "don't worry."

Finally, a call came to arrange a meeting with a doctor who had seen my husband. "Don't worry; he has been evacuated to a nearby military hospital a thousand miles away, and his vision should return in a few weeks. There's no way for you to contact him, but we'll be in touch, so don't worry."

They were absolutely correct; they continued to stay in touch, his vision did return, and with all of that support, how could I have possibly worried?

Chinese Style Corn and Crab Soup

1 (12 oz.) can creamed corn
2 (14.5 oz.) cans chicken broth
2 chicken bouillon cubes
1 cup crab meat (imitation
  may be used)

2 tablespoons cornstarch
1 cup cold water
5 egg whites, beaten slightly
few dashes soy sauce, to taste

In a large pot, combine creamed corn, chicken broth, bouillon cubes, and crab meat. Cook over medium heat, stirring often, until hot.

Stir cornstarch into cold water; mix well to form smooth paste. Add mixture to hot soup; mix well to thicken slightly. Bring to boil; slowly add egg whites, one at a time, stirring well after each addition. Add soy sauce. Serve immediately.

Per serving (based on 4 servings per recipe): Calories 152 (8% from fat), Carbohydrates 20.8 g, Protein 15 g, Total Fat 1.5 g, Sodium 1349 mg, Saturated Fat 0.3 g, Cholesterol 23 mg, Diabetic Exchanges: starch 1, meat 1

LET THERE BE LIGHT

Any family assigned overseas learns to adapt, and as a wife who was sent to a safe haven for several years during the Vietnam War, I learned to adapt a lot.

I remember moving to a small town to be closer to my husband. Actually, it was really no more than a "camp town," made up largely of bars, massage parlors, jewelry shops, and houses of ill repute! Since we had a genuine "red light" house on the corner of our dirt street, I used to pray that our children would never ask about the "people in their neighborhood!" But while that was certainly an interesting aspect of life there, it was the logistics of daily life that made our stay memorable.

My first real lesson came the very first night we spent in the house. When I went upstairs to put the kids to bed, I couldn't get more than one very weak light bulb to come on, and none of the fans would work. I walked around turning switches on and off several times, thinking, I suppose, that if I tried enough times something would finally happen. I checked the fuses (unlike anything I've ever seen before and another story in itself!) and finally gave up and did the only thing left to do—went to bed. The first night in a new house is always a little unsettling, but never had I ever had one like this. Around midnight, I jerked awake to blazing lights, an overhead fan whirling like a chopper blade, and a very loud buzzer. I literally didn't know which way to go, but it didn't take long to think "turn it off now!" It took a little longer to locate the buzzer and figure out how to shut it off. By then, of course, everyone was awake and I had no answers as to what had happened, but clearly we now had electricity upstairs. I later discovered that the box on top of the refrigerator was a step-up/step-down transformer (with a buzzer power surge alarm), and I quickly became very adept at its use. The problem was that all the bars in town turned on their air conditioners around 4:00, just in time for the 4:15 quitting time on the nearby military base. All those air conditioners pulled every bit of available electricity, and then at midnight when the bars closed down because of the curfew and the air conditioners were turned off, all that electricity surged back in to the rest of the town. We learned to step-up our transformer before 4:00 and turn on any lights and fans we thought we would need. We also learned to step-down the transformer before going to bed to prevent the alarm sounding at the power surge at midnight.

I was to learn many more lessons before it was all over, and I will always be grateful for those experiences, because while they often didn't seem very funny then, they always make me laugh now.

Oriental Chicken Salad

For dressing/marinade:

½ cup rice wine vinegar	1 tablespoon honey
2 cloves garlic, minced	1 tablespoon chili paste (sambal oelek)
⅓ cup creamy peanut butter	2 tablespoons grated ginger root
¼ cup lime juice	or 1 teaspoon ground ginger
2 tablespoons cider vinegar	2 tablespoons soy sauce

For the salad:

4 halves chicken breast,
  skin and bones removed
3 ounces uncooked vermicelli
4 cups torn romaine lettuce
2 cups Chinese cabbage,
  thinly sliced

2 carrots, shredded
1 large sweet red bell pepper
¼ cup chopped cilantro
1 medium cucumber, sliced
peanuts, chopped (optional, for garnish)

In a blender or food processor fitted with steel blade, process all dressing ingredients until smooth and well blended. Marinate chicken breasts in 3 tablespoons of dressing, tossing to coat. Cover and refrigerate for 8 hours.

Cook vermicelli according to package directions; drain well. Place vermicelli in a medium bowl; stir in 3 tablespoons dressing, tossing to coat well. Cover and refrigerate 8 hours.

When ready to serve, grill chicken breasts over medium heat, turning once, until juices run clear. Slice into thin strips.

In a large bowl, combine lettuce, cabbage, carrots, pepper, and cilantro. Arrange salad on serving platter. Transfer vermicelli onto salad; top with chicken slices; arrange cucumber slices around vermicelli. Sprinkle with chopped peanuts if desired. Pass remaining dressing separately.
Makes 4 to 6 servings.

Per serving (based on 6 servings per recipe): Calories 290 (39% from fat), Carbohydrates 27.2 g,
Protein 18.8 g, Total Fat 13.3 g, Sodium 470 mg, Saturated Fat 2.6 g, Cholesterol 27 mg,
Diabetic Exchanges: starch 1, lean meat 2, veg 1, fat 1.5

CHARLIE FOUR, WHERE ARE YOU?

The unmistakable "crruump" of exploding ordnance interrupted our dinner. After combat service in the Italian campaign during the Second World War and in Korea, the sound was familiar enough. The first round, followed immediately by a second, then a third, fell somewhere off to our left in the city, stopping my first forkful in mid-air. Communists, among other things, are boors. No respect for the civilities.

The city of Can Tho squats alongside the Bassac River, sweating in the hot, humid air like an old whore, near the mouth of the Mekong Delta in Vietnam. I was billeted in the ground-floor apartment of a four-story building across the street from the American Consulate. The niece of a high-ranking ARVN general who was visiting me from Saigon and whom I was later to marry, had prepared the dinner. Thanks to the NVA, it would go to waste that evening.

Ngoc Hoa, my future bride, was remarkably unperturbed. I was less sanguine. Already, the radio was hissing and squawking like an outraged goose. "Anybody know what's going on?" The rounds continued to fall. A mixture of mortars and rockets; I wasn't sure. "Is everybody all right?" There was no let-up. "What's happening?" Then, "Charlie Four. Get up on the roof. We need damage reports." I was Charlie Four.

I got a mattress from the bed and pushed Hoa into the bathroom. "Stay here," I told her, "under the mattress. Don't go near the window." She nodded happily. Ignorance is bliss, as the feller said. I ascended the outside stairs to the roof.

There was a babble of voices on the radio. The least secure spot in the bombardment of an urban area is out in the open, up on a roof. To be safe, you want to be under cover, close to the ground. Nevertheless, the order to go to the roof was propitious. Half the city was burning; sparks from the fires were falling on the roof. Together with some of the other residents, we stamped them out.

A crowd of frightened citizens was moving towards us to get away from the shelling. The building was surrounded by a wall. The guard at the gate was armed, but it seemed that this sole deterrent to penetration of the compound might well need reinforcement, if not, at the least, encouragement. Also, I had run out of cigarettes. (This was before the rise of the antismoking campaign.)

I descended the stairs to my apartment for a smoke and to check on Hoa. No Hoa; the apartment was empty. I ran to the gate and found her talking excitedly to the guard, as if they were spectators at a horse race, not facing a throng of panicking citizens bearing down on them. She would later recall that it was great fun.

I had not been paying much attention to the radio. As the shelling subsided, I heard my call sign and recognized the querulous voice of my Base Chief. "Where's Charlie Four? Anybody know if he's okay?"

"This is Charlie Four," I said into the mike. "All's well here."

"Where have you been?" The Base Chief's tone of voice left no doubt as to his state of mind. "Why didn't you report in sooner?"

"There was so much traffic on the air," I replied, "I could hardly get a word in edgewise."

What was the dinner we missed that evening? Hoa had prepared Langouste á la Maison, which goes something like this:

Langouste á la Maison

Figure amount of ingredients according to taste:

carrots (1 to 2 per serving)   crayfish or giant prawns

For sauce:

butter   cognac
garlic

Dice carrots. Boil some crayfish (or giant prawns) about 6 to 8 minutes, then sauté them with the carrots in a sauce of butter, garlic and cognac, until carrots are tender.

Serve with a tossed salad with oil and vinegar dressing and French bread (to mop up the sauce; but you will not find French bread in most places the like of that brought home still warm from the bakery in Can Tho).

Mortar and rocket fire is optional.

Dietitian's note: Because ingredient proportions vary according to taste, nutritional values have not been determined.

MUSSEL-BOUND PAELLA

Having grown up in the West Indies, it was with pleasure that I discovered during our postings in several Southeast Asian countries that many familiar foods were available, including ingredients for favorite dishes. Take paella, for instance. At one post I found the market could provide the basic tomatoes, onions, garlic, green peppers, coriander leaves, shrimp, rice, etc. needed. In our commissary, American chicken and an acceptable sausage were obtainable. I didn't know about the mussels (but they're not essential) until the day we ate at a lovely old hotel on the banks of the major local river. We were served an excellent bouillabaisse with, lo and behold, tasty mussels with shiny deep blue shells. After a tête-á-tête with the waiter to ascertain their availability and the local name, I was armed to tell our foreign national cook that "moules" were procurable at the morning market on Tuesdays and Fridays with prior ordering and sent him forth, as I already had a glowing vision of serving this special dish at a party the following Friday night. He returned from his foray all smiles and did I prefer round or oval, and how may dozen? I went about a busy week confident of the sensational culinary coup we were going to pull off. On Friday noon, the cook told me with a glint that he had purchased the three dozen oval moules, and I reminded him to put them in the pot in the last minutes of cooking so they wouldn't get tough, and to be sure they were standing up in the rice when the dish was presented.

Imagine my surprise (horror?) when he proudly delivered a large casserole of perfect paella with three dozen tin molds for tart shells sticking up arranged in a pattern!!

Herewith the recipe. Be sure of your fishmonger and that you and your cook speak the same version of the third language you communicate in.

West Indies Paella

1 chicken (2½ to 3 pounds), cut in 12 pieces (cut breasts in 4 pieces)
⅓ cup Spanish olive oil
1 medium onion, sliced
2 cloves garlic, crushed
1 green pepper, cut in one inch pieces
½ teaspoon salt
1 cup uncooked long-grain rice
1 cup stewed tomatoes (or canned), cut up
1 (about ¼ pound) chorizo or garlic flavored sausage
1 dozen raw shrimp, shelled and cleaned (optional)
1 cup chicken broth (make from backs, wingtips, neck, giblets, or use canned)
1 cup Spanish sherry
¼ teaspoon Spanish saffron (optional)
1 package (10 oz.) frozen green peas or frozen artichoke hearts
1 dozen mussels (optional)

Wash and dry chicken pieces. Brown in heated oil in a large skillet until golden on all sides. With tongs, remove from skillet and set aside. To drippings in skillet, add onion, garlic, green pepper, and salt; sauté until lightly browned; add saffron and salt and cook until vegetables are soft. Add rice, stir to coat evenly with oil. Return chicken to skillet. Add tomato pieces, chorizo, chicken broth, sherry, and shrimp; bring to boil. Lower heat and simmer, covered, stirring once or twice, for about 20 minutes or until half the liquid is absorbed. Add the frozen peas or artichokes and simmer about 15 minutes longer, or until all ingredients are tender and most of the liquid is absorbed. If using mussels, you can steam them in a little water until the shells open and use as garnish.

This is a very basic recipe for paella. There are endless variations and combinations that accommodate any taste or availability. Hot peppers, canned pimientos, and/or capers suit some tastes. Ground coriander (½ teaspoon) or oregano (1 teaspoon) can be used in seasoning. Clams can be substituted for mussels, and often one finds both shrimp and clams and mussels in a good paella. Fresh coriander leaves on top are a fine addition. Good accompaniments are fried plantains, green salad, French bread.

Serves 6.

Per serving: Calories 586 (44% from fat), Carbohydrates 35.9 g, Protein 45.2 g, Total Fat 28.2 g, Sodium 836 mg, Saturated Fat 6.8 g, Cholesterol 139 mg, Diabetic Exchanges: starch 2, lean meat 5, veg 1, fat 2.5

FOREIGN TO FAMILIAR

After five tours of duty in Africa and Asia, I remember many dinners, lunches, and receptions given in challenging conditions. Adapting our family's lifestyle—including familiar recipes—to the customs and foods available in undeveloped countries often proved to be unexpectedly difficult. Water had to be boiled and filtered, vegetables scrubbed and soaked in bleach. Suitable ingredients were often hard to come by. American-made stoves and ovens turned "crotchety" with fuel supplies of uncertain quality and quantity. And, most difficult of all, one had to learn what foods local customs would permit guests to eat.

However, despite these difficulties, cooking overseas often generated pleasant surprises; being forced to use local ingredients in the place of more familiar ones sometimes produced results which turned ordinary recipes into new favorites. After returning to the U.S. those new flavors were missed just as much as the old familiar ones had been while overseas.

Today, many of the ingredients familiar to overseas cooks are becoming more available in American supermarkets, making the following recipes easy to prepare at home or abroad.

Mango Pie (I)
(walnuts add flavor and texture to this pie prepared in a pie shell)

1 10-inch prepared pie shell
5 ripe mangoes, sliced
1 cup sugar
3 tablespoons cornstarch

1 egg, lightly beaten, or ¼ cup
   liquid egg substitute
1 cup heavy cream
1¼ teaspoons vanilla extract

⅛ teaspoon salt
½ teaspoon cinnamon
¼ teaspoon nutmeg

4 tablespoons butter or margarine
½ cup coarsely chopped walnuts

Bake pie shell for about ½ time suggested in directions or recipe for shell (this step avoids shell becoming soggy from fruit filling). Let cool completely.

Preheat oven to 350° F.

Arrange mango slices in lightly baked pie shell; set aside. In a small bowl, combine sugar, cornstarch, salt, and spices. In a medium bowl, blend together egg, cream, and vanilla. Gradually add sugar mixture; mix well. Pour mixture over mangoes. Dot with butter, sprinkle with walnuts.

Cover pie with aluminum foil. Bake in preheated oven for one hour until filling is firm. Uncover pie for last 10 minutes of baking time. Serve with ice cream.

Makes 6 to 8 servings.

Per serving (based on 8 servings per recipe): Calories 519 (47% from fat), Carbohydrates 66.2 g, Protein 5.2 g, Total Fat 28.6 g, Sodium 383 mg, Saturated fat 10.1 g, Cholesterol 77 mg, Diabetic Exchanges: starch 1, fruit 3.5, fat 5

Mango Pie (II)

(tapioca mix speeds the preparation of this two-crust pie)

2 tablespoons quick-cooking
   tapioca mix (such as
   Minute® Tapioca)
⅔ cup granulated sugar
½ teaspoon ground cinnamon
¼ teaspoon ground nutmeg

4 ripe mangoes, peeled and
   sliced (5 to 6 cups)
prepared dough for a two-crust 9" pie

Preheat oven to 450° F.

In a large bowl combine tapioca, sugar, cinnamon, and nutmeg; add mango slices; mix. Let stand 5 minutes.

Line pie plate with pastry for bottom crust. Fill with fruit mixture. Place top crust over fruit mixture, seal and flute edge. Cut slits in pie crust to allow steam to escape. (The top crust may be brushed with milk and sprinkled with sugar before placing in the oven.)

Bake in preheated 450° F. oven; reduce heat to 350 degrees F.; continue baking for 45 minutes more or until crust is golden and pie is done.

Per serving (based on 10 servings per recipe): Calories 281 (35% from fat), Carbohydrates 44.3 g, Protein 2.5 g, Total Fat 11.3 g, Sodium 175 mg, Saturated Fat 2.8 g, Cholesterol 0 mg, Diabetic Exchanges: starch 1, fruit 2, fat 2

Mango Sauce for Ice Cream

3 ripe mangoes, peeled and
chopped
1 tablespoon lemon juice

2 tablespoons orange juice
1 tablespoon granulated sugar

Place all ingredients in a blender or food processor fitted with steel blade; puree until smooth. Strain puree into bowl. Refrigerate 2 hours or up to 2 days. Serve over toffee vanilla ice cream (recipe below).

Per 2-fluid ounce servings: Calories 59 (44% from fat), Carbohydrates 15.3 g, Protein 0.4 g, Total Fat 0.2 g, Sodium 2 mg, Saturated Fat 0.1 g, Cholesterol 0 mg, Diabetic Exchanges: fruit 1

Toffee-Vanilla Ice Cream

⅓ cup granulated sugar
2 tablespoons water
¼ stick unsalted butter

¼ teaspoon baking soda
½ - ⅔ cup roasted nuts, chopped
1 quart vanilla ice cream

Combine sugar, water, and butter in small saucepan. Cook over medium heat until sugar dissolves and butter is melted. Increase heat to medium-high; bring syrup to boil, stirring constantly, 3 to 4 minutes until candy thermometer reaches 290° F. Add baking soda; stir in nuts. Pour mixture onto buttered cookie sheet and spread with a spoon. Allow to cool.

Remove ice cream from freezer and allow to soften slightly. When candy is cool, break into pieces and add to softened ice cream. Refrigerate. Serve in individual bowls topped with mango sauce. Pass additional sauce if desired. Makes 6 servings.

Per serving (using 1/2 cup English walnuts): Calories 330 (54% from fat), Carbohydrates 33.6 g, Protein 4.6 g, Total Fat 19.7 g, Sodium 163 mg, Saturated Fat 8.9 g, Cholesterol 49 mg, Diabetic Exchanges: fruit 2, milk 0.5, fat 4

THE KING AND I—SHALL WE DANCE?

In the 50s, the influx of diplomats in newly independent Indonesia created many housing problems in Djakarta. The U.S. Government, in its wisdom, decided that the solution to this would be to send only single personnel; three or four women could share one house (apartments were unheard of) and the same for the men. During the first 24 months I was there, there were 26 weddings among this group (mine was one), and then there was a real housing problem.

Vientiane in the early '60s was feeling the repercussions of the war in Vietnam, but during the time I was there only one serious fight took place between various elements hoping to control the government. And only one shot was fired into the compound where couples without children and single personnel of the Embassy were living. Fortunately, no one was hurt by that bullet, but it did go through the closet of one of the single women—right through the middle of every dress she owned! She said later that for a while it was rather fascinating wearing a dress with a patch just at the waistline, but it got boring after a bit.

Travel in Vientiane, in those days, was out of the question, but the King arrived from the capital for an official visit by the diplomatic corps, and officers and wives were invited to the palace to meet him. The diplomatic corps, at that time, was semi-ruled by lots of protocol, and all the wives were given lessons by a British expert on how to do a proper curtsy. I practiced hard, as we all did, and felt that my curtsy was very elegant in my long dress, and when I climbed the marble staircase to be greeted by a resplendent man in very formal dress, I was sure my curtsy was superb. The only problem was that the resplendent man was not the King, but the Major Domo, and I noted the King ahead holding back a smile. I suspected kings were happy to find errors like this were possible, because he later asked me to dance.

Chicken with Tofu

1 pound ground chicken breasts (3 to 4 boneless, skinless breasts ground in food processor)	4 cakes tofu, diced
	2 tablespoons soy sauce
	¾ cups water
1½ tablespoons safflower or canola oil	1 tablespoon corn starch
	2 tablespoons water
1 tablespoon ground ginger	½ teaspoon black pepper
1 tablespoon minced garlic	1 teaspoon sesame oil
1 tablespoon bean paste with chili	1 tablespoon minced onions
1 teaspoon chili paste (sambal oelek)	

Heat oil in a large skillet, and cook chicken in hot oil until the meat is white. Add the ginger, garlic, bean paste and chili paste; stir; continue cooking until fragrant. Add tofu; heat through. Add soy sauce and ¾ cups water; bring to a boil; reduce heat to low. Mix corn starch and 2 tablespoons water; stir into chicken mixture; simmer, stirring, for 1 to 2 minutes or until slightly thickened. Pour into serving bowl.

Garnish with pepper, sesame oil and minced onions. Serve plain or over rice.

Per serving (based on 4 servings per recipe): Calories 373 (49% from fat), Carbohydrates 9.1 g, Protein 38.9 g, Total Fat 20.9 g, Sodium 598 mg, Saturated Fat 3.6 g, Cholesterol 69 mg, Diabetic Exchanges: lean meat 5, veg 2, fat 1

Szechwan Gherkin Slices

1¼ pounds cucumbers, unpeeled
1 teaspoon salt
5 cloves garlic, thinly sliced
1 teaspoon black peppercorns
1 to 2 teaspoons bean paste with chili

1 teaspoon chili paste (sambal oelek)
2 tablespoons cider vinegar
2 tablespoons sesame oil
2 teaspoons granulated sugar

Cut off tips of cucumbers; cut each cucumber lengthwise into four or six sections. Do not peel; with a spoon remove seeds. Sprinkle cucumbers with salt and let stand for at least 1 hour. Rinse in cold water; drain; pat dry on paper towels; transfer to deep bowl or baking dish. Combine remaining ingredients in a small bowl; pour over cucumber slices. Cover and refrigerate for 24 hours.

Per serving (based on 8 servings per recipe): Calories 59 (51% from fat), Carbohydrates 6.6 g, Protein 1 g, Total Fat 3.5 g, Sodium 11.7 mg, Saturated Fat 0.5 g, Cholesterol 0 mg, Diabetic Exchanges: veg 0.5, fat 1

NO CAVITY CAKE

I had the good luck to draw an exciting Asian city for my first overseas tour. When I arrived, my luck continued as I was able to hire an excellent Chinese cook who had worked for a couple just departing. The cook's skills included the ability to make his dishes as pleasing to the eye as to the stomach. This talent was especially evident on my birthday, when he surprised me with an elaborately decorated cake. When I asked how he managed to make some of the more intricate designs in the frosting, he said proudly, "I use toothbrush."

I paled, and he immediately understood my cause for alarm. "No worry, Missy," he said; "I no use your toothbrush—I use my tooth brush."

Here's a cake recipe that avoids the problem of decorating—it has no frosting:

Coffee Cake

For the pecan topping:
¾ cup brown sugar
1 tablespoon flour
1 teaspoon cinnamon

2 tablespoons butter
1 cup chopped pecans

For the cake:
½ cup butter
1 cup sugar
3 eggs
1 cup sour cream
2 cups flour

1 teaspoon baking powder
1 teaspoon baking soda
¼ teaspoon salt
1 cup chocolate drops or chips

Prepare pecan topping by combining brown sugar, flour, and cinnamon. With a pastry blender or 2 knives, cut in 2 tablespoons butter until mixture crumbs into pieces smaller than corn meal. Stir in chopped pecans. Set aside.

Preheat oven to 350 ° F. Grease and flour 9x13-inch baking pan.

In a large bowl, cream butter and sugar. Add eggs one at a time, beating well after each addition. In a small bowl, combine flour, baking powder, baking soda, and salt. Add flour mixture alternately with sour cream to the butter-sugar-egg mixture. Stir in chocolate. Pour batter into prepared pan. Sprinkle pecan topping over top of cake batter.

Bake in preheated oven for 30 minutes. Let cool before cutting into serving size squares. Serve fresh with coffee or tea.

Variation: Use 1 cup blueberries instead of the chocolate in the cake.
(My son won a prize using this variation at a Fourth of July bake-off!)

Per serving (based on 16 servings per basic recipe): Calories 340 (50% from fat), Carbohydrates 40.4 g, Protein 4.3 g, Total Fat 19 g, Sodium 238 mg, Saturated Fat 8.9 g, Cholesterol 61 mg, Diabetic Exchanges: starch 1, fruit 1.5, fat 3.5

LUNCH TIME SURPRISE!

1958 was a big year for my husband and me, for we married and received our assignment to an interesting Asian city less than three months later. It was an extended honeymoon despite the teasing of his coworkers that taking a wife to such a city was like taking a sandwich to a banquet. We adapted quickly to the beautiful locale, finding the diversity of culture fascinating. Since friend husband was quickly immersed in his "sphere of influence," I began looking about for something to occupy my time and was happy to accept a position teaching English to students at a local college. Several other foreign women were also employed there, and we struck up a warm friendship. It was lunch at one of their homes where I discovered the recipe listed below. It was not only delicious but could be easily prepared and increased to feed a large group. It was this feature that resulted in a most embarrassing moment for me.

I was approached by a charming English acquaintance who asked if I would be interested in chairing a style show featuring the children of the city's official foreign community as models of her children's store fashions and costumes flown in by the international airlines represented in town. The proceeds of all ticket sales would be donated to the Boys and Girls Club, a charitable organization which aided the legions of street children of refugees from mainland China so prevalent in the city at that time. It sounded like a worthwhile and interesting project and I accepted, setting about to choose a committee to help with the myriad details. All were invited to lunch to be followed by an organizational meeting. I selected my friend's recipe for the large gathering and instructed my housekeeper, Ah Choy, on its preparation.

My committee arrived, introductions were made, and we all sat down at table and Ah Choy began to serve. The guest of honor was the 80-year-old honorary chairman of the Boys and Girls Club, a much revered and distinguished member of both the Chinese and British communities. I noticed that she passed the offered serving and picked about on her salad. Ah Choy, my ever perceptive amah whispered in my ear, "Missy, Buddhists no eat meat. I fix egg for lady." I thanked Ah Choy and she hurried away returning shortly with a lovely vegetable omelet which my guest attacked with gusto. I had learned an important lesson, and you can bet that in the future I made it a point to learn the dietary preferences of any guests who might be invited to lunch or dinner.

Buffet "Stroganoff"

1 to 1½ pounds lean ground beef	½ pound fresh mushrooms, cleaned and sliced
salt and pepper, to taste	1 cup sour cream
1 large green pepper, sliced	½ cup beef bouillon (optional)
1 large onion, sliced	4 cups warm cooked rice

Brown beef, mixing with a fork, in a large skillet until all redness completely disappears. Pour off accumulated fat. Season beef with salt and pepper; top with green pepper, onion and mushrooms, arranged in layers. Cook, covered, over medium heat until vegetables are tender-crisp, about 15 to 25 minutes (cook longer if you prefer softer vegetables). Stir in sour cream (add bouillon if gravy sparse), and remove from heat. To serve, spoon over rice.

This goes well with a tossed salad and a fresh fruit cup seasoned with Grand Marnier or Marsala.

Serves 4 to 6. Can be multiplied to increase number of servings.

Per serving (based on 4 servings per recipe): Calories 596 (48% from fat), Carbohydrates 42 g, Protein 35.9 g, Total Fat 31.5 g, Sodium 740 mg, Saturated Fat 14.8 g, Cholesterol 121 mg, Diabetic Exchanges: starch 2, meat 4, veg 1, fat 2

RENDEZVOUS

Mr. X had been stationed in a large Asian city for two years. His work involved dealing with a variety of travelers who visited nearby countries, usually referred to as "denied areas." He often conducted his work away from home, staying in hotels frequented by businessmen, and using an alias.

On one occasion, having been living in a hotel for most of the week and missing his family, he had a brilliant idea. Why not invite his wife to meet him near his hotel and have dinner on an evening when he expected to finish business early.

His wife's reaction was enthusiastic. They both agreed it would be adventurous for a wife to date her husband in his other persona—it might even be romantic.

Arrangements were made, and they enjoyed an excellent dinner with a touch of their courtship days. He and his wife avoided raising issues involving the children's schooling or discussing any problems from home, and just enjoyed each other's company. Swept away by the feelings of the moment, Mr. X decided to invite his wife to visit his nearby hotel room.

Their pleasant reunion was interrupted briefly by an officious hotel roomboy offering champagne or other libations for the occasion. Mr. X declined and thought no further of the intrusion. When the time came to escort his wife to a taxi, they both agreed it had been a most enjoyable evening.

When he returned home a few days later, he couldn't wait to tell his wife about his encounter with the roomboy the next morning on his way to breakfast. "Do you know what he said to me? He said that the next time I wanted a Western woman to visit me, to let him know, because he could arrange something much better than I had done on my own last night."

The wife hesitated a moment, then laughed as she responded, "I doubt that very much!"

The editors suggest the following menu to create a romantic mood at home.

Tortellini Soup with Hot Pepper Sauce

1 small yellow onion, peeled
 and halved
2 medium carrots, scraped
 and trimmed
2 tablespoons olive oil
1 (14 oz.) can peeled Italian
 plum tomatoes, undrained
1 cup tomato puree

3 cups water
1 pound frozen or dried tortellini
½ cup heavy cream
salt and pepper, to taste
1 teaspoon fresh parsley
Creamy Hot Pepper Sauce (recipe follows)

Coarsely chop onion halves and carrots. Heat oil in a large pot; sauté onion and carrots in hot oil for 3 minutes until softened, but not browned. Stir in tomatoes and liquid from can, breaking up tomatoes with a wooden spoon. Add tomato puree and 3 cups water; cover and bring to a boil. Lower heat; add tortellini; simmer over low heat 10 to 12 minutes until tortellini is tender. Add cream; season with salt and pepper. Serve in individual soup bowls; top each serving with a spoonful of creamy hot pepper sauce and ¼ teaspoon parsley. Pass extra sauce.

Makes 4 servings.

Per serving (not including Creamy Hot Pepper Sauce): Calories 447 (52% from fat), Carbohydrates 40.5 g, Protein 13.9 g, Total Fat 26.6 g, Sodium 750 mg, Saturated Fat 10.9 g, Cholesterol 188 mg, Diabetic Exchanges: starch 3, meat 1, fat 4

Creamy Hot Pepper Sauce

2 cloves garlic
1 (4 oz.) jar roasted red peppers,
   drained and chopped
1 tablespoon fresh lemon juice

3 egg yolks
½ teaspoon cayenne pepper
½ teaspoon crushed red pepper flakes
1 cup olive oil

Press garlic into a small bowl. In a food processor with steel blade, process garlic, peppers, lemon juice, egg yolks, pepper, and pepper flakes until smooth. With motor running, add oil slowly, stopping frequently to scrape down sides of container. Process a few seconds until smooth. Pour sauce into small saucepan; simmer over low heat, stirring frequently, for 10 minutes to cook egg yolk. Do not boil. Add salt to taste. Pour sauce into a bowl and cover tightly until needed.

Per 2-tablespoon serving: Calories 179 (96% from fat), Carbohydrates 1.1 g, Protein 0.9 g, Total Fat 19.3 g, Sodium 113 mg, Saturated Fat 2.8 g, Cholesterol 53 mg, Diabetic Exchanges: fat 3.5

Caesar Salad

For the salad:
1 large carrot, scraped and trimmed
1 small head romaine lettuce, washed, trimmed and torn into bite-size pieces
4 to 5 cups washed, torn spinach, stems removed
small bowl ice water
Parmesan cheese, to taste
freshly ground black pepper, to taste

For the dressing:
⅓ cup olive oil
3 tablespoons water
1 egg
2 tablespoons fresh
   lemon juice

4 to 6 flat anchovy fillets, rinsed
   and chopped
2 garlic cloves, minced
pinch of salt
few dashes Worcestershire sauce

For the croutons:
2 cups ½ inch cubes cut from Italian or French bread
2 tablespoons olive oil

Using a vegetable peeler, cut long, thin strips from carrot. Curl strips around finger; drop strips into ice water. Chill in refrigerator at least 1 hour.

Wash greens and dry thoroughly. Place in plastic food storage bags; seal, chill in refrigerator.

Prepare dressing by whisking together all ingredients in a saucepan. Cook slowly over low heat 5 minutes until slightly thickened; do not allow to boil.

Remove from heat and let cool. Pour into cruet or screw top jar. Chill in refrigerator at least 1 hour.

Prepare croutons by pouring oil onto a jelly-roll pan or shallow baking dish. Add bread cubes and toss to coat evenly with oil. Bake in preheated 350° F. oven for 15 minutes until crisp and golden. Remove croutons from pan and set aside.

To serve: Drain carrot curls. Combine chilled greens in large salad bowl. Add carrot curls. Shake chilled dressing until smooth and well-blended. Pour dressing over salad; toss gently. Add Parmesan cheese, ground pepper, and croutons; toss again. Serve with fresh bread.

Per serving (based on 8 servings per recipe): Calories 188 (70% from fat), Carbohydrates 8.9 g, Protein 5.4 g, Total Fat 15 g, Sodium 287 mg, Saturated Fat 2.8 g, Cholesterol 29 mg, Diabetic Exchanges: starch 0.5, meat 0.5, veg 0.5, fat 2.5

Wine and Berry Compote

1 to 1½ pounds (4 to 6 cups) mixed fresh berries
1 cup red wine
1 cup water

¼ cup granulated sugar
6 tablespoons fresh lemon juice
1 vanilla bean

Wash and drain berries, remove any stems; set aside. Combine remaining ingredients in a small saucepan. Bring to a boil; cook, stirring, until sugar is dissolved and liquid is reduced to 1¼ cups. Remove bean; scrape seeds into syrup. Pour syrup into large bowl; add berries, stirring to mix. Cool several hours in refrigerator to blend flavors. Serve cold in individual glass dessert bowls or cups.

Per serving (based on 4 servings per recipe): Calories 162 (4% from fat), Carbohydrates 37.3 g, Protein 1.5 g, Total Fat 0.8 g, Sodium 8.5 mg, Saturated Fat 0.1 g, Cholesterol 0 mg, Diabetic Exchanges: fruit 2.5

TOP SECRET SOUP

This is a recipe I acquired in Asia. While my husband was assigned there, we frequently ate in a rooftop restaurant which primarily served Spanish food. At that time, I was a subscriber to *Gourmet* magazine and wrote them to obtain the recipe for me. More than a year later, *Gourmet* wrote me that the restaurant refused to release the recipe. The last week before we left the country, some three years later, my husband and I went there for dinner. As usual, I ordered the soup, remarking to the waiter that I liked the soup so much that I wished I had the recipe. A few minutes later, he brought it to me with the compliments of the cook.

Sopa de Ajo Blanco (Cold Garlic Soup)

1 medium size white onion, chopped
1 whole head of garlic, peeled, separated, and chopped
3 slices of French bread, broken into bits
1 jigger (3 tablespoons) white wine
1 egg yolk or ¼ cup liquid egg substitute
1 cup crushed ice
salt to taste
ground white pepper to taste

Put all ingredients in blender and blend until well mixed. Refrigerate and serve very cold.

Per serving (based on 2 servings per recipe, using egg substitute): Calories 193 (8% from fat), Carbohydrates 36.3 g, Protein 6.1 g, Total Fat 1.7 g, Sodium 676 mg, Saturated Fat 0.4 g, Cholesterol 0 mg, Diabetic Exchanges: starch 2, veg 1

SEEING IS NOT BELIEVING

I always thought that being tall had its advantages—one can breathe in elevators, see parades, and reach top shelves in cupboards. Being tall in Asia, though, can be painful. I didn't fit in doorways and I didn't fit at tables—forehead and knees were always covered with bruises.

Shopping for clothes was a deflating experience—there was very little designed for a woman of my height, but I needed a dress for a dinner party. A dressmaker was the answer.

Armed with the material and a picture from a magazine, I arrived at the recommended shop. The standard procedure was a discussion of the picture and the fabric, then a step up on a platform to be measured. Problems arose when it became obvious that even with a ladder, the dressmaker could not reach to measure anywhere above my waist while I was on the platform. I like to think of myself as a relaxed individual, but thought it a bit early in my relationship with the community to appear at a formal function topless.

Much whispering and giggling preceded my descent from the platform, and continued throughout the laborious and thorough job of measurement-taking. At last I was instructed to return in five days.

Five days later I trotted back to the shop and was presented with a glorious creation to try on. Behind a curtain, in a tiny cubicle, I stepped into the dress and proceeded to pull it on. It became painfully clear, even before the exquisitely hand-stitched hem of the floor-length gown rose over my knees, that I could not continue. There was nothing to do but present myself to the seamstress and her assistant, and beg their forgiveness for being so tall.

1,2,3,4,5 Spareribs
(for appetizer)

5 pounds meaty spareribs, cut into 2-inch long sections
1 tablespoon rice wine
2 tablespoons dark soy sauce
3 tablespoons vinegar
4 tablespoons sugar
5 tablespoons water

Combine all ingredients in a heavy saucepan, mix well. Set on a high heat until boiling, then reduce heat to low. Cover and simmer for 45 minutes until ribs are tender. Stir, and turn spareribs, from time to time. At the end of cooking time there should be very little sauce left.
Makes 12 servings.

Per serving: Calories 590 (68% from fat), Carbohydrates 4.7 g, Protein 42 g, Total Fat 43.5 g, Sodium 305 mg, Saturated Fat 15.9 g, Cholesterol 174 mg, Diabetic Exchanges: lean meat 6, fat 5

Bean Sprouts and Tofu

3 tablespoons sunflower oil
3 cloves garlic, minced
1 (10 ounce) piece firm tofu,
  cut in half then ⅛ inch slices
1 pound fresh bean sprouts
2 green onions, with some tops,
  cut into 1-inch pieces

1 tablespoon fish sauce
1 teaspoon salt
1 teaspoon granulated sugar

In a small bowl combine fish sauce, salt and sugar; set aside. Heat oil in a large skillet until hot; add garlic and sauté until lightly browned. Add tofu; stir until oil coats each piece. Add bean sprouts and seasoning sauce; stir until well mixed. Stir in green onion.
Serves 4.

Per serving: Calories 240 (57% from fat), Carbohydrates 12.1 g, Protein 15.8 g, Total Fat 16.7 g, Sodium 891 mg, Saturated Fat 2.2 g, Cholesterol 3 mg, Diabetic Exchanges: meat 2, veg 1, fat 1.5

EAST IS EAST, BUT DESSERT IS BEST

The ancient Asian capital in January was monochromatic at best. This gray-brown introduction did not bode well for my next 2-1/2 years. Although I had anticipated an exhilarating immersion into an ancient civilization, I felt instead that I was in purgatory. This culture shock was compounded by the fetid odors of partially-thawed cabbages neatly stacked on every other street corner. Butchered sheep carcasses were dumped on the sidewalk where toddlers were potty-trained and their elders spit. Even the grocery store reserved for the privileged offered only slimy onions and half defrosted meat of questionable pedigree. It seemed that the Asian cooking techniques I had mastered in San Francisco would be useless during this tour. It could only get better.

And it did. Spring came along with dust storms from the desert. Bird markets and free markets provided a source of fresh produce and exotic spices that camouflaged the real merchandise: antique porcelains and cricket cages. Cuisine of some description became a possibility.

My first culinary challenge was to entertain a half-dozen host country businessmen at a proper luncheon. I was not up to the scrutiny of pros and hastily eliminated Oriental fare from consideration. After all, I rationalized, the guests might enjoy a respite from sea slugs and beef tendon, and besides, we should be ambassadors of American cuisine as well as philosophy and government.

Thirteen years after the party, I cannot remember what I served for the main course though I'm sure I agonized over it and they politely consumed it. Dessert was another story.

Mao himself must have promoted the notion in his Little Red Book, "Life is uncertain; eat dessert first!" Our once reticent, somewhat dour guests descended on a buffet of sweet concoctions with uninhibited schoolboy exuberance. When they could eat no more, their exquisite almond eyes said "yes" to my suggestion that they carry home the remaining morsels of mousses and cakes. The moral of this story is obvious: dessert is the Ambassador of Good Will.

This recipe will leave your guests saying, "Mao!!"

Chocolate Angel Pie

For the crust, prepare a meringue for a 9-inch pie:

whites of 4 eggs

⅛ teaspoon cream of tartar (optional)

1 teaspoon vanilla extract

1 cup powdered or superfine sugar, sifted

Bring egg whites to room temperature; beat until foamy; add vanilla and cream of tartar. Continue beating whites while gradually adding sifted powdered or superfine sugar until the mixture forms stiff peaks. Do not overbeat. Spread the meringue in a pie plate or pipe it from a pastry bag for a decorative effect. Bake in preheated oven** until very dry but not browned. Turn off oven and let crust dry until oven is cool.

**editors recommend baking at 350° F. on the lowest rack for 15 minutes.

For the filling, use your favorite chocolate mousse or this one:

6 oz. semisweet chocolate morsels   4 eggs, separated

¼ cup water   1 teaspoon vanilla extract

½ cup light brown sugar   1 teaspoon Kahlua, cognac or other liqueur

Combine semisweet morsels, water and light brown sugar over low heat until chocolate has melted. Beat until smooth and let cool slightly. Beat egg yolks with vanilla and liqueur, and stir into chocolate. Beat egg whites just until stiff peaks form. Stir ⅓ of beaten egg whites into chocolate; then gently fold in remaining egg whites. Fill cooled baked meringue with the mousse and refrigerate.

Per serving (based on 8 servings per recipe): Calories 252 (37% from fat), Carbohydrates 35.4 g, Protein 6.4 g, Total Fat 10.7 g, Sodium 61.7 mg, Saturated Fat 5.1 g, Cholesterol 187 mg, Diabetic Exchanges: meat 1, fruit 2, fat 1.5

AMERICAN AS APPLE PIE

My family was given a recipe for mock ice cream many years ago by an old friend; simple enough for children to make, good enough to serve as dessert at a dinner party. The recipe has special meaning for me because I had the opportunity to share it with the local community in an Asian capital city during an international conference in 1978.

A representative from the British side asked if I would represent the United States during the week of the conference by participating in an international cooking event at a major department store. My task was to cook before a local audience and share with them two "all-American" recipes. The two recipes I chose were apple pie and the mock ice cream dessert.

With an interpreter close at hand, we talked about American and Asian cuisine and these two recipes in particular. I learned that the local people cook their apples first before they use them in cakes or pies.

Samples had to be made prior to the show so that people could taste. We did two shows so the recipes used in the first show were served at the second show. The audience seemed to enjoy both dishes. The mock ice cream had been a favorite for years in my family, and maybe it has become a favorite for another family somewhere in Asia!

Mock Ice Cream Dessert

1 (5 oz. or 6 servings size) box instant vanilla pudding

milk as required by directions on pudding box

12 to 16 oz. container whipped topping

1 (1 pound) box honey graham crackers

chocolate frosting (enough for one cake)

In a large bowl, whisk together pudding mix and milk; beat, according to package directions. Fold in whipped topping.

Empty box of graham crackers onto wax paper; divide into 3 equal portions. This step can be skipped if you use a box of three wrapped packages of crackers;

each pile or package will be used for one layer of the dessert.

In a 9x13-inch baking pan, spread one portion of graham crackers. On top of the graham crackers, add a layer of one-half of pudding mixture; add another layer of graham crackers; continue with a layer of the remaining half of pudding; add a final layer of the remaining crackers on top. Place pan in freezer for several hours or overnight.

When dessert is set, cover the top layer with chocolate frosting and return to freezer. To serve, remove from freezer and let sit about 20 minutes to soften slightly. Cut into square serving pieces.

Per serving (based on 24 servings per recipe): Calories 177 (37% from fat), Carbohydrates 26.4 g, Protein 2.3 g, Total Fat 7.5 g, Sodium 229 mg, Saturated Fat 4.1 g, Cholesterol 1 mg, Diabetic Exchanges: starch 1, fruit 0.5, fat 1

MANY MINUTE RICE

One of the best things about this vagabond life style of ours is all the people you get to know and the stories and recipes that you acquire. One of my very favorite stories came from a friend in East Asia who hated to give dinner parties. I was never quite sure why, because she was a wonderful hostess when she did and one of the best storytellers I ever knew.

Ann and I worked in the same office, so when the time came that she had to give a dinner party for her husband's office, I heard about it well in advance. It was a huge ordeal to her and one which she worked at for weeks. Every Monday morning she would tell me what she had prepared and frozen over the weekend for the forthcoming dinner party. Well, on the Monday morning after the dinner party, I could hardly wait to ask how it had gone. She said, "You know I never have a drink until everything is ready," and then she told me the following story.

Everything was ready, her husband was preparing the sates and the guests were seated in the living room. All that remained to be done was to cook the rice. So Ann put the rice on the stove, poured herself a drink, and went in to sit down with her guests. Twenty minutes or so later, she went to check the rice and found that she had put the rice on one burner but had turned on another! She quickly moved the rice and turned on the burner, poured herself another drink, and told her guests that dinner would be ready in 20 minutes. Well, 20 minutes later she discovered that she when she had moved the rice, she had turned on the wrong burner, again. The dinner was served later than planned, but no one seemed to mind.

Fried Rice

3 tablespoons vegetable oil
3 cloves garlic, diced
1 cup small shelled shrimp
   (optional)
1¼ cups diced pork
1 tiny hot red pepper, diced

1 onion, sliced
1½ cups frozen peas and carrots
4½ cups cold cooked rice
   (1½ cups uncooked)
2 tablespoons double-black soy sauce
   (no substitutes)

1 teaspoon MSG
  (monosodium glutamate)
½ teaspoon black pepper

1½ tablespoons fish sauce (no substitutes)
lemon juice, to taste
1 medium lemon, sliced into wedges

Heat oil in a wok; add garlic and sauté over high heat until lightly browned. Add shrimp, if desired; stir fry shrimp 3 to 4 minutes. Remove shrimp and set aside.

Add meat, red pepper, MSG, and black pepper to wok; cook until meat is no longer pink. Add onions and vegetables; continue cooking 2 to 3 minutes more. Stir in rice; reduce heat. Return shrimp, if using, to wok. Add soy sauce, fish sauce and lemon juice; stir until all rice is evenly coated. Serve with lemon wedges.

Makes 4 to 6 servings.

Variations: Chicken or beef may be used instead of pork.

Per serving (based on 6 servings per recipe): Calories 273 (32% from fat), Carbohydrates 33.2 g, Protein 13.2 g, Total Fat 9.9 g, Sodium 583 mg, Saturated Fat 2.1 g, Cholesterol 33 mg, Diabetic Exchanges: starch 1.5, meat 1, veg 2, fat 1

Cucumber and Onion Salad

1 medium cucumber,
  peeled and sliced thinly
1 medium red onion, sliced thinly
1 to 2 small hot red "bird's eye"
  or chili peppers, chopped
  (optional)

1 tablespoon fresh coriander leaves (cilantro)
½ cup white vinegar
2 teaspoons granulated sugar
¼ teaspoon salt

Combine cucumber, onion, peppers, and coriander leaves in a salad bowl; toss. In a small bowl mix together vinegar, sugar, and salt; pour over salad. Refrigerate until ready to serve.

Makes 4 servings.

Per serving: Calories 39 (3% from fat), Carbohydrates 8.6 g, Protein 0.9 g, Total Fat 0.1 g, Sodium 136 mg, Saturated Fat 0 g, Cholesterol 0 mg, Diabetic Exchanges: veg 1

PERFECT BIRTHDAY CAKE

In East Asia in the mid-50s, foreigners could afford to hire help in the home. My husband and I welcomed the efficient, pleasant, and very helpful pair we were fortunate to employ in our large Asian-style house. Getting our daughter to junior high, our almost four-year-old son to the local neighborhood nursery school, and our youngest boy, still a baby, out into the crisp October air were the main duties of the two. But the houseboy's special talent for cooking, including help with the preparations for any special meal or family occasion, became apparent within the first two months after our arrival.

I'd been planning our oldest son's fourth birthday for days. A tricycle and some unique local gifts, already purchased, were in a closet awaiting wrapping. Balloons and cone hats had been bought. The maid had extended an invitation to small neighborhood children for our nursery school son's birthday party. She'd put Baby in his crib for his nap and then left for the day. The houseboy was away on an errand. I had the house to myself. I'd prepare the birthday cake!

I remembered my mother's expertise at making and decorating birthday cakes for her many children. I collected the ingredients. But you haven't unpacked your recipe books yet, I'd tried to reason with myself. Oh, but I'd remember as I mixed. After lots of butter and sugar I started beating in the eggs. Was it eight or ten? Ten would be better. This would be no boxed cake-mix cake. I visualized my mother whipping in egg after egg, alternating with a bit of flour. I added a large tablespoon of vanilla. The mix was ready! Oh yes, preheat the oven. "Remember," she had always said, "bake a cake slowly." With the mix poured into a prepared tube pan and popped into a most erratic (but today I knew I could trust it) 200° oven, I determined that I'd not start the sugar-water and whipped egg whites frosting yet. I wanted to get the tricycle and other gifts wrapped. Uh-oh! Baby announced his naptime was over! I abandoned the gift wrapping. After dealing with 3-month-old Baby's usual helpfulness, I took him out into our serene garden for his daily viewing of the goldfish in the small pond, an outing he loved. Actually, I did too. It was a time when I could dream of becoming a student of oriental design and perhaps other arts of Asian culture.

I closed the screen separating us from the house and relaxed contentedly. I was brought back to reality some time later by the sound of the houseboy's return and his polite inquiry regarding the finished cake. Quickly handing Baby over to him, I rushed to the kitchen. The opened oven door revealed the flattest, saddest looking cake I'd ever seen. As was customary with local manners (at least in those days), the houseboy laughed heartily to cover, he reasoned, my great loss of face. He quickly tried to cheer me up by saying that it was OK, no problem. Then he added: "We have dessert to dinner tonight. You know, Madame, like pudding! I go early and buy cake at bakery." To purchase a cake at the bakery for tomorrow's birthday boy would suit me just fine.

Mother's Pound Cake

2 cups butter (preferably unsalted)
3 cups granulated sugar
8 medium eggs
4 cups white flour

¼ teaspoon baking powder
1 tablespoon vanilla extract
   (or the juice of one large lemon)
¼ teaspoon salt

Preheat oven to 200 ° F. Lightly butter and flour 10-inch tube pan or a 10-inch fluted bundt pan; set aside.

Sift flour together with baking powder onto sheet of wax paper. Set aside. Cream butter and sugar in a large mixing bowl. Add eggs, one at a time, each followed by ½ cup of flour, while beating the mixture continuously. When all the eggs and flour have been added, stir in vanilla or lemon juice. Pour batter into prepared pan. Bake in preheated oven, increasing oven temperature by 50° every 8 to 10 minutes, until temperature reaches 350° F, and cake has baked 30 minutes. Continue baking at 350° for another 1½ hours or until golden on top and a wooden pick inserted in the center comes out clean and dry.

Allow to cool in pan on wire rack for 10 minutes. Gently loosen sides of cake and invert onto cooling rack, then invert again to cool right-side-up. To serve, cut in thin slices.
Makes 30 servings.

Per serving: Calories 265 (46% from fat), Carbohydrates 32.9 g, Protein 3.3 g, Total Fat 13.6 g, Sodium 44 mg, Saturated Fat 8.1 g, Cholesterol 83 mg, Diabetic Exchanges: starch 1, fruit 1, fat 3

CHILLY CHILI

One snowy New Year's Eve in East Asia, we tripled the family's favorite chili recipe to take to a party. Along with the chili, I prepared a huge pot of saffron rice.

When it was time to go to the party, we carefully rested the large casserole dish containing the chili on the hood of the car while working open the icy door. Blocked by the door which made rescue impossible, we watched helplessly as the dish slid off the hood and smashed on the parking lot. So much for six pounds of stew meat. We took the rice.

Chili Colorado

5 tablespoons vegetable oil
2 pounds beef, cut into
   1-inch cubes
1½ cups chopped onion
1 teaspoon salt
¼ teaspoon pepper

1 teaspoon crushed red pepper (or to taste)
1 package taco seasoning mix
1 (10 oz.) can tomatoes and green chilies
1 to 2 (4 oz.) cans green chilies, to taste
1 cup water or beef broth

Heat oil in large skillet or Dutch oven; brown beef on all sides in hot oil; remove beef from skillet. Sauté onion in hot oil until soft and lightly browned;

remove from heat. Combine next four ingredients together in small saucepan; add tomatoes, green chilies, and water or broth; cook, stirring constantly, for 5 minutes. Return beef to skillet; add green chili mixture; cook, covered, over low heat for 1½ hours.

Remove cover and cook until thickened. Serve over saffron rice or with flour tortillas.

Makes 4 servings.

Per serving: Calories 606 (58% from fat), Carbohydrates 45.3 g, Protein 45.3 g, Total Fat 37.7 g, Sodium 2120 mg, Saturated Fat 10.3 g, Cholesterol 156 mg, Diabetic Exchanges: meat 6, veg 1, fat 1

East Asian Short Ribs

In the summer, we enjoyed staying home and preparing barbecued meat—it only has to be transported from the grill to the plate!

4 pounds beef short ribs
2 tablespoons peanut oil
2 tablespoons sesame seeds, toasted
2 green onions, chopped
freshly ground black pepper

3 tablespoons sugar
½ cup soy sauce
¼ cup water
2 cloves garlic, chopped

Cut through meat at ½-inch intervals lengthwise and crosswise on meaty side of ribs. Combine remaining ingredients and marinate ribs in mixture for several hours.

Grill over hot coals (or broil) for 8 to 10 minutes or until brown and crispy. Serves 4 or 5 . . . depending on how hungry they are!

Per serving (based on 5 servings per recipe): Calories 805 (56% from fat), Carbohydrates 8.1 g, Protein 77.7 g, Total Fat 49.3 g, Sodium 967 mg, Saturated Fat 19.8 g, Cholesterol 230 mg, Diabetic Exchanges: starch 0.5, meat 10

SOME HOLIDAYS DON'T TRANSLATE

We were living in a very modern, clean, efficient Asian city. Multistoried chrome and glass department stores, with crowded elevators, competed with one story "Mom and Pop" shops crammed to the ceiling with goods for sale. Anything and everything was available.

American-style holiday celebrations, with a local touch, were a commercial boon—especially at Christmas. Artificial snow, decorated palm trees, and skinny St. Nicks were everywhere. We were sure that Halloween, a great commercial success in the U.S. and a favorite at our house, would certainly already be well known.

When Halloween evening approached, the children were very excited and happily submitted to make-up and elaborate costumes. Monsters, skeletons, and gruesome ghosts were the preferred choices. Flashlights and bags for the goodies completed the outfits.

We proceeded along our quiet residential lane to the first house. No answer; apparently no one at home. Not discouraged, we walked on to the next house. A bright front-door light was a great encouragement, and we knocked politely.

The door was opened slowly by an ancient woman. She took one look at our group of goblins, screamed, and slammed the door. We were somewhat startled and were about to turn away when the door opened again. A large bucket of water was thrown on us accompanied by more screams. We fled.

Dirt Cake

(fun for birthday parties, garden parties, and, of course, Halloween)

1 large package (20 oz.) chocolate
   sandwich cookies
½ stick (¼ cup) margarine
1 (8 oz.) package cream cheese
¼ cup powdered sugar

2¼ cups milk
1 (6 servings size) package instant
   chocolate pudding
1 (12 oz.) container whipped topping

Using a rolling pin, crush cookies between two pieces of wax paper. In a small bowl, cream together margarine, cream cheese, and sugar; set aside. Mix milk and instant pudding. Combine with margarine-cream cheese mixture. Fold in whipped topping. In clean, small clay pots (for plants) or paper cups, layer first the crushed cookies and then the pudding mixture. Chill overnight. Top with gummy worms or other suitable garden friends.

Per serving (based on 12 servings per recipe): Calories 452 (52% from fat), Carbohydrates 49.4 g, Protein 5.6 g, Total Fat 26.1 g, Sodium 565 mg, Saturated Fat 14.2 g, Cholesterol 71 mg, Diabetic Exchanges: starch 2, fruit 1, fat 5

BLACK TIE ETIQUETTE?

While attending a black tie dinner at the U.S. Ambassador's residence, I noticed a large beetle crawl out from beneath the lettuce on my salad. I attempted to be "discreet" in removing the offending bug, but as I scooped it up with my spoon, the female guest to my left took notice. With a quick smile to her, I catapulted the bug over my left shoulder and quickly (and terminally) finished the matter with my heel. What could I say to the Ambassador's guest? "They don't teach you that in Miss Manners." We had a good laugh and the rest of the guests (and the Ambassador) were unaware.

Spinach Salad

1 pound fresh spinach
4 hard boiled eggs, chopped
1 red onion, sliced

½ pound bacon, cooked, drained,
   and crumbled
croutons

Dressing:
⅓ cup brown sugar
⅓ cup vinegar
3 tablespoons catsup

1 clove garlic, crushed
salt to taste

Prepare dressing: combine ingredients in a screw-top jar; mix well. Refrigerate 1 hour or longer to blend flavors. Shake well before serving.

Wash spinach; cut off tough stem ends; remove bruised or wilted leaves; dry. Tear large leaves into bite-size pieces; refrigerate.

When ready to serve, put in a salad bowl. Add eggs, onion, and bacon; toss lightly. Add dressing; toss. Top with croutons. Serve at once.

Beetle optional!

Per serving (based on 8 servings per recipe): Calories 260 (39% from fat), Carbohydrates 28.5 g, Protein 12.6 g, Total Fat 11.6 g, Sodium 779 mg, Saturated Fat 3.5 g, Cholesterol 115 mg, Diabetic Exchanges: starch 1, meat 1, fruit 0.5, fat 1.5

MORE IS BETTER

Each of our postings had a unique food story, but one of my favorites is the incident that reinforced the "more is better" theory. We were serving a "reward" tour in the Southern Pacific in the first and only house that I was allowed to find and select myself. It was in a beautiful setting, overlooking a huge expanse of reserve lands. We decided to show off our new home by hosting a dinner party for several of my husband's local counterparts who were on their way to assignments in Washington. Feeling a sense of power and abandon brought on by the fresh air and lovely surroundings, I decided that a buffet dinner for thirty-two was not out of the question. We worked all day, setting up tables of eight throughout the house, making sure everyone had a view from the windows overlooking the range. I chose a menu that was colorful and filling and a recipe for chicken cacciatore that could be easily multiplied.

To make a painfully long story short, two of the guests of honor arrived very late with their two small children in tow because they could not get a babysitter. Unfortunately, our two children chose to spend the night out with friends, probably in anticipation of the massive clean-up that would follow dinner for thirty-two. So, no in-house babysitters, either. These were new age parents who wanted their children to be seated with them at the table—so much for four tables of eight. By this time, the other guests were ravenous, and as the buffet line formed, it was apparent that my chicken recipe should have been multiplied by eight instead of just quadrupled. Guests were taking the three and four pieces of chicken and piling on the pasta. By the time guest number twenty-four was serving himself, we were down to a lonely stick of broccoli. I ran around to those of my fellow Americans who had already helped themselves, but had not, thank goodness, begun to eat, and literally regrouped the food. Some of my countrymen ended up with about a tablespoon of Cacciatore sauce on four strands of pasta—tasty, but not too filling. It was one of the longest nights of my life.

What follows is the recipe which has been quadrupled for your convenience. Because of my past experience, I never make less than sixteen servings. If you are not planning to feed the multitudes, it can be reduced to its original four servings. Buon Appetito, and remember, more is better.

Chicken Cacciatore

4 pounds boneless, skinless
   chicken breasts, halved
1 cup all-purpose flour
¼ cup olive oil
6 tablespoons chopped shallots
4 cloves garlic, minced
1 cup tomato paste
2 cups dry white wine

1½ teaspoons salt
1 teaspoon white pepper
3 cups chicken broth
2 bay leaves
½ teaspoon dried thyme
½ teaspoon dried marjoram
2 cups sliced mushrooms

Dredge chicken with flour. In a large Dutch oven, heat oil; sauté chicken, shallots, and garlic in hot oil until golden brown. Lower heat; add remaining ingredients; simmer, covered, for about 1½ hours or until chicken is tender. Remove bay leaves. Serve with your favorite pasta.

Per serving (based on 8 servings per recipe): Calories 483 (25% from fat), Carbohydrates 27 g, Protein 51.2 g, Total Fat 21.1 g, Sodium 1031 mg, Saturated Fat 2.7 g, Cholesterol 125 mg, Diabetic Exchanges: starch 1, lean meat 6, fruit 0.5, veg 1

ELEVENSES

When my husband was assigned to an English speaking post in the Southern Pacific, I was both delighted and apprehensive. It was a wonderful career change for him but I wasn't sure what it meant for me. Here I was, a middle-aged woman who had been a stay-at-home mom with seven children, about to find myself literally halfway around the world, quite separated from family. There was a lot to learn. At the first function we attended, I wore a red silk dress, thinking it would be quite appropriate, only to have a woman say: "My, a red dress. I've never before seen a red dress at this sort of occasion!" I looked around the room and, sure enough, there was everyone in their discreet black or white dresses. Ah, first lesson.

However, I was determined to jump in and take part in as many activities as possible. I joined the Woman's International Club, the American Embassy Association, and an association of American and host country men and women. The friendships I began with these groups continue to this day. They have enriched my life beyond measure.

Fortunately, it was an English speaking country—sort of. The first time my neighbor said to come for "elevenses," I had to ask what that meant. Of course, she meant coffee at eleven. It was wonderful. She served those lovely, melt-in-your-mouth scones spread with clotted cream and jam. I then knew one of the reasons the city was known as a 20-pound post; you were sure to leave 20 pounds heavier than when you arrived!

This neighbor gave me insights into local life and customs that I would never have found in books. Our hosts were very much their own people, and wanted to remain so, no matter how much they liked Americans.

As for our children, they managed quite well without Mom hovering over them. We did receive SOS calls at 5:00 A.M. on occasion; they never could get the different day and time zones sorted out. Three college sons benefited greatly from educational leave on their visits to us, and whined only a little about no snow at Christmas.

Scones

4 cups self-rising flour
pinch of cream of tartar
1 teaspoon salt

1 teaspoon powdered sugar
2 cups lukewarm whole milk (no substitutes)
2 tablespoons cream (no substitutes)

Preheat oven to 450° F.

The secret of these scones is to work quickly, handling the dough as little as possible.

Sift into a large bowl the flour, cream of tartar, salt; add the powdered sugar. Using a knife, mix in the milk and cream to make a soft dough.

Turn out onto a floured board, gently flatten, and cut into triangular shapes. Place on greased cookie sheet. Brush tops with milk. Bake in preheated oven about 15 minutes until golden brown. Allow to cool slightly, about 5 minutes. Serve warm. Scones are traditionally served with clotted cream and jam. Makes 10 servings.

Per serving: Calories 215 (12% from fat), Carbohydrates 40 g, Protein 6.6 g, Total Fat 2.9 g, Sodium 873 mg, Saturated Fat 1.5 g, Cholesterol 9 mg, Diabetic Exchanges: starch 2, fat 0.5

SALAD OR SWEETS?

Thirty years ago in Australia, we were warned that Australians didn't think of Jell-O or frozen-type salads as salad; they were "sweets" (dessert). Nevertheless, at an international potluck supper, we fearlessly introduced our frozen salad onto the salad table, then went and took our place in the food line. Moments later we saw our salad pass by in the hands of a young man (not Australian). My husband and I exchanged some humorous comments between us in lowered voices about the fate of our salad. Another young man, an Australian standing just in front of us, overheard and inquired about it, and we explained about our "frozen salad." He promptly went to the sweets table, rescued the salad, and headed back toward the salad table. The absconder who had originally moved our salad and was unknowingly standing near us noticed and asked him what he was doing, to which our rescuer replied that it was an American frozen salad, and he was putting it back on the salad table. The absconder blurted out, "Well, there's no accounting for some people's taste!"

Frozen Fruit Salad

1 (3 oz.) package gelatin
   (mixed fruit, strawberry,
   lemon or pineapple-grapefruit)
1 cup boiling water

⅓ cup mayonnaise
1 cup heavy cream, whipped
1 medium banana, thinly sliced
½ cup seeded and halved grapes

1 can (8.75 oz.) pineapple tidbits   ¼ cup diced maraschino cherries
   or crushed pineapple   ¼ cup chopped walnuts or pecans
¼ cup lemon juice

Dissolve gelatin in boiling water. Drain pineapple, reserving syrup. Measure syrup; if necessary, add enough water to make ½ cup. Stir into gelatin with lemon juice. Blend in mayonnaise. Chill several hours until very thick.

Fold whipped cream, fruit, and nuts into gelatin. Pour into a 9x5x3-inch loaf pan or shallow 7x10-inch pan. Freeze until firm—at least 3 to 4 hours.

To serve, slice or cut into squares and serve on lettuce.

Per serving (based on 8 servings per recipe): Calories 278 (65% from fat), Carbohydrates 22.8 g, Protein 2.8 g, Total Fat 20.6 g, Sodium 94 mg, Saturated Fat 8.1 g, Cholesterol 46 mg, Diabetic Exchanges: fruit 1.5, fat 4

ONE DAY IN NOVEMBER

One beautiful, sunny November day on the Asian subcontinent, the American Women's Club was planning a charity fashion show and tea around the swimming pool at the American Club inside the embassy compound. The executive board members were providing the food, each bringing two trays ready to put on the table. My fellow board member and neighbor had a family emergency in the U.S. and had to leave on a British Airways flight on the morning of the party. In spite of her worry and hurry, she prepared the promised food and brought two beautiful silver trays laden with delicious-looking canapés to my house on the way to the airport. I planned to take them and my two to the club later in the day.

Other people had different plans for the afternoon. Around noon, a bus load of students from the nearby university began arriving at the embassy compound to stage an angry response to a radio broadcast by Ayatollah Khomeini of Iran regarding a takeover of the sacred mosque in Mecca, supposedly by American terrorists. This angry response quickly escalated into storming the embassy building, knocking down the compound walls, and "borrowing" weapons from the local national guards who were protecting the compound. The Embassy was set on fire and the employees inside took refuge in the vault. Two Americans and a local national employee were shot dead as the students rampaged through the compound, burning cars and taking hostages from the apartments and the American Club. After spending time in a local jail and elsewhere for "protection," all were released.

My husband was at home for lunch when the events began. The Ambassador was also lunching at home. He went directly to the Foreign Ministry to protest the attack and to ask for protection of U.S. life and property. My husband went to the British Embassy, located across the street from the U.S. Embassy. He set up a phone line to Washington. The siege dragged on, since no assistance was forthcoming from the military or civilian authorities.

In the meantime, students were arriving at the International School six miles away to burn it. Some cars and windows were damaged and the children were terrified. That assault was aborted by a courageous local national colonel whose child was a student. He confronted the students and demanded that they kill him first and then proceed with their plans against the foreigners.

In mid-afternoon, my husband and a colleague from the British Embassy appeared at our door, looking for food for the Americans when they were rescued and brought to the British Embassy for safe haven. I immediately loaded four beautiful trays of food into the British officer's car. He looked at the food, then looked at me, and said, "My God! I thought we Brits knew how to show grace under pressure! While you watched smoke rising from your burning Embassy, were you preparing food for the survivors?" Not waiting to hear my logical explanation as to why I had the food on hand, he and my husband disappeared into the afternoon—my husband proud that I had risen to the occasion and the Brit amazed and admiring.

The Americans rescued themselves, and the next day all nonessential personnel were evacuated to the U.S. for seven months, and bilateral relations took another turn.

There are many true tales of heroism that came out of that afternoon.

Keema Seekh Kebab (Ground Beef/Lamb Kabob)

This has become one of our family's favorite recipes. It can be served as an appetizer or as part of a meal, even as a canapé (if we can stretch the meaning a bit).

1 pound ground beef or lamb	1 teaspoon finely grated fresh ginger
2 tablespoons besan	1 teaspoon salt
1 medium onion, finely chopped	1 teaspoon garam masala
1 clove garlic, crushed	¼ cup yogurt
2 tablespoons finely chopped	
fresh coriander leaves (or 1 tablespoon dried coriander)	

In a large bowl, combine meat with all ingredients, except yogurt. Mix thoroughly; knead until smooth. Form portions into sausage shapes around skewers. (I use bamboo sate sticks, available at Asian markets). Beat the yogurt slightly and coat the meat with it. Grill over hot coals or under preheated broiler until browned on all sides and cooked through. Serve as an appetizer with beer or cocktails. Or, serve with rice, pita bread, and vegetables.
Serves 8.

Per serving: Calories 180 (13% from fat), Carbohydrates 2.6 g, Protein 16 g, Fat 11.3 g, Sodium 57 mg, Saturated Fat 4.5 g, Cholesterol 58 mg, Diabetic Exchanges: meat 2.5

A LETTER HOME

During an assignment in Asia, living conditions for Americans became unsafe, and non-essential personnel and families were evacuated. A close friend and I were among those who departed post, leaving behind our husbands. This is a message forwarded to me from my husband, relaying his attempts at entertaining with my friend's husband, during the time they we were without us:

Dear "P.,

This is a message from your husband penned while comfortably seated in Jack's living room; the ceiling fan is gently stirring the air and the sun is caressing the front garden which is in full spring fashion. The colors of red, purple, white, orange, green, and yellow are right off the cover of House Beautiful. What is obviously missing are a couple of lovely memsahibs to grace the occasion!

In addition to the obvious decorative value of memsahibs in subcontinental gardens, Jack and I are finding that the organizational skills of the seasoned memsahib are hard to replace. You see, we are currently in the process of planning what will undoubtedly be the most decorous event here since the evacuation.

One evening, while engaged in global thought, Jack turned to me and said, "Let's have a few people in." This started a train of events that have firmly established the irreplaceable value of memsahibs.

I said, "Who?"

"Oh, you make out the list; some people you'd like," he cheerfully replied.

"How many?" I cooperatively rejoined.

He suggested, "Maybe 18—but invite 20 to 25 since many will refuse."

I eagerly put together the list of 30 and dutifully called them all since Jack cheerfully suggested, "Why don't you contact them," as he dashed out the door to the office.

So, I did, and was really surprised at how eager people were to come. I'd like to think it was the expectation of sharing the warmth and affection Jack and I were prepared to dispense—but I think everybody's bored silly and any social event is eagerly embraced!

At any rate, we now have to plan the menu. After considering the obvious possibilities of champagne punch and liver paté, we decided upon a help-yourself bar in the garden with peanuts!! Next comes the master meal. Such an occasion demands vichyssoise, beef Wellington, and lobster Newburgh, with spinach soufflé and wild rice pilaf—but we couldn't find the right vintage wine to serve with it; so, we settled on sliced salami, sliced corned beef, sliced undercut, potato salad, green beans, and green salad with lemon meringue pie and coffee—no wine or after dinner drinks!

This has been an exhausting experience. Tell Memsahib R. that you both could find meaningful work here!!!!

J."

The two party planners might have added some excitement to their menu with this easy-to-prepare salad.

Artichoke-Rice Salad

1 package chicken flavored
  rice mix or 2 cups rice,
  cooked in chicken broth
4 thinly sliced scallions
½ green pepper, seeded
  and chopped

12 sliced pimento-stuffed olives
2 (6 oz.) jars marinated artichoke hearts
¼ teaspoon curry powder
⅓ cup mayonnaise

Cook the rice as directed on the package, omitting the butter. Cool rice in a large bowl. Add the scallions, green pepper, and olives. Drain artichoke hearts, reserving marinade. Cut the artichoke hearts in half; add to the rice salad.

Prepare dressing: in a small bowl combine artichoke marinade with the curry powder and mayonnaise; mix well.

Pour dressing over rice salad and toss. Chill. Adjust curry powder to taste.

Variation: Add cooked shrimp for a more substantial salad.

Per serving (based on 8 servings per basic recipe): Calories 212 (51% from fat), Carbohydrates 22.3 g, Protein 4.6 g, Total Fat 12.4 g, Sodium 599 mg, Saturated Fat 1.9 g, Cholesterol 5 mg, Diabetic Exchanges: starch 1, veg 1, fat 2

THE EQUALIZER

Michael, our cook, was not native to our host country. As a Catholic, he was able to cook pork and other foods which would have been taboo to most cooks in a Muslim setting. This versatility, combined with his experience as a chef, made him a real treasure, and I was happy to hire him when we arrived at post. Skilled in dishes of the subcontinent, he was also adept at western cuisine, and our dinner table developed a reputation for excellence, which was a great help in entertaining.

Michael, had only two flaws, as I saw them. One, to which I soon became accustomed, was his slight padding of the accounts for his market shopping. I learned to understand and accept this as his personal version of "baksheesh," a routine part of life on the Subcontinent.

The other was a bit more difficult to live with—his temperament. Whenever I said anything which offended him (and who could anticipate what and when that might be?) he would retaliate by adding extra chili to the curry. Normally, his curries were spectacular, but heaven help us on one of his "get-even" days. In time, we did learn to live with each other, but rest assured that all the concessions were made on my side.

One memorable incident occurred when I began to notice that the walls in the kitchen, where Michael cooked on a kerosene stove, were terribly greasy and blackened. I mentioned this to him and requested him to clean them when he had some time. Highly offended, he immediately reminded me that, "Memsahib, I cook. I not sweeper!"

"Very well," I replied, "then call the bearer's son. He is young and strong." Now I was reminded that the bearer's son was a Muslim and could not touch any pork residue, and besides, he, too, was not a sweeper.

Finally, determined to get the walls clean, I gathered a ladder, a mop, and a bucket of suds. Then, assisted by our 14-year-old and 11-year-old sons, I washed the kitchen walls. It was wonderful fun and so gratifying to see the grime come off and the clean, white paint emerge. The household help stood and watched in amazement. They could not believe that the sahibs would stoop to physical labor. I tried to explain that in my country all honest work is good in the eyes of God and each other. I seriously doubt, though, that my lesson in democracy penetrated.

The following is Michael's basic curry recipe. Individual cooks may vary some of the spices, according to their own taste.

Michael's Chicken Curry

1 large onion, minced
2 large cloves garlic, minced
2½ to 3½ pounds chicken,
   cut into serving pieces
2 oz. ghee*, or 2 oz. margarine,
   melted
3 teaspoons ground coriander
2 teaspoons ground cardamom

1 teaspoon ground cloves
1 teaspoon ground ginger
1 teaspoon ground cumin
1 teaspoon mustard seed
1 teaspoon ground chilies
   (or less according to taste)
pinch of salt

Sauté onion and garlic in ghee or margarine in a large, deep skillet or kettle. Combine spices and salt; add to skillet. Sauté spice mixture over low heat for 3 or 4 minutes. This step, known as "bhoon" is very important. Stir frequently to prevent sticking. Add the chicken pieces; mix well. Cook slowly, covered, about 1 hour, until chicken is tender. Check frequently, adding water if necessary, and draining accumulated fat. Serve chicken and sauce, accompanied by a rice pilaf.

Variation: Add 1 or 2 tomatoes for a different flavor.
Substitution: Use lamb, pork, or shrimp in place of the chicken.

*Ghee is clarified butter. If unavailable, melt butter over low heat, then remove from heat and let sit 5 minutes until contents separate. Skim off fat; strain remaining liquid into a cup and use in recipe, or substitute margarine.

Per serving (based on 8 servings per recipe): Calories 242 (41% from fat), Carbohydrates 2.9 g, Protein 32.3 g, Total Fat 10.7 g, Sodium 71 mg, Saturated Fat 5.4 g, Cholesterol 102 mg, Diabetic Exchanges: lean meat 4

UNDER EVENING SKIES

Vultures are among the many fascinating sights encountered on the Asian subcontinent. Whether soaring gracefully high in the bright blue sky or sitting menacingly on
the domed Lodi tombs watching the daily activities taking place in the garden, they are an
ever present reminder of the circle of life. They are always vigilant to life and death as they
observe those taking a brisk early morning constitutional, sitting quietly in meditation, or
enjoying a twilight stroll. They follow the constant movement, watching for a slowing
down which might indicate the possibility of a meal. The plodding cow lawnmower
moving slowly back and forth over the rolling lawns of the garden might also be a meal in
the making. Sometimes the vultures gather in groups on the broad berms, attacking their
own...the frail, the infirm, the aged. Somehow it was a long time before I made the
association between these creatures and the bones we occasionally found in the driveway.

The Director was making a visit to the area, and our garden was to be the setting for a
dinner for his entourage to meet the community. The evening was lovely and some of our
guests were amazed to see the flight of huge fruitbats as they left the trees on Shah Jahan
Road. Dusk became night, the moon was high, and, not unexpectedly, all the guests were
present with the exception of the Director, my husband, and a few of the official group.
Dinners are customarily late there so none of the guests was surprised that we did not sit
down until about 10 P.M. Those at my table did not seem to notice that I excused myself
almost immediately and did not return for an hour. They didn't realize that just as I sat
down a vulture flew over and dropped his evening meal on me. At last I understood the
bones in the driveway.

The following recipes are from my cookery teacher at the time.

Potatoes with Cauliflower

2 to 3 tablespoons vegetable oil
1 teaspoon cumin seeds
1 whole brown cardamom*
2 red chili peppers
½ teaspoon ground turmeric
2 medium potatoes, peeled
   and quartered

½ pound cauliflower, cut into pieces
⅓ inch length fresh ginger, peeled
   and thinly sliced
2 teaspoons salt
generous pinch of black pepper
fresh coriander for garnish

In a large skillet, heat oil. In a small bowl grind together cumin seeds,
cardamom, and chili peppers, to form a paste. Add paste to hot oil; add turmeric.
Sauté for 3 to 4 minutes, stirring constantly. Add potatoes, cauliflower, ginger,
and salt. Cook for 5 minutes over medium heat, stirring occasionally. Cover;
reduce heat to low; simmer 5 to 15 minutes or until vegetables are tender and dry.
Sprinkle with water, if necessary, to keep vegetables from sticking to skillet.
Remove from heat. Season with black pepper. Garnish with coriander leaves.

Per serving (based on 4 servings per recipe): Calories 161 (47% from fat), Carbohydrates 19.4 g, Protein 10 g, Total
   Fat 8.9 g, Sodium 1089 mg, Saturated Fat 1.2 g, Cholesterol 0 mg, Diabetic Exchanges: starch 1, veg 1, fat 2

Shah Jahani Pilau

(a multilayered dish of rice, chicken, cream, and yogurt)

I. Prepare the rice:

2 cups Basmati or
   other long grain rice
3 cups chicken broth
1 medium onion, chopped
6 to 7 whole green cardamom*

1-inch stick cinnamon
4 whole cloves
3 tablespoons vegetable oil
2 teaspoons salt

Rinse rice. Soak in cold water for 5 minutes; drain. Heat oil in a large saucepan; sauté onions in hot oil until soft. Add drained rice, spices, and broth. Cover, cook over medium heat about 15 minutes. Transfer rice mixture to large platter; spread evenly on platter to cool.

2. Prepare the chicken:

1½ to 2 pounds skinless, boneless chicken breasts
4 to 5 tablespoons vegetable oil
2 medium onions, sliced into thin rings
1 inch length fresh ginger, peeled and shredded
6 to 8 cloves garlic, chopped
¼ teaspoon ground coriander
¼ teaspoon ground cloves
½ teaspoon ground cardamom
1 teaspoon salt
pinch of saffron, soaked in 1 tablespoon hot water
1½ cups chicken broth

Cut chicken into bite-size pieces; set aside. In a large skillet heat oil. Sauté onion rings in hot oil until soft but not browned. Add chicken pieces, ginger, garlic, coriander, cloves, cardamom, and salt. Cook covered over medium heat, sprinkling occasionally with water until chicken is a uniform golden brown. Add chicken broth. Lower heat; cook slowly until broth is evaporated and chicken is tender. Sprinkle with saffron water.

3. Assemble the pilau:

5 oz. cream
¾ cup plain yogurt

blanched almonds for garnish (optional)

Preheat oven to 350° F.
Lightly grease large ovenproof mixing bowl. Arrange in layers in bowl as follows:

layer 1 - ½ of the yogurt

layer 2 - ¼ of the rice mixture

layer 3 - ½ of the cooked chicken

layer 4 - ¼ of the rice mixture

layer 5 - ½ of the cream

layer 6 - ¼ of the rice mixture

layer 7 - remaining cooked chicken

layer 8 - remaining yogurt

layer 9 - remaining rice mixture

layer 10 - remaining cream

Set mixing bowl in a pan of hot water in preheated oven for 20 minutes until all ingredients are thoroughly heated through. To serve, run a knife around the edge of the rice to loosen it from bowl; turn out onto serving platter. Garnish with blanched almonds.

Per serving (based on 8 servings per recipe): Calories 451 (55% from fat), Carbohydrates 22.4 g, Protein 28.1 g, Total Fat 27.8 g, Sodium 1313 mg, Saturated Fat 7.7 g, Cholesterol 82 mg, Diabetic Exchanges: starch 1, meat 2, veg 0.5, fat 4.5

*whole cardamom, brown or green, can be found in markets specializing in Asian or Middle Eastern food. If unavailable, substitute ¼ teaspoon ground cardamom for 1 whole cardamom; adjust to taste.

PRESIDENTIAL SUITE

When we were living in Asia from 1958 to 1962, our daughter's room doubled as our guest room. Furnished with twin beds, it was easily converted by removing the toys and wardrobe of a small girl and adding suitable adult conveniences. Kathy was quite accustomed to this system and was perfectly happy to share quarters with one of her older brothers whenever her room was given over to guests. Since we had frequent houseguests coming from Washington and elsewhere to confer with her daddy, she had become accustomed to accepting the change of quarters with equanimity.

In December 1959, the entire American community at post was very excited. President Dwight Eisenhower was coming on an official visit, and the Embassy personnel, including the CIA station, would be extremely busy. Hearing the impending visit discussed at the family dinner table, Kathy asked what was for her a very natural question:

"Oh. And is the President going to sleep in my room?"

Perhaps if the President had stayed in her room, Kathy might have left him a plate of cookies to snack on.

Fail-Safe Chocolate Chip Cookies

2¼ cups unsifted all-purpose flour
1 teaspoon salt
1 teaspoon baking soda
¾ cup butter, melted and
    cooled until just warm
    (this part is critical)
1 cup brown sugar, firmly packed

½ cup granulated sugar
1 large egg
1 egg yolk
2 teaspoons vanilla extract
1 cup chocolate chips or chunks of broken
    dark chocolate candy bars

Adjust oven racks to the two middle positions. Preheat oven to 350° F.

Lightly grease cookie sheets or line with parchment. Set aside. Combine flour, salt, and baking soda in a large bowl. In a small bowl, blend thoroughly melted warm butter and sugars; add egg, yolk and vanilla. Add mixture to dry ingredients; mix until just combined; stir in chips.

Drop batter from a teaspoon onto prepared cookie sheets; space cookies about 2 inches from edges and from each other. Bake 15 minutes until golden. Remove sheets from oven and cool for 1 or 2 minutes; with a spatula remove cookies from cookie sheets to wire racks and let cool completely. Store in airtight container. Makes 2 to 3 dozen cookies.

Variation: Dough can be frozen and then sliced and baked.

Per serving (based on 3 dozen cookies per recipe): Calories 115 (43% from fat), Carbohydrates 15.7 g, Protein 1.3 g, Total Fat 5.6 g, Sodium 137 mg, Saturated Fat 3.3 g, Cholesterol 22 mg, Diabetic Exchanges: starch 0.5, fruit 0.5, fat 1

AS YOU WISH, MADAME

People from all foreign service agencies who have served in places where servants are affordable usually have one or more memorable stories involving those servants, and these stories are often shared and swapped with other foreign service people. The following story is one such shared account. It was not experienced directly by the writer. It was told to the writer on the occasion of a sit-down dinner in the writer's home at the time in Southern Asia. In the dining room one of the guests pointed out the "butler's window" or "pass-through," i.e., one of those 14x20-inch openings that connect the kitchen with the dining room. This butler's window prompted the guest to relate her servant story.

The storyteller described a foreign assignment of a few years before and the standard two months of settling in—temporary quarters for one month, anxieties about the arrival of household effects and the car, selection and hiring of servants and meeting new friends and work-related contacts. After these difficult two months passed, she was ready to host her first social entertainment occasion, a sit-down dinner for 12. She devoted a couple of days to coming up with the menus and instructing the newly hired servants on procedures that would be required for this dinner. One of her last such instructions, shortly before the guests arrived, was to the head servant and waiter for this dinner, and that instruction was that all courses—absolutely everything—was to come through the butler's window. The head servant's reply was a polite, "As you wish Madame."

The guests arrived and the usual first one and one-half hours were devoted to cocktails, conversation, and finger food. As planned, "dinner is served" was announced at 2100 hours, and 12 people made their way to the dining room, which was beautifully arranged. The first course was soup. The hostess executed a signal for the first course by ringing a chic little silver bell. The butler's window opened and a soup tureen came through, followed by an arm. The arm was followed by a foot and a leg. Then came the head servant's head and upper torso, the other foot and leg and arm. In a very athletic maneuver, he was able to bring the first course and himself through a rather small space— and, without spilling a drop of the soup. Ten awestruck guests broke into a spontaneous and sustained applause. The remaining courses came through the butler's window, but in the standard and prescribed manner. The hostess concluded this story by saying that the experience was obviously the result of a slight language problem, plus a very literal interpretation.

Catch/Grab Soup

Thinking about the soup in this story brought to mind a sort of recipe for soup from my experience of studying Russian language for one year at the Agency's language school. One particular lesson, in the lesson book, dealt with the Russian peasant and his circumstances and surroundings. In winter, which is a rather long and cold period, a Russian peasant house has a large pot of soup simmering on a wood burning stove in the kitchen day and night. It is a sort of perpetual, ever changing soup-of-the-day. When the children come home from school, they are given a bowl as a snack to warm them. The soup is also served at virtually every meal.

Ingredients:
Water
Bones from chicken, duck, turkey, beef, pork, or wild game and some of the meat
Potatoes, cabbage, beans, beets, carrots, onions or whatever other vegetables
    were available that day
Herbs, spices and seasoning to taste

The ingredients constantly changed, depending on what was around, but the flavor and taste remained rather consistent. A simple method of making soup.

My wife and I have served this Russian peasant soup at dinners overseas many times and, of course, told the story about the soup course coming through the butler's window on each occasion.

Dietitian's note: Because ingredients and proportions vary, nutritional values have not been determined.

WHICH COOK RULES THE KITCHEN?

When our Philippine friend and his wife were preparing to leave our mutual overseas post for Los Angeles, where he would be the consul general, we planned a special farewell party for them— "special" because I planned to make lasagne, since he really enjoyed my lasagne. Making lasagne on the subcontinent was a challenge. Making the sauce and filling from scratch was no big deal as long as the commissary had the ingredients. The local market could not help me. Creating the noodles from flour and water without benefit of a pasta machine was another story. The first hurdle was to convince my excellent cook that I, Memsahib, was going to make six pans of lasagne for our 24 guests. He insisted he could do it. No doubt he could, but I stubbornly insisted that I would. I had not yet outgrown my Southern upbringing which urged me to have a personal hand in a meal meant to honor friends.

The second challenge was creating this culinary masterpiece in a kitchen without air-conditioning when it was at least 97° F. outside. Our house was comfortably air-conditioned, but the Embassy assumed that only servants used to the heat worked in kitchens, so A.C. was not necessary—and besides, "They don't like the artificial cold air."

Undaunted by cook and climate, I spent six hours creating my famous lasagna. As I stowed the six pans in the fridge, I asked the cook to have them ready, along with the rest of the meal, on the table at 8 o'clock.

Guests arrived at 7 o'clock and we had cocktails in our garden. We enjoyed our drinks and the fabulous view of the hills which began literally across the street. These beautiful foothills flowed onward and upward ending many miles away—a perfect setting for a farewell party.

A few minutes before eight it was time to inspect the table before inviting the guests in to dinner. As usual, the table was perfect: beautiful flowers, bright candles, sparkling silver and crystal, appetizing food. I wondered if the bearer had remembered to put pads under the hot pans to protect the table, but naturally I didn't want to embarrass him by asking, implying that he didn't know his job. So I checked it out myself. To this day I don't know if the pads were there or not, but hot pads were not necessary. My expert cook had obeyed my orders perfectly and put the lasagne on the table for the 8 o'clock dinner. Of course, because Memsahib had not specifically said to cook them first at 350° F. for 45 minutes, he hadn't.

The final challenge of the evening was to enter the kitchen and politely ask the cook to please bake the lasagne and then put it on the table. I silently accepted the blame for the late dinner. Indeed, I deserved the blame. I had violated the unwritten code between cook and mistress of the house. I never again prepared food except on the cook's day off. He had trained his Memsahib well!

By the way, the party was a success. By the time we ate, everyone was so happy with the extra round of drinks that the dinner could have been cold or uncooked and no one would have noticed!

The Late Lasagne

1 pound lasagne noodles (you don't have to make your own), cooked

For cheese filling:

2 eggs, well beaten (you can use ½ cup liquid egg substitute if desired)

8 oz. cottage cheese (nonfat or low-fat is best)

black pepper to taste

pinch of dried basil leaves

2 cups shredded mozzarella cheese

For meat sauce:

1 pound ground beef*

1 onion, finely diced

1 green or red pepper, diced

minced garlic, to taste

10 fresh tomatoes, peeled and diced, or 1 (28 oz.) can tomatoes, cut up

1 (15 oz.) can tomato sauce

1½ tablespoons dried oregano

1 teaspoon dried basil

1½ teaspoons black pepper, or to taste

grated Parmesan cheese

1. Preheat oven to 350° F.
2. Prepare meat sauce: In a large skillet or kettle stir together meat, onion, garlic and diced pepper; cook over medium heat for about 10 minutes, or until meat loses its pink color. Add remaining ingredients and simmer over low heat for 30 minutes until flavors are blended. Note that this sauce does not need oil or salt.
3. Prepare cheese filling by mixing together all ingredients in a large bowl.
4. In a 9x13-inch baking dish, spread a thin layer of sauce, followed by a layer of cooked noodles, and a layer of half the cheese filling. Repeat with another layer of sauce, noodles, and cheese, topped with an additional layer of sauce. Sprinkle grated Parmesan cheese on top. Bake in preheated oven for 45 to 60 minutes until thoroughly cooked and bubbling. Let sit for 10 minutes before cutting and serving.

This recipe makes a large lasagne to serve 4 generously or up to 6.

*I have used ground water buffalo, and, once, camel, but my family prefers ground beef.

Per serving (based on 6 servings per recipe): Calories 442 (56% from fat), Carbohydrates 15.2 g, Protein 33.8 g, Total Fat 27.6 g, Sodium 1002 mg, Saturated Fat 12.8 g, Cholesterol 163 mg, Diabetic Exchanges: meat 4.5, veg 2, fat 1

ONE MAN'S TRASH IS ANOTHER MAN'S TREASURE

When we were overseas we would often take the opportunity to travel to interesting places we otherwise might not have been able to visit. One such trip took us through the renowned Khyber Pass to Peshawar in Pakistan. We had packed a picnic lunch before starting out that day because we knew that nowhere along the way would we find fast food restaurants (indeed any restaurants!) where we could stop to eat. We had decided we wanted to eat at a spot where we would be away from any semblance of civilization and finally chose a desolate boulder-strewn strip of road without a town or human in sight. We stopped the van and began unloading our picnic lunch, but within seconds we were surrounded by about 30 Afghans, adults and children alike. They sat at the perimeter around us, watching each mouthful of food we ate and tittering among themselves.

When we finished our awkwardly eaten lunch, we began to collect the paper plates, plastic cups and utensils, and empty soda cans to dispose of our trash. At that point, however, the children came shyly forward and asked for our trash. We distributed it among them and watched as adults and children delighted in their new "treasures."

As we left, we mused at how our audience had seemed to materialize from nowhere and, once again, we searched for signs of houses or tents but still could find none. This may be one of the reasons why the British and Soviets were so unsuccessful in their respective attempts to take over Afghanistan!

Best Ever Banana Bread
(simple to make and easy to take along on a picnic)

3 to 4 ripe medium bananas,
  broken in pieces
2 eggs, beaten
1 cup granulated sugar

1 teaspoon salt
2 cups all-purpose flour
1 teaspoon baking soda
½ cup vegetable oil

Preheat oven to 350° F. Line a loaf pan with aluminum foil. In mixer or blender, mix together first 6 ingredients. Slowly add oil; mix well. Pour dough into foil-lined pan. Bake in preheated oven for about 1 hour 10 minutes until golden brown, checking after 1 hour. Cool before slicing.

Variation: Pour dough into muffin cups, ⅔ full each. Bake 30 minutes. Makes 12 muffins. Substitutions: ½ cup liquid egg substitute can be used instead of eggs to lower cholesterol; ½ cup applesauce can be used instead of vegetable oil to lower calories and fat. Bread made with applesauce should be stored in the refrigerator.

Per serving (based on 24 servings per basic recipe): Calories 131 (34% from fat), Carbohydrates 20.2 g, Protein 1.7 g, Total Fat 5.1 g, Sodium 146 mg, Saturated Fat 0.6 g, Cholesterol 16 mg, Diabetic Exchanges: starch 0.5, fruit 1, fat 1

MAZEL TOV, MEMSAHIB!

Our second post was on the Asian subcontinent. Two weeks after we arrived I became pregnant.

My last pregnancy had been in Africa, and no ultra-sound facilities were available there. My husband, a regional medical officer, had followed me through the pregnancy until I had been sent on medical evacuation orders to the U.S. at 34 weeks' gestation because that post was not considered a safe place to have a baby.

This time, the American Embassy had a four-bed hospital, and pregnant Federal employees or spouses delivered there. And at 20 weeks, midway through the pregnancy, I went to a small local lab for an ultra-sound.

Because I had never had an ultra-sound before, it never occurred to me that the technicians might discern the sex of the baby, nor did I think about whether I wanted to know before the baby was born. So I was shocked when the technician gleefully said, "Yes, there's the testes!" "You mean it's a boy?" I said with disappointment. I wanted another little girl to round out our family: two boys and two girls. Of course, to the technician, it was wonderful news, because in that culture, sons are desired, not daughters.

All right, so if we were going to have a son, then we had to plan the brit milah (covenant of circumcision), also known as the bris. According to Jewish law, the bris occurs on the eighth day of life. The day begins at sunset in the Jewish calendar, so if a baby is born before sundown on Monday, the bris is held the following Monday during the day. If a baby is born after sundown on Monday, the bris is held during the day on Tuesday.

The baby was due February 28, but by early February, I was sick and tired of being pregnant. We decided to induce labor and get it over with because all physical signs indicated that I was ready to deliver. We wanted to have as many of our friends as possible at the bris, so I went into the hospital on Monday, February 9, 1987, and hoped the baby would be born before sundown. Then the bris would be on the following Monday, President's Day.

It worked! Joel was born at 3:15 P.M.

That week our cook Lena was busy making challah, cake, and chickpea salad for the bris. Chickpeas (nahit, or arbis) are a traditional food to welcome a newborn baby boy. The chickpea salad recipe is one I still use today.

The bris was quite an affair. It was held on the roof of our house near the Embassy. About 75 people from the Embassy attended, including the Ambassador and his wife. The head of the local Jewish community brought the special Elijah's chair from the small synagogue in town. He said it was the first bris in the city in 25 years. In Jewish law, the father is obligated to circumcise his son, but because most fathers are not capable of this, a mohel, or ritual circumciser, is hired to act as his agent. In our case, my physician husband was qualified to perform this mitzvah (commandment). And it was a lot cheaper than flying in the mohel from another city!

Chickpea Salad

Use your judgment as to quantity of ingredients:

cooked chickpeas   mayonnaise
sliced pimento-stuffed   pepper
   green olives

Combine chickpeas and olives. Use enough mayonnaise to bind. Season with pepper.

Dietitian's note: Because ingredient proportions vary according to taste, nutritional values have not been determined.

PATRIOTIC POTATOES

Ahmed came to us fresh from his village in 1962. His English was sufficient, but he had a sponsor who described his ability as a cook as outstanding. It was our first tour and we were still gullible. We hired Ahmed. Outstanding was, to say the least, an overstatement. Nevertheless, Ahmed was a quick learner and after the initial month with its culinary trials and errors, we decided to keep him on. He was delighted and strove mightily to please us.

Ahmed realized his moment of greatest achievement when, on July 4th, he placed on the table a bowl of mashed potatoes—in red, white, and blue stripes! How could we fault him? He beamed as we applauded his handiwork.

These potato recipes may not be as colorful, but they would be welcome at any holiday table.

Party Potatoes

10 medium potatoes   1 teaspoon baking powder
1 (8 oz.) package cream cheese   chives (optional)
1 cup sour cream or crème fraiche   pats of butter, to taste
salt and pepper, to taste   paprika, to taste
garlic salt, to taste

Preheat oven to 350° F.

In a large covered pot, cook potatoes in boiling water to cover, 20 to 40 minutes, until tender; drain well; peel. Transfer potatoes to a large bowl; mash potatoes with a masher or a fork; set aside. Using an electric or hand mixer in a large bowl, beat cream cheese and sour cream together until blended. Gradually add hot potatoes, beating constantly until light and fluffy (if mixture is too stiff, add a little milk). Season to taste with salt, pepper, and garlic salt. Stir in baking powder. Mix in chives, if desired. Spoon potatoes into an 8-cup casserole. Dot with butter, sprinkle with paprika. Bake in preheated oven 30 minutes until browned.

May be refrigerated before baking for up to 2 days. Bake in 350° F. oven about 1 hour before serving.

Makes 8 to 10 servings.

Per serving (based on 10 servings per recipe): Calories 292 (53% from fat), Carbohydrates 30 g, Protein 5.3 g, Total Fat 17.1 g, Sodium 394 mg, Saturated Fat 10.9 g, Cholesterol 48 mg, Diabetic Exchanges: starch 2, fat 3

Oven-Roasted Potato Skins
(serve as an appetizer or side dish)

5 large Russet potatoes (2½ to 3 pounds)
⅓ to ½ cup butter, melted
salt (optional)

Preheat oven to 400° F.

Scrub potatoes and pierce each with a fork. Place directly on oven rack. Bake, uncovered, in preheated oven about 1 hour until potatoes are soft enough to squeeze. Remove from oven and let cool.

Preheat oven to 500° F.

Cut each cooled potato in half lengthwise; cut each half in half crosswise. Scoop flesh from skins with a spoon, leaving ⅛-inch shell. (Discard scooped out flesh or use for mashed potatoes or potato pancakes.) At this point, skins can be held at room temperature for up to 6 hours; then continue as follows.

Brush potato skins inside and out with melted butter. Arrange, cut side up and side by side, on a baking sheet. Bake, uncovered, in preheated 500° F. oven about 12 minutes until crisp. Serve hot, and salted, if desired.

To make one day ahead: after baking, let shells cool, then cover and refrigerate until next day. To reheat, arrange on baking sheet and bake, uncovered, in a 400° F. oven until crisp (about 8 minutes), then serve as above.

Per serving (based on 5 servings per recipe): Calories 275 (48% from fat), Carbohydrates 33.7 g, Protein 3.2 g, Total Fat 14.9 g, Sodium 584 mg, Saturated Fat 9.2 g, Cholesterol 40 mg, Diabetic Exchanges: starch 2, fat 3

HAPPY BIRTHDAY

My husband had come from a fairly austere family and he had never had a birthday party, so one year I decided to give a large birthday party for him. At the time we were living in an underdeveloped country of mountains and deserts in Southwest Asia.

Our guests colored on paper tablecloths with crayons and played a variation of "Pin the Tail on the Donkey." The culmination of the party, however, was the giving of presents. In a country where it is difficult to obtain suitable gifts, our guests had come up with a remarkable selection of items. Among a variety of other nonsense, my husband received a canary, a large ram with enormous horns (a gift from the Seabees, whose mascot is a ram), the largest donkey a good friend could find, and, from the Marine Guards, a very large and

UGLY camel! Much fun was had by all as our guests attempted to wrestle the ram and ride the donkey and the camel.

Within a week, however, we already felt we had to do something with the camel, as he was constantly trying to eat the snow-white hair off the heads of our four children. We gave him back to the Marines, suggesting they sell him and put the proceeds into the Marine Corps Ball fund.

We ultimately traded in the donkey for a bicycle for our houseboy. The ram met an untimely demise, unfortunately, one day while we were out, when our German Shepherd decided he had put up with all the abusive butting he intended to take. The canary, however, continued to entertain us with his lovely song throughout the rest of our assignment, and we passed him on to a new family when it was time for us to leave.

Soda Fountain Dessert

Scoop out or cut into small cubes: vanilla, chocolate, and strawberry ice cream. Put in large individual bowls and keep well frozen until serving time.

Along with ice cream, set out on buffet table, small bowls with the following choices of toppings:

sliced bananas

Maraschino cherries

shredded coconut

chopped nuts

crushed pineapple, well drained

sprinkles or chocolate candy pieces

chocolate, caramel, butterscotch, or
    other favorite topping

whipped cream or whipped topping

Invite guests to create their own banana splits or sundaes.

Dietitian's note: Because ingredient proportions vary according to taste, nutritional values have not been determined.

HOME SWEET HOME

This recipe is near and dear to my heart. I was a young bride, never having lived THAT far from home or family, now finding myself living in the hinterlands of Southeast Asia, and certainly far from anywhere that would have caramel-covered popcorn. When the boss's wife sent a homemade batch up to our site, the reality hit: if I wanted to have many of the things I had mistakenly taken for granted to be available in the local grocery store, I had better have a recipe that I could put together from scratch.

Caramel Popcorn

12 quarts popped popcorn, unsalted

1 cup margarine

2 cups brown sugar

½ cup light corn syrup

1 teaspoon salt

¼ to ½ cup molasses or honey

½ teaspoon baking soda

2 teaspoons vanilla extract

2 cups unsalted peanuts (optional)

Preheat oven to 250° F.

Mix margarine, brown sugar, corn syrup, salt and molasses (or honey) in a large saucepan over medium-high heat; boil for 5 minutes. Add baking soda and vanilla; mix well. Pour mixture over popcorn to which peanuts, if using, have been added, and stir well to coat each piece. Works well to put everything in brown paper bag, close bag, and shake to mix. Place in 2 shallow pans. Bake in preheated oven for 1 hour. Stir every 15 minutes. Place in airtight containers. Before serving, crisp in 250° F. oven for 10 to 15 minutes.

Per serving (based on 20 servings per recipe, using air-popped corn, 1/2 cup molasses and 2 cups dry roasted unsalted peanuts):   Calories 341 (44% from fat), Carbohydrates 44.2 g, Protein 5.9 g, Total Fat 17.2 g, Sodium 235 mg, Saturated Fat 2.6 g, Cholesterol 0 mg, Diabetic Exchanges: starch 1, meat 0.5, fruit 2, fat 3

Dietitian's note: Corn popped in oil will increase both the caloric count and the fat count.

Ohio Buckeyes
(chocolate and peanut butter treats named for the nuts produced by the state tree of Ohio; similar to horse chestnuts but inedible. The name "buckeye" is a translation of a Native American word for eye of a buck.)

1 stick (½ cup) margarine	1 pound powdered sugar
1 (18 oz.) jar crunchy style peanut butter	1 (12 oz.) bag chocolate chips
1 teaspoon vanilla extract	

Cream margarine and peanut butter; add vanilla. Stir in powdered sugar; mix well. Form into 1-inch balls. Place balls on wax paper and freeze at least one hour.

Melt chocolate chips in microwave or on top of double boiler. Using a toothpick, dip peanut butter balls almost completely into melted chocolate, leaving small portion at top uncovered by chocolate. Place on wax paper to set. Remove toothpick and smooth over hole with a wet spoon. Store in freezer or refrigerator.

Variations: Add 1 cup packed coconut and/or 2 cups graham cracker crumbs with the sugar.

Per serving (based on 75 servings per basic recipe): Calories 113 (51% from fat), Carbohydrates 12.9 g, Protein 1.6 g, Total Fat 6.8 g, Sodium 66 mg, Saturated Fat 2.1 g, Cholesterol 0 mg, Diabetic Exchanges: fruit 1, fat 1

Holiday Shortbread

1 pound butter, softened (no substitutes!)

2 cups all-purpose flour

1 cup cake flour

1 cup powdered sugar

Preheat oven to 350° F.

If butter is coming straight from the refrigerator, soften it by placing in microwave on low, 1 to 2 minutes. Combine all ingredients. Drop by spoonful on cookie sheet, or spread out on sheet for one major cookie. Bake in preheated oven for 10 to 15 minutes or until golden.

Per serving (based on 36 servings per recipe): Calories 138 (66% from fat), Carbohydrates 10.7 g, Protein 1 g, Total Fat 10.3 g, Sodium 104 mg, Saturated Fat 6.4 g, Cholesterol 28 mg, Diabetic Exchanges: starch 0.5, fat 2

A WALK IN THE MORNING

What a morning! The air was almost cool. Birds were singing, not yet silenced by the heat and lack of oxygen. It was early, before the soporific humidity and numbing din of motorized vehicles closed in.

A walk down the narrow street behind the house seemed a grand idea. The lane was bordered on one side by garden walls, some plain and some decorated, and on the other side by a small canal. Multiple shades of green interrupted by bright flowers met the eyes.

A few vendors, the ever present monks with their too-orange robes, a thin, everyday dog, and a man on a bicycle were the only creatures stirring.

Farther down the lane a thick, gnarled tree pushed against a wall and intruded onto the path. A heavy branch stretched across the road all the way to the canal. There was a bunch of fruit hanging from the branch—or maybe it was a lantern—there were flashes of color. On closer view, it seemed to be a doll or a large puppet. Closer still, and you could see it was a young man in a red and black dress, hanging by the neck.

What a morning.

Central & South America

A Conversation with Julia Child

I think the thing is that if you're feeling good about life, you can just have a marvelous time in the service overseas. If you have good health . . . if you have children and they are well and happy and so forth, then I think the more that you can learn about where you are and the people that you are meeting, the more full and wonderful an experience you'll have.

Yes. Absolutely.

Learn the language!

THE LOIN THAT BECAME A CROWN

When we arrived in South America in 1970 we had two children and my mother in our household. Mother, in her lifetime, had had a great deal of experience with entertaining and I relied on her for advice for all my dinner parties. She was an excellent cook and always had a knack for menus.

Beef in our region was of questionable quality in those days. Often tough, it was best marinated or slow-cooked. Pork, on the other hand, was exquisite: light in color, tender, not fatty.

The time came for us to give our first dinner party, and mother and I began discussing the menu. Because we could not depend on the beef to be suitable, we thought of pork for the main course. In Mother's generation, the only acceptable cut of pork to serve at a formal dinner party was a crown roast. Unfortunately, I had seen no such roasts displayed in the local butcher shops, but Mother and I agreed that it was worth a try.

The day before our party, our housekeeper and I set off to find the proper crown roast. With my few words of the local language I usually managed to gesture my way through most situations, and the housekeeper understood a lot of English and could serve as interpreter. We went from butcher shop to butcher shop trying to explain what we wanted, with no success.

We returned home and I told Mother that we would have to change the menu. Mother was not going to give up so easily. She spoke even less of the local language than I, but she took the housekeeper and set off down the street, determined to come back with a crown roast. And she did!

Mother simply marched into a butcher shop and, spying a rack of pork hanging from the ceiling, she went behind the counter, pulled it down, grabbed a cleaver, and proceeded to show the butcher how to make a crown roast! The housekeeper—indeed, probably everyone in the shop—was thunderstruck. Mother paid the butcher for the meat and arrived home with a beautiful crown roast, which was an enormous hit at my dinner party.

To this day, I wonder if that butcher went on to make his fortune as the only butcher in town selling crown roasts for elegant dinner parties. He has my mother to thank!

A more usual presentation of pork in parts of South America is boned loin. In our house it is often served with black beans, traditionally accompanied by white rice, collard greens, and fresh orange slices.

Black Beans
(two equally tasty versions)

For meatless version:

1 pound dried black beans	1 tablespoon vegetable oil
2 bay leaves, crushed	1 medium onion, chopped
pinch of salt	3 to 4 cloves garlic, chopped

Soak beans overnight. In the morning, drain them and put in a large pot with enough fresh water to cover. Add bay leaves, and salt. Cook over medium heat about 2 hours until beans are tender.

While beans are cooking, heat oil in a large skillet; sauté onion and garlic in hot oil until transparent.

When the beans are thoroughly cooked, remove about one cup of beans and add them to skillet with the onion and garlic; mash mixture with a potato masher. Return the bean-onion-garlic mixture to the pot of beans and stir.

Serve with rice, collard greens (see below), and fresh orange slices.

Per serving (based on 8 servings per recipe, version 1) Calories 186 (4% from fat), Carbohydrates 33.7 g, Protein 12.3 g, Total Fat 0.8 g, Sodium 29 mg, Saturated Fat 0.2 g, Cholesterol 0 mg, Diabetic Exchanges: starch 2

For version with meat, to above ingredients add:

1 teaspoon ground cumin	2 large smoked ham hocks
black pepper, to taste	1 pound pork sausage or smoked sausage
1 medium onion, chopped	carne seca (dried beef)* (optional)

After adding bay leaves and salt in above recipe, add cumin, pepper, onion, and meats. Bring to a boil; reduce heat and simmer until meat and beans are tender. Continue as above. Serve as above.

The author of this version offers these suggestions:

Although many people do not do so, I always prepare black beans one day ahead to let the beans absorb the flavors. For those who like it hot, I add some hot peppers.

*dried beef is not the same as beef jerky; it can be found in markets specializing in Latin American foods.

Per serving (based on 8 servings per recipe, version 2): Calories 437 (44% from fat), Carbohydrates 34.4 g, Protein 27 g, Total Fat 21.5 g, Sodium 803 mg, Saturated Fat 7.4 g, Cholesterol 61 mg, Diabetic Exchanges: starch 2, meat 2, fat 3

Collard Greens Latin Style

Wash the leaves, and cut out the center stem. Stack a couple of leaves together, and roll them up like a tight cigar. With a sharp knife, cut crosswise into paper-thin slices. Five minutes before serving the black beans, fry the sliced collard greens. Add salt, fresh garlic and pepper to taste.

Per 1-cup serving: Calories 40 (5% from fat), Carbohydrates 7.9 g, Protein 1.7 g, Total Fat 0.2 g, Sodium 21 mg, Saturated Fat 0.1 g, Cholesterol 0 mg, Diabetic Exchanges: veg 1

GOOD DOG

Everything was ready for our first diplomatic reception in this small Latin American country. The guest list included several Ambassadors, including our own. The house seemed to glow with crackling fires in all three fireplaces.

I was waiting by the door to greet our Ambassador right at the front steps. Then, quite unexpectedly, Freddy, our miscreant mutt who disappeared for days at a time, was there at the front door, apparently home for a good meal or two and even a bath, given his coat matted with dirt. Naturally, at that moment, the Ambassador's car drove up and he quickly got out. I opened the door and scooted Freddy into a far corner of the foyer.

Whirling back to the door, I was just in time to greet the Ambassador and shake his hand, and he hurried past me to say hello to the other guests who were chatting just off the foyer. He never made it. The very feisty Freddy just hated to see people striding away from him, perhaps because he decided early on that little dogs need to mount sneak attacks. Before I could react, Freddy's teeth had firmly sunk in the Ambassador's right ankle, ripping the pant leg slightly. This, of course, caused the Ambassador to stumble into three of his colleagues, who in turn spilled their drinks all over their pin-stripes. The Ambassador didn't stay long after that. Others did, however, well into the night. The laughter over the "dog bites Ambassador" incident kept resounding throughout the house, as the guests took turns speculating over different ways my Chief of Mission would be torturing me over the coming months. I was not amused. (By the way, the bite did not draw blood).

Appetizer Empanadas

2 pounds ground meat
½ pound chopped green onion,
    whites with some tops
3 cloves garlic, crushed
2 tablespoons ground cumin
1 tablespoon pepper
2 (6 oz.) cans tomato paste
½ pound raisins

2 pounds all-purpose flour
pinch of salt
1 pound margarine or shortening
1 egg
1½ cups water
oil for deep frying
bottled hot pepper sauce

Filling:

In a large bowl, mix together ground meat, green onion, garlic, cumin, and pepper. Sauté mixture in a large skillet over low heat until meat is browned. Stir in tomato paste; simmer for 20 minutes. Add raisins; mix well. The meat mixture should be slightly dry.

Dough:

Combine flour, salt and margarine in a large bowl. Add egg; mix well. Add water, about 1½ cups, or enough to form dough. Turn out onto floured board and roll out into thin sheet. Cut into 3-inch circles with floured cookie or biscuit cutter. Drop 1 tablespoon of filling into center of each circle. Fold over and shape into half moons. Use fork to seal edges. Deep fry in hot oil (about 365° F.) until golden brown. Remove from oil and drain on several layers of paper towels on a platter. Serve warm with hot pepper sauce.

Makes 100 bite-size empanadas. Larger circles, filled with more meat, can be made into meal-size empanadas.

Per serving (2 bite-size empanadas each): Calories 196 (47% from fat), Carbohydrates 20.3 g, Protein 6 g, Total Fat 10.3 g, Sodium 167 mg, Saturated Fat 2.3 g, Cholesterol 15 mg, Diabetic Exchanges: starch 1, meat 0.5, fat 1

Seafood Stew
Any type of fish and seafood may be used in this dish.

½ cup olive oil
4 onions, sliced
3 cloves garlic, crushed
5 medium tomatoes, peeled, seeded, and chopped
3 sprigs parsley, chopped
2 bay leaves
salt, to taste
freshly ground pepper, to taste
¼ teaspoon nutmeg

dash bottled hot pepper sauce
½ pound total of 3 varieties of fish fillets, cut into 1-inch chunks
½ pound squid, cleaned, and cut into 1x2-inch pieces
18 mussels
½ cup dry white wine
2 tablespoons white vinegar
2 tablespoons melted butter
6 thick slices of bread, crusts removed

Preheat oven to 350° F.

Heat oil in a large pan. Sauté onions and garlic in hot oil until onions are transparent. Add tomatoes, parsley, bay leaves, salt, pepper, nutmeg, and hot pepper sauce; simmer over low heat for 15 minutes.

In a heavy casserole, arrange layers of fish, squid, and mussels, alternating with the tomato-onion-garlic sauce. Stir in wine, vinegar, and butter; place bread slices on top; cover casserole; bring to boil. Lower heat; simmer 5 minutes until mussels open and fish is tender.

You may wish to bake, uncovered and without bread, in preheated 350° F. oven for 10 minutes until bubbly and fish is lightly golden (but do not overcook fish or mussels). Serve hot with rice. Good accompanied by "Manioc Mash" (recipe follows).

Makes 6 servings.

Per serving: Calories 430 (56% from fat), Carbohydrates 26.4 g, Protein 21.1 g, Total Fat 26.8 g, Sodium 847 mg, Saturated Fat 5.7 g, Cholesterol 45 mg, Diabetic Exchanges: starch 1, meat 2, fruit 3, veg 2

Manioc Mash

1 medium tomato, chopped
3 tablespoons chopped onion
oil or butter
salt and pepper, to taste
1 bay leaf (optional)

2 cups ground manioc meal (raw preferred,
    but toasted may be used)
4 cups boiling water
3 tablespoons finely chopped parsley
dash bottled hot pepper sauce

In a large saucepan, sauté tomato and onion in very little oil or butter, over medium-high heat, until onion is transparent. Add salt, pepper, and bay leaf, if using. Reduce heat to low. Add manioc meal; gradually stir in boiling water using a wooden spoon to mix well to avoid lumps. If desired, add some liquid from the Seafood Stew above. Simmer over low heat, stirring often, until mixture thickens; add hot pepper sauce; adjust seasonings. Transfer to serving bowl. Liquid from Seafood Stew may be drizzled on top, or passed separately.

Per serving (based on 8 servings per recipe): Calories 70 (21% from fat), Carbohydrates 10.5 g, Protein 1.3 g, Total Fat 1.7 g, Sodium 370 mg, Saturated Fat 0.9 g, Cholesterol 4 mg, Diabetic Exchanges: starch 0.7, fat 0.3

CHICHA AL FRESCO

My first and last taste of Chicha was from a different recipe than the one which follows below. Truth be told, I can't provide the exact ingredients, but it involved the mastication of corn by Jivaro women, which after a time would be spit into wooden gourds containing pieces of sugar cane and allowed to ferment. At some point in the process, water and other local ingredients were blended in to add some flavor to the alcohol kick. This recipe was all that Kurt, my Prussian guide on my trip through Jivaro country in South America in 1959, could tell me and, indeed, more than I really wanted to know at the time.

The Jivaros were the famed head-shrinkers who lived in the rain forests in the southernmost part of the Amazon jungle, then virtually untouched by civilization. The all-knowing Kurt, who visited the rain forests periodically to gather orchids for his nursery, said they only shrank the heads of monkeys, as missionaries had convinced them that it was wrong to use humans. I'm not so sure. The shrunken heads I saw sure didn't look like monkeys. Of course they didn't look very human either, being very small and grotesque, but they did have long hair, and I don't recall seeing many long-haired monkeys. Also, Kurt said that the Jivaros did not shrink just anybody's head; it had to have been an enemy who had been bested in battle. The shrunken head was then worn around the waist as a warrior's trophy. I couldn't picture the Jivaros being that mad at monkeys, so I really didn't buy the missionary story. Just to be on the safe side, I smiled a lot, trying to appear friendly. I think they thought I was strange; they didn't smile back. Anyway, I kept my head.

The great Chicha experience occurred during the first week of our two-week journey. We stopped our canoe at a village (5 to 7 huts) along a river whose water would ultimately reach the Amazon River. We had purchased a pig up river and offered to share it that evening with our Jivaro hosts. In appreciation, the local chief ordered a young woman to bring in the Chicha. She held the gourd in one hand as she raised it to my lips, while she used the other hand to pull away the corn pulp. This was good as it left both my hands free to put pressure on my stomach, which was undergoing some rather strong convulsions at the time. The Chicha looked like a mixture of dirty dishwater and skim milk and tasted the way it looked. I definitely didn't want to offend the Jivaros and perhaps qualify as an enemy. I got the Chicha down. And I kept smiling, although at the time it probably looked a bit strained. After the fact, it was a wonderful first tour adventure, although I have never had any desire to use that first Chicha recipe.

Chicha Morada

1 pound red corn
3 sticks cinnamon
5 unpeeled apples, quartered
½ cup sugar

16 cups water
6 cloves
1 fresh unpeeled pineapple, cut in
    large pieces
½ cup lemon juice

Wash corn and place whole in large saucepan with water, cinnamon, cloves, apples and pineapple. Simmer for 2 hours. Strain and add sugar and lemon juice. When cold, store in refrigerator for future use. If served in a punch bowl, add a diced apple.

Per serving (based on 24 servings per recipe, using yellow corn): Calories 61 (6% from fat), Carbohydrates 15.3 g, Protein 1 g, Total Fat 0.5 g, Sodium 8.17 mg, Saturated Fat 0 g, Cholesterol 0 mg, Diabetic Exchanges: fruit 1

FIRST TOUR REMEMBERED

My first tour began in South America in 1965. It was a time of instability throughout the region, and political demonstrations were commonplace, especially after the capture of the guerrilla leader Che Guevara in nearby Bolivia. At my post, two unsuccessful coup attempts were followed by a successful one. Among other significant events, the new military junta created a 200 mile fishing limit which resulted in an international crisis, and the U.S. Ambassador was declared Persona non Grata and had to leave.

The most significant memory of all for me was meeting a very beautiful young lady who arrived at post on the day of the Marine Corps Birthday Ball in November 1967. This was also the day on which I originally had planned to depart end-of-tour, but my departure had been rescheduled. Three months later that young lady and I were wed. Fortunately for us, we were allowed to use the elegant but now unoccupied Ambassador's Residence, complete with household staff, as our "honeymoon cottage" until we departed at Easter time. We are still very happily married and still use for special brunch occasions, the following recipe given to us during that assignment in South America.

Spice Pancakes

2 cups all-purpose flour
2¾ teaspoons baking powder
¾ teaspoon salt
1 teaspoon ground cinnamon
½ teaspoon ground allspice

½ teaspoon ground cloves
½ teaspoon ground nutmeg
2 eggs, beaten
1⅔ cups milk
3 tablespoons vegetable oil

Sift flour, baking powder, salt, and spices into a medium-sized bowl. Combine eggs, milk, and oil in a small dish; add to dry ingredients and stir quickly to moisten.

Pour about 2½ tablespoons batter onto a hot griddle (or into a skillet), greased, if necessary. Cook until bubbles appear on surface and pancake is golden brown underneath; turn with a spatula and cook on other side until golden brown on both sides and done. Serve immediately or keep warm in a preheated 250° F. oven until ready to serve. Serve with hot fruit sauce.
Makes 12.

Per serving: Calories 140 (36% from fat), Carbohydrates 18.2 g, Protein 4.2 g, Total Fat 5.5 g, Sodium 272 mg, Saturated Fat 1.5 g, Cholesterol 36 mg, Diabetic Exchanges: starch 1, fat 1

Hot Fruit Sauce

¾ cup granulated sugar
3 tablespoons cornstarch
¼ teaspoon ground cinnamon
pinch of salt

1 cup chopped peaches, fresh or canned, drained
1 tablespoon lemon juice
1 cup water or juice from canned peaches

Combine sugar, cornstarch, cinnamon and salt in a medium saucepan. Add remaining ingredients. Bring to boil, stirring constantly; boil 1 minute.

Per serving (based on 12 servings per recipe): Calories 62 (<1% from fat), Carbohydrates 16 g, Protein 0 g, Total Fat 0 g, Sodium 23 mg, Saturated Fat 0 g, Cholesterol 0 mg, Diabetic Exchanges: fruit 1

CHOCOLATE-COVERED ICE

Many years ago, when my husband and I arrived in South America, I knew no Spanish because in those days Uncle Sam did not provide language training for spouses. We had a cook who spoke no English and was even weak in Spanish.

For our first dinner I asked the cook to make ice cream balls, later to be covered with chocolate sauce and nuts. Fortunately, I checked things out before the guests arrived. I found the freezer full of beautifully shaped ice balls prepared by the cook and her daughter. I had said "balas de hielo" instead of "balas de helado." A quick trip to the nearby ice cream store saved the guests from crunching into ice balls covered with chocolate sauce.

We liked the following dish, based on a recipe in a bilingual cookbook prepared by a nearby American Women's Club:

Carbonada Criolla

1 large pumpkin (about 10 pounds)
3 tablespoons butter
2 cloves garlic, minced
1 large onion, chopped
2 large tomatoes, coarsely chopped
1 large green pepper, chopped
1½ pounds lean beef, cut in cubes

salt and pepper to taste
½ teaspoon granulated sugar
4 fresh peaches, peeled and diced
3 white potatoes, peeled and cubed
3 sweet potatoes, peeled and cubed
6 ears corn, cut off cob (not grated)
1½ cups beef broth or bouillon

Preheat oven to 375° F.

Prepare pumpkin: Scrub outside of pumpkin under cold running water. Cut across and down into top of pumpkin to create a lid, about 6 inches in diameter. Do not remove stem. Scrape seeds and stringy fibers from lid and inside of pumpkin. Brush inside with softened butter and sprinkle with salt. Place in a large, shallow pan and bake in preheated oven for 45 minutes or until just tender and shell is still firm enough to hold filling.

For the carbonada: Heat butter in 5-quart (or larger) pot; sauté garlic in hot butter until well browned; remove and discard. Add chopped onion; sauté until tender but not browned; add tomatoes, green pepper, beef, salt and pepper, and sugar. Cook, over medium-high heat, stirring, for 15 minutes. Stir in peaches and potatoes. Reduce heat; add corn and beef broth. Simmer, covered, 40 to 60 minutes until meat and potatoes are tender. Add more broth if mixture becomes too dry.

To serve, pour carbonada into prepared pumpkin, and place on a platter. Ladle carbonada from pumpkin onto serving plates.

Per serving (based on 10 servings per recipe): Calories 369 (30% from fat), Carbohydrates 43 g, Protein 23.9 g, Total Fat 12.5 g, Sodium 859 mg, Saturated Fat 5.6 g, Cholesterol 64 mg, Diabetic Exchanges: starch 1.5, lean meat 3, fruit 1, veg 0.5

A SHAKY FIRST TOUR

Our first overseas tour was in South America; we arrived with our two-year-old daughter not knowing exactly what to expect, or the language. We immediately fell in love with the people, and soon after getting settled we met some neighbors and started having them over each weekend for dominoes.

About six months later my husband's new boss arrived and checked into a hotel with his wife and two children. The following night we had a dinner party to welcome them and, just as the guests were arriving, we had an earthquake. Luckily, no damage was done to our house (except a few small cracks in the walls), so we continued the dinner.

After dinner, we turned the radio on and heard the stations calling for doctors, nurses, and other medical personnel to please report to the hospitals. Still wondering how serious and widespread the damage was, everyone eventually went home and we went to bed. We were awakened at 3:00 A.M. by a phone call from the new boss; his hotel had been condemned because of the earthquake (as had many others in the area), and those not damaged were full and he had nowhere to go with his family. Naturally, we invited him and his family to stay with us until they could find a house. We were only then beginning to understand the severity of the quake.

There were many buildings down, mud slides, apartment buildings damaged, and many people killed or trapped in debris. After a sleepless night, we received another phone call on Sunday morning from a friend with whom we played dominoes. He told us that he and his wife (and dog) had been evicted from their damaged apartment building and that his parents and sister had been in one of the buildings that had fallen. He wanted to know if they could come over, along with two other friends. There I was, serving coffee and breakfast to whoever could eat. Our local friends left that evening with our friend, still not knowing the fate of his family. Sadly, on Wednesday of that week he received the news that his parents and sister had perished in the earthquake. I had terrible nightmares for quite a while after the quake. Eventually, of course, life did get back to normal and we started enjoying the beauty of the country again, the beaches, fishing, clam digging, snorkeling, food, climate, etc. (and no more earthquakes!) It really ended up being a very good tour.

Here are two of my favorite recipes from those days. Enjoy them!

South American Paella

¼ cup olive oil
3 cloves garlic, chopped
3 cups long grain white rice
2 medium onions, chopped
5 cups chicken broth
2 teaspoons saffron
salt and pepper to taste

3 red sweet peppers, cut into large pieces
2 cups stewed chicken, skin removed, cut into large pieces
1 (10 oz.) box frozen green peas, thawed
1 to 2 cups as desired: artichoke hearts, mushrooms, hearts of palms, shrimp, clams, crab meat, mussels

Preheat oven to 350° F.

In a large ovenproof pan or baking dish, heat oil. Sauté garlic in hot oil until soft but not browned. Remove garlic. Add rice and chopped onions to hot oil; cook over high heat, stirring constantly, until rice is slightly brown. Add chicken broth and saffron, mixing well. Add salt and pepper to taste. Cook over medium heat until ¾ of the liquid is gone. Add red pepper. Cover and place in preheated oven for 30 minutes.

Remove from oven; mix in chicken and green peas; add remaining ingredients, except seafood. Cover and continue to bake another 30 minutes. Remove from oven; top paella with seafood (if using mussels, steam separately in water until shells open; add to paella before serving). Cover and continue to bake 20 to 30 minutes longer, until all ingredients are tender, but chicken is not overcooked.

All you need is a salad with it for a complete meal.

Per serving (based on 6 servings per recipe): Calories 482 (36% from fat), Carbohydrates 35.3 g, Protein 41.2 g, Total Fat 19.1 g, Sodium 1571 mg, Saturated Fat 3.8 g, Cholesterol 110 mg, Diabetic Exchanges: bread 1.5, lean meat 4, veg 1, fat 2

Ceviche

1 pound white fish, cut
   into bite-size pieces (1 inch
   or smaller) of white meat only
2 hot peppers, chopped
1 clove garlic

2 tablespoons cilantro
juice of 6 limes (Key West limes, preferred)
lettuce leaves, for serving platter
2 medium onions, sliced and rinsed
   in water, for garnish

Wash fish and dry. In a blender, combine hot peppers with a little water and garlic clove. In a bowl, mix together fish, cilantro, and lime juice. Pour blended pepper-garlic mix over fish mix. Let sit in refrigerator for one hour.

To serve, remove from refrigerator and place on serving platter which has been lined with lettuce leaves; top with onion slices. Serve accompanied by hot baked sweet potatoes.

Per serving (based on 4 servings per recipe): Calories 307 (26% from fat), Carbohydrates 27.4 g, Protein 30.4 g, Total Fat 8.8 g, Sodium 96 mg, Saturated Fat 1.4 g, Cholesterol 88 mg, Diabetic Exchanges: starch 1, lean meat 4, veg 1

A colleague adds the explanation that in much of Latin America, ceviche is second only to expresso coffee as a social facilitator. Restaurants serve it with meals, but, in general, it is served as a morning or afternoon break. Businessmen use it to close deals. Workers use it (when they can afford it) to catch their breaths. It is so often employed as a social tool that officers have used it extensively to mask more meaningful contacts.

Ceviche has its basic ingredients, but every self-respecting region has its own recipe, which is, of course, the only way to make it. In the early '60s there flourished a ceviche palace called the Wonder Bar, renowned for its ceviche. At 10:30 A.M. and 3:30 P.M. it was always crowded with workers, businessmen, and others taking a ceviche break. The following is another ceviche recipe based on the one served at the famous Wonder Bar. It has been simplified and made milder for U.S. cooks. It is, however, just as tasty. It is usually served sprinkled with toasted corn kernels, but plain popcorn will do just fine. A batch of ceviche will last for days covered in the refrigerator, but please pop the corn fresh each time you serve it.

Simple Ceviche

1 pound firm, white fish*
juice of 9 to 12 lemons

1 large white onion
1 (28-oz.) bottle ketchup

In a ceramic or glass bowl (no metal of any sort) cut fish into ½-inch cubes. Cover (literally) fish with lemon juice. Cover bowl (plastic wrap will do); refrigerate for at least 24 hours.

The day before serving, slice onion into long, thin strips; blanch by placing onion slices in a colander and pouring boiling water over the slices. Add blanched onion to marinated fish; add ketchup; mix thoroughly. Refrigerate for another day. Good accompanied by plenty of popcorn.

*corvina (sea bass) is the fish generally used in Latin America. Neither flounder, sole, nor halibut are firm enough; orange roughy may be used, but make an effort to find corvina.

Author's note: This is the sissy ceviche relished by many Americans who cannot take real picante, the hot, spicy taste for which ceviche is known. If a hotter version is desired, add sliced and diced chili peppers, jalapenos, or Louisiana hot sauce to taste at the time the ketchup is added. For real sports, try a tiny, green Bolivian product called ulupica, perhaps the hottest ají I have ever eaten, available at Latin American grocery stores. Remember, though, that these additions will increase the picante during the days of refrigeration, and, if not used carefully, will make the ceviche excessively hot. This recipe comes without warranty for burned tongues or fiery throats. Beer is the best quencher.

Per serving (based on 4 servings per recipe): Calories 435 (16% from fat), Carbohydrates 65.5 g, Protein 25.9 g, Total Fat 7.7 g, Sodium 2079 mg, Saturated Fat 1.2 g, Cholesterol 70 mg, Diabetic Exchanges: lean meat 3, fruit 3.5, veg 2

DINNER AT 8: . . .

My most embarrassing dinner party took place while we were in South America. I had a live-in cook/maid, and the night of the dinner party I had her prepare everything except the main dish. Two hours before the guests arrived, I put the finishing touches on the meat dish and placed it in the oven to cook slowly for two hours.

After the guests arrived, we sat around the living room having drinks and hors d'oeuvres. I soon excused myself from the room to get the food on the table to serve dinner. When I got into the kitchen and opened the oven door, I was shocked to find the oven COLD and my meat dish sitting there just as I had put in it two hours earlier, cold and uncooked. I frantically checked the oven. It was turned on but definitely not working, and I was stumped as to what had happened to my well planned dinner. When I checked the electric stove (for the tenth time), I finally saw the problem. Apparently when the oven had been cleaned earlier in the day the time switch had been accidentally turned on. My oven was set to start cooking in a couple of hours.

The large group of people from the American Embassy were sitting in my living room waiting for my home cooked meal. What could I do but sheepishly go in and explain the situation and apologize. Luckily, everyone thought it was funny! Except me!! We all climbed into our cars and drove to the Chinese restaurant. That was probably the most expensive dinner party I ever had.

Here are some recipes which are always hot!

Ají de Gallina (Spicy Chicken)

1 (3 to 4 pounds) chicken, cut up

1 onion, quartered

3 carrots, sliced

2 stalks celery, sliced

4 tablespoons chopped parsley

hot peppers*, to taste

¼ cup olive oil

2 cups chopped onion

5 garlic cloves, finely chopped

½ teaspoon ground cumin

salt and pepper, to taste

½ cup ground pecans

4 slices of bread, soaked in a little milk

1 cup Parmesan cheese, grated

In a large pot, bring to boil about 5 quarts water. Add chicken, onion quarters, carrots, celery, and parsley. Return to boil, skim, then simmer covered for 1 to 2 hours until chicken is tender. Remove chicken and cool. Reserve chicken broth.

While chicken is cooling, in another pot, cook hot peppers in boiling water for 10 minutes. Drain. Grind peppers.

When chicken is cool, shred finely with fingers. In a large, deep skillet or Dutch oven, heat oil; sauté chopped onion and garlic in hot oil until soft but not browned. Add cumin, salt, and pepper. Add ground hot peppers, ground pecans, and soaked bread; mix well; sauté 3 to 4 minutes. Lower heat; stir in shredded chicken; mix well. Add chicken broth. Cook slowly over low heat, stirring often, and adding more broth (½ cup at a time) if needed, for 1 hour.

Add Parmesan cheese; mix well. Continue cooking slowly for 1 more hour, again adding broth if needed. Taste; adjust spices.

Serve over rice or boiled potato halves.

Per serving (based on 6 servings per recipe): Calories 589 (57% from fat), Carbohydrates 28.4 g, Protein 35.5 g, Total Fat 37.4 g, Sodium 870 mg, Saturated Fat 9.9 g, Cholesterol 85 mg, Diabetic Exchanges: starch 1, meat 4, veg 2, fat 4

Picante Sauce for Potatoes or Eggs

1 tablespoon olive oil

1 large garlic clove, sliced

hot peppers*, to taste

¼ pound fresh farmer's cheese

¼ to ½ cup evaporated milk

1 cup crackers

1 to 2 teaspoons lemon juice

In a small skillet, heat oil; sauté garlic slices in hot oil. Let garlic and oil cool.
. In a saucepan, cook hot peppers in boiling water 30 minutes; drain. In a blender or food processor fitted with steel blade, combine drained peppers with half of the cheese. Add ¼ cup milk, ½ cup crackers, and cooled garlic and oil, processing after each addition until incorporated into mixture. Add remaining cheese and crackers; process until blended. Add a little more milk if necessary to

get a thick consistency. Pour into serving bowl. Add lemon juice to taste.
Serve over hot or cold boiled potatoes or hard boiled eggs.

Per serving (based on 4 servings per recipe, using Ritz® crackers): Calories 203 (66% from fat), Carbohydrates 7.6 g,
Protein 8 g, Total Fat 15.5 g, Sodium 386 mg, Saturated Fat 7.5 g, Cholesterol 34 mg,
Diabetic Exchanges: meat 1, veg 0.5, fat 2.5

Sopa a la Crilla

2 tablespoons vegetable oil
1½ cups finely chopped onion
4 garlic cloves, minced
1½ cups lean beef, cut into
small pieces
5 large tomatoes, halved,
skinned, and grated
½ teaspoon ground cumin

1 tablespoon chopped cilantro
dash oregano
hot peppers*, to taste
8 to 10 cups water
salt and pepper, to taste
1 (8 oz.) package fine noodles

Heat oil in large stockpot or kettle. Add onions and garlic; sauté until tender,
but not browned. Push onions and garlic to the side; add meat. Brown meat on all
sides. Add remaining ingredients except noodles. Cook slowly about 2 hours until
meat is tender. Add noodles to soup; continue cooking until noodles are done.
Serve with toast or croutons.

Per serving (based on 4 servings per recipe): Calories 358 (42% from fat), Carbohydrates 31.2 g,
Protein 21.6 g, Total Fat 17.2 g, Sodium 516 mg, Saturated Fat 4.2 g, Cholesterol 69 mg,
Diabetic Exchanges: starch 1, meat 2, veg 2, fat 1

* best made with orange hot peppers from South America. If unavailable, substitute 2 to 3
tablespoons yellow chili sauce (not paste) available in Latin American markets. Do not
cook the chili sauce separately, as for fresh peppers. Other hot peppers, such as red
jalapenos, may be used, but taste will be milder.

A NIGHT TO REMEMBER

One of my most memorable dinner parties took place in Latin America where my
husband was assigned to a U.S. military command during a period of political turmoil. One
day he informed me that we had the "honor" to host a buffet dinner at our home for some
65-plus military and embassy personnel and spouses. The dinner was to welcome the
Deputy Director of Operations (DDO) and our division chief, who were making an official
visit on short notice. The guest list would include the General who served as the
Commander-in-Chief of the Command (CINC). If my memory serves me correctly, I was
given approximately 3 or 4 days' notice. My husband usually followed up this kind of
announcement with the statement that he knew I loved entertaining, and thrived on this
type of challenge. He was sure that I would come through without any sign of what he and
his colleagues called the "pucker factor" (their term for stress-causing wrinkles in well-
made plans).

The big night arrived with only minor crises. Even the weather was cooperating—no rain. I had spent the weekend preparing food for the large crowd, and all was ready for the visitors. Following military custom, we had set an early hour for the party. Our military and embassy guests had arrived promptly, and only the CINC and our senior Washington visitors were among the missing when the "pucker factor" began to make its appearance. At approximately 1900 hours military time, we heard a loud rumbling noise. Most of the guests had already gravitated to the glassed-in porch which extended across the wide front of the house and around each side, and from where we watched in awe as 13 Armored Personnel Carriers (APCs) slowly drove up the street and passed directly in front of our house. The noise grew deafening with the rattling of the windows adding to the commotion as the APCs passed by and circled the entire block. From our vantage point we could see armed soldiers deploying throughout the Command and, particularly, around the CINC's house across the street.

One of our embassy guests, a young officer who had only recently arrived at post, was standing to my side as the APCs rolled by. He watched with amazement, then turned to me and asked, "Does this happen every night?" Having no idea what was going on, I quipped, "Only when the CINC comes to dinner." Just then the smiling CINC walked up the front walk. He was immediately besieged by the Chargé, among others, seeking information. The General had a well-deserved reputation as a hard-nosed military commander whose voice was rumored to peel bark off a tree and known to reduce grown men to jelly. He was also a gracious host and guest and a charming individual in a social setting.

The CINC patiently explained that the Command had received information that a drug cartel was planning to attack U.S. military bases in our region using car bombs, similar to those being used at the time in other Latin American countries. As a result, stringent security measures were being implemented to protect U.S. personnel and installations, to include sealing off all bases to prevent the entry or departure of vehicles. With a gracious smile, the General said he did not want to interrupt the dinner party and that we should enjoy ourselves, particularly since—for the time being, anyway—there could be no movement in or out of the Command.

At this point, the CINC was informed that our senior visitors had not yet arrived and, indeed, were likely to be en route or perhaps even at the gate to the Command, unable to pass through. The look on my husband's face indicated his "pucker factor" was in overdrive, as was mine. He may have been thinking about his career or the possibility of its sudden end, but I was focused on more immediate concerns, wondering how long I could delay dinner without ruining the food.

The CINC, meanwhile, immediately dispatched to the gate an officer with enough stars on his collar to ensure an immediate response, and shortly thereafter our guests of honor arrived. They were somewhat bemused at having been stopped by a machine gun outpost in front of the Command gate, impolitely ordered out of their car and questioned by a rather intense soldier as to the nature of their business. Not exactly the kind of welcome we had planned!

All's well that ends well, they say. The dinner party was a great success, although possibly more beverages than usual were consumed. In any event, conversation was not a problem that night. Upon leaving, the CINC said the party was so enjoyable and the food so delicious he would arrange to provide a tank escort anytime I wished to give a dinner party. I politely declined, but gave him a hug and a kiss for being so understanding and helping avoid a potential social disaster. I later received a lovely thank you note from the DDO that this was definitely one party he would always remember—as do I.

The great bomb scare? It turned out be a hoax. It did turn our lives upside down for a couple of weeks, and gave us a few more chances to deal with the "pucker factor"!

The following two recipes are among my favorites and were served at the dinner.

Roasted Peppers

3 large red bell peppers
3 large green or black bell peppers
3 large yellow or orange
   bell peppers
¼ cup fresh orange juice
1 tablespoon Dijon mustard

1 tablespoon grated orange peel
6 tablespoons olive oil
salt and pepper, to taste
⅓ to ¼ cup chopped toasted
   nuts (pine or hazelnuts)
fresh cilantro, minced

Turn oven to broil. Place peppers on large cookie sheet and broil until all sides are blackened. Carefully remove charred peppers and place in paper bags; close loosely; allow peppers to steam in bags for approximately 30 minutes.

When cool enough to handle, peel and seed peppers (if necessary, rinse in water and pat dry). Slice peppers into even strips about ½ inch wide. Arrange on round platter.

Prepare dressing by combining orange juice, mustard, and orange peel in small bowl. Gradually whisk in oil; add salt and pepper to taste.

Pour dressing over peppers. (If desired, this recipe can be prepared to this point up to one day ahead and refrigerated. Bring to room temperature before continuing.) Garnish with nuts and cilantro.

Makes 10 to 12 servings.

Per serving (based on 12 servings per recipe): Calories 118 (62% from fat), Carbohydrates 10.1 g, Protein 2 g, Total Fat 8.6 g, Sodium 124 mg, Saturated Fat 1.1 g, Cholesterol 0 mg, Diabetic Exchanges: veg 1.5, fat 1.5

Black Bean and Rice Salad

4 cups water

1½ cups dried black beans

5 whole cloves

1 3-inch cinnamon stick

1 tablespoon cumin seeds

6 cups cooked brown rice
(about 1¼ cups uncooked)

1 cup minced onion

1 cup minced fresh cilantro

7 tablespoons fresh orange
juice or lemon juice

¼ cup olive oil

3 tablespoons rice vinegar (brown preferred)

¼ teaspoon orange peel

salt and pepper, to taste

½ cup pine nuts, toasted

2 oranges, peeled, seeded, and sliced
crosswise into rounds

fresh cilantro leaves for garnish

bottled hot pepper sauce

Early in the day, combine black beans, water, cloves, and cinnamon stick in a large saucepan. Cover and simmer about 2 hours or until beans are tender (time depends on freshness of beans). When beans are tender, drain. Discard spices. Set aside 1 cup beans.

In a small skillet, stir cumin seeds over medium-low heat until aromatic, about 3 minutes. Crush in mortar with pestle or on a board with a mallet.

Transfer remaining drained beans to a large bowl; add rice; mix. Stir in cumin seeds, onion, minced cilantro, orange juice, oil, vinegar and orange peel; season with salt and pepper. (If desired, recipe can be prepared to this point up to two days ahead. Cover separately the bean-rice mixture and the set aside 1 cup of beans. Refrigerate. To serve, remove from refrigerator and bring to room temperature, or rewarm if preferred; continue as follows.)

Stir pine nuts into bean-rice mixture. Transfer mixture to round bowl; press firmly into bowl. Invert onto serving platter. Arrange reserved beans and orange slices around beans and rice. Garnish with cilantro. Serve at room temperature (may also be served warm). Pass bottled hot pepper sauce separately.
Makes 12 servings.

Per serving: Calories 253 (30% from fat), Carbohydrates 36.5 g, Protein 8.5 g, Total Fat 8.7 g, Sodium 11 mg, Saturated Fat 1.52 g, Cholesterol 0 mg, Diabetic Exchanges: starch 2, fat 1

FLAMING FONDUE

My first posting was in November 1967 to South America. I worked for a single male workaholic and consequently had little time to acquire any culinary experience at my new post. I do, however, vividly recall a very small dinner party I gave for a VIP who was visiting our post. There were four in attendance: my boss, the visitor, a female co-worker, and myself.

Because I was working long hours and would not have much time for preparations, I decided that beef fondue would be the way to go. I had received a fondue pot as a gift just before coming to post, and this would be its first use. It was supposed to be fueled by sterno, but as is often the case overseas, a substitute was required. I purchased what I had been told was an acceptable alternative: "white gasoline."

As my guests and I began to prepare our beef fondue, I noted that the flame was too high and tried to adjust the cover over the fuel container. Suddenly, flames shot toward the ceiling of my dining room. The flame underneath the pot must have reached the cooking oil in the pot and set it on fire. I took the pot to the kitchen with the intention of putting it in the sink, but the sink was too full from my dinner preparations, so I put the pot down on the gas stove. Unfortunately, the gas pilot was enough to cause more fire.

One of the men grabbed the pot and threw it into the sink. Although I cannot remember for certain, I believe the hero also threw a cloth over the pot to stifle the fire.

The next day my boss ordered fire extinguishers for all of our kitchens.

When the VIP wrote to thank us for our hospitality, he wrote that the fire at my home had been the high point of his visit.

I've rarely used a fondue pot since then, but when I have, I've always made sure to use only sterno as the fuel.

Chicken in Cognac

4 pounds chicken parts, skin and bones removed	1 bay leaf
flour for dredging	1 to 2 teaspoons salt
¼ cup vegetable oil	pepper to taste
2 cloves garlic, chopped	white wine
	1 cup cognac

Dredge chicken lightly in flour. Heat oil in a large, deep skillet or Dutch oven; reduce heat; add chicken and brown slowly on all sides. Add garlic, bay leaf, salt and lots of pepper. Add wine to cover; add cognac. Simmer over low heat about 2 hours until alcohol has evaporated. Remove chicken from broth. Serve with biscuits accompanied by the broth in small cups.

Per serving (based on 12 servings per recipe): Calories 299 (33% from fat), Carbohydrates 0.5 g, Protein 43.8 g, Total Fat 13.5 g, Sodium 398 mg, Saturated Fat 3.4 g, Cholesterol 135 mg, Diabetic Exchanges: lean meat 5

Mango Mousse

For the mousse:

3 large mangoes

1 tablespoon powdered
   sugar, or to taste

1½ envelopes unflavored gelatin

¼ cup cold water

½ pint heavy cream

1 to 2 egg whites (optional)

For the sauce:

1 passion fruit

2 tablespoons lime juice

sprigs of fresh mint, for garnish

Lightly oil glass or metal loaf pan; line with greaseproof paper. Set aside.

Peel the mangoes and remove the large seed. In a blender or a food processor fitted with steel blade, puree mangoes until smooth. Reserve 1 cup of puree for the sauce. Add sugar to the remaining puree to sweeten to taste; pour into large mixing bowl; set aside.

Pour ¼ cup cold water into a small, heatproof bowl; sprinkle gelatin over water. Let stand 5 minutes. Place bowl in a pan of very hot water to dissolve gelatin. Let cool 2 to 3 minutes. Stir dissolved gelatin into sweetened mango puree.

In a medium bowl, whip cream until soft peaks form; carefully fold into the mango-gelatin mixture. (If desired for added volume, in a clean bowl, whisk egg whites until stiff but not dry; fold into mango mixture using a large metal spoon.) Pour mousse into prepared loaf pan; chill in refrigerator until set.

Prepare sauce: Cut passion fruit in half; scoop seeds and any juice into food processor fitted with steel blade; process for a few seconds. Press mixture through a sieve to remove the seeds. Add resulting strained passion fruit juice to reserved mango puree. Stir in lime juice.

To serve, remove mousse from loaf pan; slice and arrange on individual chilled plates. Spoon a little passion fruit sauce around mousse slices. Garnish with sprigs of fresh mint.

Substitutions: 3 (14-oz.) cans of mangoes in syrup may be substituted for fresh mangoes. Bottled passion fruit juice may be used instead of fresh fruit; add lime juice to taste.

Per serving (based on 8 servings per recipe): Calories 162 (61% from fat), Carbohydrates 15.9 g, Protein 2.8 g, Total Fat 11.2 g, Sodium 26 mg, Saturated Fat 6.9 g, Cholesterol 41 mg, Diabetic Exchanges: fruit 1, fat 2

CASSEROLE COMMITTEE

I cannot remember why, but the Embassy Wives' Club at my South American post decided to have a luncheon for 60 at the Ambassador's Residence, and we could not depend on the staff to prepare anything. We were trying to think of something easy that could be prepared in individual homes and transported to the Residence, something that would require only a bit of heating up before serving.

I remembered a reliable recipe that a friend of mine, whose husband was a Naval officer, used for large gatherings of this sort. It required lots of American canned goods, but, fortunately, those were readily available at the embassy commissary. We were able to assign the casserole to several people to prepare in advance. The casseroles were transported to the Residence and then warmed to serving temperature in the kitchen there. Other people brought tossed green salads and some French rolls, and the meal was complete.

The recipe was a hit, and no one who tasted it could believe that we hadn't worked all day to prepare it.

Chicken Curry Casserole

1 (5 oz.) can chow mein noodles
2 (10.75 oz.) cans cream of
    chicken soup
1 cup mayonnaise
2 (14 oz.) cans Chinese
    vegetables, drained
1 (8 oz.) can water chestnuts,
    drained and sliced

1 (8 oz.) can button mushrooms,
    drained and sliced
2 tablespoons lemon juice
2 tablespoons curry powder
1½ pounds cooked chicken
    or shrimp

Preheat oven to 350° F.

In a large bowl combine all ingredients, except chow mein noodles. In a casserole dish, spread a layer of mixture; add a layer of noodles on top of mixture; continue alternating layers of mixture with layers of noodles, ending with a noodle layer on top.

Bake in preheated oven for 45 minutes.

Per serving (based on 12 servings per recipe): Calories 447 (60% from fat), Carbohydrates 27.4 g, Protein 18.4 g, Total Fat 30.5 g, Sodium 1164 mg, Saturated Fat 5.6 g, Cholesterol 51 mg, Diabetic Exchanges: starch 1, meat 2, veg 1, fat 4

CHICKEN NUGGETS, THEY'RE NOT

Diplomatic receptions abroad, like cocktail parties everywhere, often provide enough food to allow one to skip dinner that evening. The wife of the Soviet Ambassador clearly was pursuing such a goal at a reception in an upscale hotel in a Latin American capital in the mid-'70s. She was eating, to put it uncharitably, with both hands from a large platter of what could appear to be small pieces of chicken. Taking a breather when she noticed me standing alongside her, she turned and commented that the chicken was delicious.

"Yes, it is," I said, and then to be truly uncharitable, added, "Except it's not chicken; it's cui, a South American rodent."

"What? You're crazy!" she blurted, and began calling her husband from across the room filled with about 100 diplomats and government officials. He quickly arrived at her side, and I watched the blood drain from her face as he told her, in Russian, that unfortunately I was right. She had been eating with some verve pieces of a rat-sized rodent that is considered a delicacy and does indeed taste like chicken. She kept shaking her head "nyet", but he kept saying, "da, da," as she fled the room with him in close pursuit. I never had another conversation with the Ambassador's wife in the entire year we remained in that city. Actually, I never even made eye contact with her again, try as I might.

I do not have the recipe for that scrumptious cui, but here is one of my favorite recipes for genuine chicken.

Soft Fried Chicken

flour	vegetable oil
salt and pepper	pat of butter
chicken parts, as desired	

Mix together in a bag, flour, salt and pepper. Add chicken parts to bag and shake to coat with flour mixture. Heat small amount of oil in a skillet; brown coated chicken in hot oil. Remove chicken from pan. Melt a pat of butter in same pan and return chicken to pan. Lower heat, simmer, covered, over low heat about ½ to 1 hour until chicken is done.

Dietitian's note: Because ingredient proportions vary according to taste, nutritional values have not been determined.

IT'S ALL IN THE INTERPRETATION

We had to ship our car from Europe to South America. The trip involved loading the car onto a ship in Bremerhaven, Germany, for a trans-Atlantic crossing, shipment through the Panama Canal, and finally down the western coast of South America by boat to Antofagasta, Chile. From there it traveled on a railroad car until it came to a lake where it was placed on a small steamer. Once it had crossed the lake, it was loaded onto a truck and brought to its final destination. This extraordinary feat took some nine months to accomplish. It was with great anticipation, therefore, that we went to the customs area to pick up our car. We were pleased to discover that the car had been completely crated to protect it in shipment and from the elements. In addition to our address, each side of the box was clearly marked with large black arrows. We were aghast to see, however, that the symbol Americans took totally for granted was open to interpretation. Somewhere along the way, an assumption was made that the arrows indicated which side should be placed DOWN! We watched with great trepidation as a large crane awkwardly turned the enormous box over once again. Upon uncrating the car, we found the roof had been caved in and the battery had fallen out of its compartment. My husband reconnected the battery and got into the back seat of the car. Placing the soles of his feet in the center of the roof, he pushed his bent knees upward and the roof miraculously popped back to its proper shape. Having accomplished that, the car was filled with gas and oil. My husband turned the key in the ignition and the car started up immediately. We left amidst cheers.

Giant Upside-Down Pecan Rolls

⅔ cup milk

1¼ cups granulated sugar, divided

¾ teaspoon salt

¼ cup butter, divided

2 packages dry active yeast

½ cup warm water

5 to 5½ cups all-purpose flour, divided

1 large whole egg

1 large egg, separated

1 tablespoon ground cinnamon

1 cup chopped pecans

For syrup:

¼ cup butter

2 tablespoons water

1 cup dark brown sugar

1 cup pecan halves

Combine milk, ¾ cup sugar, salt, and ½ cup butter in medium saucepan. Stir over high heat until butter is melted and sugar dissolved; then cool to 110° F.

Sprinkle yeast over warm water in large bowl; let stand 5 minutes to soften. Blend in cooled milk mixture. Add 3 cups flour; stir to moisten, then beat 5 minutes. Beat in 1 whole egg and 1 yolk; beat in 1 cup more flour; stir in remaining 1 cup flour.

Turn out dough onto lightly floured board and knead until smooth and elastic, about 10 minutes; an additional ½ cup flour may be kneaded into dough if it is very sticky. Place dough in greased bowl, turning to grease all surfaces of dough. Let rise 2 hours in a warm, draft-free place. Punch down and let rest 10 minutes.

Prepare syrup: Combine ¼ cup butter, 2 tablespoons water, and 1 cup dark brown sugar in a saucepan. Boil over high heat for 1 minute. Pour immediately into 9x13-inch baking pan; tilt pan until syrup is even. Arrange pecan halves, flat side up, on syrup.

Turn out rested dough onto lightly floured board; roll dough to 18x24-inch rectangle. Melt remaining ¼ cup butter; brush over dough. Combine cinnamon and remaining 1 cup sugar in a small bowl; sprinkle on dough. Sprinkle with chopped pecans. Roll up dough lengthwise, jellyroll style. Moisten edge with water; seal. Cut into 12 slices. Arrange slices, cut side up, in syrup-coated pan. Let rise until doubled.

Preheat oven to 350° F.

Brush surface of rolls with egg white, beaten with 1 teaspoon water. Bake in preheated 350° F. oven about 30 to 40 minutes until brown. Invert pan onto serving platter immediately.

Per serving (based on 12 servings per recipe): Calories 632 (31% from fat), Carbohydrates 101 g, Protein 9.4 g, Total Fat 22.4 g, Sodium 241 mg, Saturated Fat 6.4 g, Cholesterol 58 mg, Diabetic Exchanges: starch 3, fruit 4, fat 4

STEW, PIONEER STYLE

This recipe, a standby in Hungarian kitchens, is easily duplicated in both the Northern and Southern Hemisphere. It saved the party one evening in 1947 in Santiago de Chile. The electric power for our electric stove had been unexpectedly turned off all day preceding what was to be an elegant dinner party featuring a gourmet menu for 30 guests. At that time few people in Chile had telephones, so there was no way to call the party off.

The stew was prepared in a large preserving kettle placed over a wood fire in the living room fireplace. Rice cooked in another large kettle was served as an accompaniment instead of the traditional mashed potatoes. Here's the recipe:

Hungarian Stew

1 medium onion, cut in ¼-inch slices
1 tablespoon bacon fat or vegetable oil
1 large green bell pepper, cut crosswise into round ⅓-inch slices
2½ cups fresh tomato chunks (2 to 3 medium tomatoes) or canned
    chopped tomatoes
1 pound frankfurters or Kielbasa (Polish sausage), cut into round ⅓-inch slices

Sauté onion slices in heated fat or oil in a deep skillet until tender; do not brown. Add pepper slices; sauté 1 minute. Add tomato chunks and sliced frankfurters or sausage. Stew, covered, over medium heat 15 minutes.

Good served with mashed potatoes which have been well seasoned with salt, pepper and butter, with some stew vegetables and sauce ladled on top. May be made one day ahead and reheated on top of stove, but best freshly prepared. Do not freeze.

Per serving (based on 4 servings per recipe): Calories 425 (75% from fat), Carbohydrates 10.2 g, Protein 16.3 g, Total Fat 35.5 g, Sodium 1254 mg, Saturated Fat 13.3 g, Cholesterol 80 mg, Diabetic Exchanges: meat 2, veg 2, fat 5

WHATEVER WORKS

The street in front of our home in a mountainous region of South America was of rustic cobblestone. In early winter it developed a hole which continued to grow from an annoying rut until, by January, it could swallow the whole wheel of a car. No one seemed to be particularly in a hurry to fix it, and those of us who lived on the street grew accustomed to swerving around the obstacle even in complete darkness (there were no street lights). However, one evening one of our guests complained long and loudly over having almost lost the front end of his car in what he described as a cavern. As it turned out, we had just taken down our Christmas decorations and our naked tree lay by the front door. As we were seeing our guests out the door, a spontaneous idea was spawned, and the men uproariously grabbed the tree and ceremoniously "planted" the 8-foot pine in the center of the hole in the street. My husband and I had a wonderful laugh the following morning as we left for work watching cars effortlessly avoiding the now clearly marked hole in their path. Our biggest laugh, however, was upon our return home that evening to find not only that the tree was gone, but the street had been miraculously repaired!

Cornbread Jalapeño

2½ cups cornbread mix
   or cornmeal
1 cup all-purpose flour
2 tablespoons granulated sugar
1 tablespoon salt
4 teaspoons baking powder
3 eggs
½ cup oil

1 cup milk
½ cup sour cream
1 (15 oz.) can cream-style corn
1 (4 oz.) can jalapeno peppers
   (or green chilies), chopped
¼ cup chopped bell peppers, red and green
2 cups grated sharp Cheddar cheese
3 slices bacon, cooked crisp and crumbled

Preheat oven to 375° F. Generously grease a 9x13-inch baking dish.

Stir dry ingredients together in a large bowl. Add eggs, oil, milk, and sour cream; mix well. Stir in creamed corn, jalapenos, bell peppers, cheese, and bacon; mix well. Pour into greased baking dish. Bake in preheated oven until lightly browned, about 45 minutes. Cut into squares or rectangles to serve.

Per serving (based on 12 servings per recipe): Calories 395 (47% from fat), Carbohydrates 41.6 g, Protein 11.8 g, Total Fat 20.6 g, Sodium 1080 mg, Saturated Fat 7.6 g, Cholesterol 75 mg, Diabetic Exchanges: starch 2 , meat 1, fat 3.5

Assignment

Europe

A Conversation with Julia Child

One thing that I do remember when we were living in Paris—that's where I really started cooking—we had a big party for Bastille Day. I had been going to the Cordon Bleu, and I was filled with all kinds of wonderful dishes. I had a tremendous stuffed breast of veal poached in wine, and one of the most delicious stocks I've ever made in my life. It had everything, and it was just divine—we had this funny old apartment in Paris; the kitchen was on the fourth floor, dining room on the third, and you had to send things up or down on a little lift that you pulled up—and I had this marvelous stock sitting on the floor in my kitchen just waiting for me, and my brother-in-law who was a very helpful fellow . . . he just rushed around cleaning up and he dumped all the garbage—

Into it?

I have never forgotten that—40 years ago! Never forgotten that. Ruined that beautiful stock and I'll probably never, ever make such a one in my life.

THE FLYING BUN

It was a black-tie affair at the Belgian Ambassador's residence in a formal European capital. The Ambassador was related to the Rothschild family, and it showed the moment we walked through the front door into a foyer that resembled a small museum. The occasion was a farewell party for a mutual Swedish friend, a young diplomat also assigned here, with family ties to his country's royal family.

Staff in white gloves hovered around the guests as they searched for their names on the seating chart. Whiskies and aperitifs were being gently pressed into waiting hands. Displayed against one wall were six white circles on a green baize background representing tables, eight name tags to a circle. My wife was assigned to one table, I to another. We didn't recognize the names of our dinner companions. The evening shaped up as desperate mime: heads nodding, hands waving, mouths chewing, eyelids drooping. I could only hope that the food was good.

A bell sounded. We entered a grand dining room. People circled the six tables like wary mallards looking for a safe water landing. "Pardon" and "Excusez-moi" filled the air as place cards were examined and rejected. Worried smiles were exchanged but slowly, inevitably, the tables were filled. We were four men and four women at my table. We could have been eight strangers in a lifeboat, scrutinizing one another with quick, darting looks, slipping into tight smiles to hide our suspicions and concerns. The men tried to lean across the table to exchange brief hand shakes, but the flower arrangements and the crystal glassware proved forbidding obstacles. Names were muttered in a way to defy comprehension. I made surreptitious attempts to read my immediate neighbor's place cards, but gave it up for fear of getting a kink in my neck.

Then, as if bidden by some secret command, everyone reached for the linen napkin folded majestically over the tier of dinner plates placed before them. As I shook mine open, a hard dinner roll concealed in the folds dropped out. Just then, out of the corner of my eye, I caught a blurred movement on the far side of the room. It was a dinner roll! Flying over heads! It hit a wall with a crisp smack. I saw a brief commotion at my wife's table. Heads were turned skyward, fingers pointing at the roll's trajectory. One guest raised a napkin and demonstrated an errant slingshot motion with it. One of the waiters appeared and marched over to the table. In his gloved hand was a platter, and on the platter was another hard roll. He used silver tongs to present it to my wife. Head held high, she took it and placed it on a dish.

No one at my table mentioned the flying bun. As for me, it never happened. And I certainly didn't know that woman across the room. The dinner began. Conversation at my table was as flat as at a religious retreat, but I observed a lively conversation going on at my wife's table.

European Hard Rolls

3½ cups (500 grams) all-purpose flour
1 cake fresh yeast
2 teaspoons granulated sugar
1 cup (250 ml) warm water or milk, 100° F. (40° C.)
½ teaspoon salt

Preheat oven to 400° F. (200° C.)

Pour flour into a large bowl; make a well in the center. In a small bowl, crumble yeast; mix yeast with sugar, a little of the warm milk or water (¼ to ½ cup), and some of the flour. Carefully pour yeast mixture into well. Cover with a cloth and let stand in a warm, draft-free place for 15 minutes. Add salt and work in the remaining flour and water with hands or use hooks. Allow dough to rise for another 20 to 25 minutes. Form into small balls of 2½-inch diameter. Make a ½-inch deep cut across top of each ball. Place on oiled baking sheet and let rise for another 10 minutes. Bake on middle rack in preheated oven for 40 minutes, or until golden brown. To achieve crispness, place a small oven-proof bowl of water in the oven underneath the baking sheet or mist frequently with water using a spray bottle.

Makes 40 rolls.

Per serving: Calories 66 (5% from fat), Carbohydrates 14.1 g, Protein 2.4 g, Total Fat 0.4 g, Sodium 28 mg, Saturated Fat 0.1 g, Cholesterol 0 mg, Diabetic Exchanges: starch 1

MYSTERY MEAL

Adapted from *Reflections in a Silver Spoon*:

Even before Pearl Harbor, my brother-in-law Colonel David Bruce had been recruited by Major General William "Wild Bill" Donovan to be the General's right-hand man in London with the task of setting up an intelligence network. While Donovan spent most of the war in the U.S. as head of the Office of Strategic Services (OSS), David ran the London office, as Chief of the organization's European Theater of Operations. By the time I arrived, David had been in his new post for several months.

Stacy Lloyd—an old friend who was working in the Special Intelligence Branch of the OSS—and I rented an apartment together for about six months and then moved into a house that we rented on Chapel Street, Belgravia. It was a convenient arrangement since we had a housekeeper who looked after things and who could cook dinner if either or both of us were in. If she was off duty, she left something for us to heat up. On one of the first nights that we both decided to stay home for dinner, we discovered a saucepan on the stove with large lumps of meat and some rice in it.

We couldn't make up our minds whether it was some sort of soup, to which we were meant to add water before heating, or a stew. Being inexperienced cooks, we filled the saucepan with sufficient water to cover the meat and then heated it over the gas ring until it had boiled for a little while before serving it up. It had a disgusting taste, and we found that we couldn't eat very much, so we thought we had better go straight on to the dessert. While searching for that, we opened the oven door and found a very nice-looking casserole, which was obviously intended as the main course.

The following day the housekeeper looked at us resentfully and said, "You absolutely ruined my cat's dinner."

The editors suggest the following easy recipe would have been much enjoyed by the two men and, most certainly, by the cat!

Fettucine with Smoked Salmon Sauce

½ stick (¼ cup) unsalted butter
3 ounces smoked salmon
   (cut into julienne strips)
¾ cup half-and-half (cream)
½ cup grated Parmesan cheese

freshly grated nutmeg, to taste
freshly ground pepper, to taste
8 oz. fettucine, cooked, drained,
   and kept warm

Melt butter over moderate heat in medium saucepan. Add salmon and cream; bring to a boil stirring constantly. Remove pan from heat; add Parmesan cheese, nutmeg and pepper; stir mixture until cheese is melted. Pour sauce over fettucine, mixing well. Serve immediately.

Per serving (based on 4 servings per recipe): Calories 467 (44% from fat), Carbohydrates 47.3 g, Protein 18.1 g, Total Fat 22.6 g, Sodium 537 mg, Saturated Fat 13.2 g, Cholesterol 63 mg, Diabetic Exchanges: starch 3, meat 1, fat 4

Reprinted with the permission of William Morrow and Company from *Reflections in a Silver Spoon*, by Paul Mellon and John Baskett. Copyright © 1992 by Paul Mellon and John Baskett.

LET THEM EAT CAKE

Support officers are the Agency's counterpart to private bankers. They are responsible for ensuring that the "world's most exclusive clients" get whatever financial and material resources they need for espionage operations. A small, tight-knit group, support officers must constantly balance the need to stay within regulations with their desire to accomplish the mission.

In his exuberance to get the job done, a field (overseas) support officer authorized an item that should have been the prerogative of his support chief in Washington. He received a cable shortly thereafter that the chief intended to pay him a visit to "discuss the matter." The field officer realized that his judgment might be in question if the support chief decided not to approve the transaction after the fact.

Protocol demanded that the field officer invite the visiting chief to dinner when he arrived in town, and the officer shared with his wife the importance of making a good impression. Their small flat was cleaned and polished to perfection, the best crystal, china, and silver perfectly aligned, candles and soft light glowed. The wife prepared a dinner of her best recipes, proven favorites with guests from many countries and cultures.

The evening was orchestrated to perfection, even to the point of the couple's long haired cat flirting with their guest during cocktails. Nevertheless, the chief maintained a polite but somewhat detached decorum throughout dinner, presumably so as to be able to discipline his charge the next morning at the office. The officer was getting worried that his dinner strategy might not do the trick, and mentioned his concern to his wife during a quick trip to the kitchen to help with the dessert.

"Don't worry," his wife said. "I've got him just where I want him. Your voucher is as good as approved."

The dessert was his wife's specialty, a liqueur cake made from scratch that she had perfected over the years. It was served with French vanilla ice cream and, in the tradition of the couple's California upbringing, accompanied by strong coffee. After his first taste of the dessert, the visitor's composure changed noticeably as he dug in with increasing relish. By "seconds," it was clear that he had surrendered.

The next morning in the office, the chief got immediately to the point. Then, smiling, he continued, "Do you suppose that your wife would give me the recipe for that cake?"

Approving Officer's Grand Marnier Cake

For the batter:

1 cup (2 sticks) butter, softened
1 cup granulated sugar
3 eggs, separated
1 teaspoon Grand Marnier
2 cups all-purpose flour

1 teaspoon baking powder
1 teaspoon baking soda
1 cup sour cream
1 tablespoon grated orange peel
½ cup chopped mixed nuts

For the topping:

¼ cup fresh orange juice
⅓ cup Grand Marnier

½ cup sugar

Lightly butter and flour a 10-inch fluted bundt pan. Preheat oven to 350° F.

Cream butter and sugar in a large mixing bowl. Add egg yolks; mix well. Add 1 teaspoon Grand Marnier; blend. Sift flour, baking powder, and baking soda onto a sheet of waxed paper; add ½ of dry ingredients to the creamed butter mixture; mix well. Add sour cream and blend. Add remaining dry ingredients. Stir in orange peel and nuts.

In a separate bowl, beat egg whites until stiff; fold into batter. Pour into prepared baking pan.

Bake in preheated oven about 55 minutes, or until a wooden pick inserted into center comes out clean. Remove from oven to wire rack; cool in pan 10 minutes. Invert cake onto a second wire rack.

While cake is baking, combine topping ingredients in a small bowl. Pour over cake while it is still warm. Cool. To serve, cut cake into medium thick slices.

Per serving (based on 12 servings per recipe): Calories 416 (50% from fat), Carbohydrates 43.4 g, Protein 5.6 g, Total Fat 24 g, Sodium 316 mg, Saturated Fat 12.6 g, Cholesterol 97 mg, Diabetic Exchanges: starch 1, fat 5, fruit 2

MACHO MAN

During the five years we spent in Europe, my husband and I developed a strong liking for escargot. After talking to a French friend at our current post about our love for the appetizer, he presented us with a gift of several cans of snails. We immediately planned for their preparation, and wanted to share them with friends who had a similar liking. We asked one of the young Marine Security Guards who had visited us often if he had eaten snails and liked them. He came back with a resounding "yes," and we included him on the invitation list. Because all of our guests were "connoisseurs" of escargot, no explanations were necessary on the ritual of eating them—or so we thought. We were all amazed when the first person to begin eating was the Marine, who did so by picking up a shell in his fingers, popping it entirely into his mouth and crunching it to shreds!

For those less adventurous, here is a shellfish recipe as given to a colleague many years ago by a hotel chef, and lovingly saved on the original hotel stationery. You will have to depend on your own preferences in determining the ingredient amounts, and you can choose for yourself whether or not to eat the shells!

Scampi Flambés (Hotel Princess Juliana Style)

scampi (6 to 8 per person) salt and pepper
butter few drops of lemon juice
chopped onions parsley
sliced mushrooms lobster sauce
Calvados (apple brandy) cream
  and brandy

"Fry some butter in a frying pan. Add the chopped onions and sliced raw mushrooms and fry them for a few minutes over low heat. Add the shrimps, increase heat. Pour a spoonful of Calvados and a spoonful of Brandy over the shrimp, onions and mushrooms and ignite to flambé. Add lobster sauce and cream with salt and pepper, lemon juice, and parsley, all to taste. Stir well."

Serve with hot buttered rice.

Dietitian's note: Because ingredient proportions vary according to taste, nutritional values
have not been determined.

ECONOMY GASTRONOMY

I have always loved to cook. In the '60s, I began planning a cookbook entitled *Economy Gastronomy* and actually wrote several chapters before I learned that someone else had snagged that title for her cookbook. There was a time when I probably fancied myself the next Julia Child. I certainly thought a stay in Paris and a Grand Dipliôme from the Cordon Bleu would be next to dying and going to heaven.

In the late '70s, I was able, at last, to follow in Julia's footsteps, earning the Grande Diplôme at the Cordon Bleu! Well, the Cordon Bleu had learned of its fame, and the dollar-to-franc exchange ratio was at a dismal low. My husband's modest government salary could not underwrite a Grande Diplôme, but it did assist with a few afternoon demonstrations at the Cordon Bleu and La Varenne.

Finally, I discovered the Ecole Hotelière de Paris on Rue Méderic in the 17th district. That is where many of France's best chefs have received their professional training. Through the American School of Paris and the U.S. Embassy, I was able to round up enough French-speaking Americans to organize a special class called "Cuisine—Perfectionnement" taught by one of the regular chef instructors.

The government-subsidized ecole offered our class at much lower cost than the privately-owned Cordon Bleu, enabling us to learn French cuisine at a reasonable price, truly Economy Gastronomy! On the other hand, the director of the ecole was delighted to discover a new paying market for their services.

We must have seemed like a bunch of dilettantes at first. We were constantly asking if things could be prepared in advance, and the usual response was, "No." Most classic French dishes are meant to be served directly from the oven or stovetop. Keeping the dishes warm while dinner guests arrive and socialize can mean disaster. Just think of a soufflé. Timing is everything.

Nevertheless, our group accumulated 50 hours of solid French cooking fundamentals and hundreds of wonderful recipes. I still depend on them for my classic French repertoire. Here is one that is a standard first course for a special dinner party.

Pâté de Saumon (Salmon Paté)
À l'Ecole Hotelière de Paris Jean Drouant

¾ cup water
1 stick (½ cup) butter, divided
pinch of salt
pinch of pepper
dash grated nutmeg
1 cup all-purpose flour, divided

3 egg yolks
3 pounds fresh salmon fillet
1 egg white
3 cups crème fraiche or
    lightly whipped heavy cream

In a saucepan heat water, 4 tablespoons butter, salt, pepper, and grated nutmeg; bring to a boil; cook until butter is melted. Add ¼ cup flour; stir constantly and quickly with a wooden spoon until mixture pulls away from sides of the saucepan; remove pan from the heat.

Add egg yolks, one at a time, stirring after each addition until yolk is completely incorporated (mixture will be thick). Chill the panade in refrigerator.

Preheat oven to 350° F. Butter a 4x12x2-inch terrine; set aside.

From the salmon fillets, cut 8 large baton-shaped pieces, approximately 1 inch by 6 inches; season each piece with salt, pepper, and nutmeg and dredge in remaining flour. Heat 4 tablespoons butter in skillet; sauté salmon pieces on all sides. Remove from skillet and set aside to cool.

Beat 1 egg white until frothy. Chop remaining salmon meat finely; transfer to a metal bowl; set bowl in a container of ice. Season lightly; stir in the egg white until completely incorporated. Gradually add crème fraiche or lightly whipped heavy cream, stirring constantly until absorbed thoroughly. Add chilled panade; keep mixture cold.

Spread ⅓ of the egg white-panade mixture on the bottom of buttered terrine, pressing mixture carefully into the pan so that there are no pockets of air. Lay 4 pieces of salmon lengthwise on the mixture; cover with another ⅓ of the mixture, taking care to smooth out any pockets of air. Lay the last 4 pieces of salmon on this layer; cover with the rest of the mixture.

Cover the terrine with aluminum foil or lid and place in a pan of water filled halfway up the sides of the terrine. Bake in preheated oven at least one hour or until a needle inserted into the center comes out clean. The paté must be hot in the middle.

Remove the terrine from the oven. Let set for 10 minutes before unmolding. Serve hot or cold.

Per serving (based on 24 servings per recipe): Calories 260 (71% from fat), Carbohydrates 5 g, Protein 14.1 g, Total Fat 20.3 g, Sodium 175 mg, Saturated Fat 10.3 g, Cholesterol 110 mg, Diabetic Exchanges: meat 2, fat 2

FIVE'S A CROWD

Early in our tour in Southern Europe, we were pleased and a little nervous (me) to host a dinner party for the Division Chief and several other senior officers from Washington, DC. We hoped they would recognize our ability to learn something of the style and culinary achievements of our host country friends.

We had just moved into our apartment three weeks before and were unfamiliar with the many quirks of our building, e.g., power outages, elevator stubbornness, water flow stoppages in the middle of showers, etc. The evening of the dinner party arrived, preparations completed and the apartment looked great. The food, the wines, the china, the stemware, and the flowers were selected with care, and we believed our preparations to be faultless.

We peered over the balcony and noted our distinguished guests arriving—five in all—and entering the building. Opening the front door, we eagerly awaited their arrival on the elevator, which was really no bigger than a very small closet. The minutes went by; where were they? And what is that muffled shouting we hear from several floors down? Suddenly, we heard footsteps of someone running up the stairs. It was one of our officers, gasping for breath, explaining the elevator was stuck between floors.

There is a warning in the elevator, albeit in the local language, stating that no more than three people should attempt to ascend in it. No way could that tiny elevator carry five adults to the 7th floor! My husband ran down to the basement to alert the portiere (our dog was running along with him to see what all the excitement was), and they proceeded to pull the set of greasy cables in an attempt to inch it to the 4th floor, all the while shouting words of encouragement to the stuck passengers.

Finally, they were able to open the doors manually, and they all piled out and climbed the remaining three floors. The visitors were good sports, and the food and wine were devoured. I guess emergencies build up a great hunger and thirst. The evening was declared a success. Although we did note that even though the portiere had in the meantime repaired the elevator, everyone walked down the seven flights to the street level when it came time to depart.

Mediterranean Beans

(a rustic dish best made with cannellini, a type of dried white kidney beans)

1½ cups dried cannellini beans or white navy or great northern beans, rinsed
1 (13 oz.) can of chicken broth
1½ cups of water
dried pepperoncini (red peppers), to taste (optional)
½ cup fresh sage leaves or 1 tablespoon dried sage plus 2 tablespoons
    fresh parsley
fresh rosemary to taste
¼ teaspoon ground pepper
1½ teaspoons minced garlic
2 tablespoons olive oil
¾ teaspoon salt

Soak beans overnight in water to cover by 2 inches. (To quick-soak: Combine beans with water to cover by two inches in a saucepan and bring to a boil. Boil for 2 minutes. Cover and let stand one hour.) Drain beans. Combine beans, broth, water, pepperoncini, sage, rosemary, and pepper in saucepan. Bring to a boil; reduce heat, cover and simmer about 40 minutes until tender. Add garlic, oil, and salt, and simmer uncovered for another 5 to 15 minutes. Makes nine ½-cup servings.

Per serving: Calories 81 (42% from fat), Carbohydrates 8.1 g, Protein 3.8 g, Total Fat 3.9 g, Sodium 321 mg, Saturated Fat 0.5 g, Cholesterol 0 mg, Diabetic Exchanges: starch 0.5, fat 1

HELEN'S MASTERPIECES

Some of my fondest memories of living overseas are those that include sharing time with friends and learning more about the culture in which we were living at the time. While living in the Mediterranean area, many an evening was spent with friends and co-workers in neighborhood restaurants. We developed a love for many of the wonderful regional dishes we sampled and wished that we could recreate those delights for our families. As luck would have it, we met a woman from Greece who agreed to teach us how to prepare some of her favorite dishes. Word spread, and soon Helen was teaching small groups the fine art of Greek cooking. We looked forward to those afternoons, laughing at each other as we awkwardly tried to pronounce the Greek names. We developed many close friendships, an understanding of a culture different from our own, and, more importantly, we allowed someone else a chance to get to know us and learned that people are basically the same, no matter where we come from. Here are some of Helen's fabulous recipes.

Avgolemono (Lemon Soup)

Stock:

8 to 10 cups water
1 stalk celery with tops, chopped
4 to 5 carrots, sliced
3 small onions, quartered
2 large (or 4 small) potatoes

½ cup rice
2 eggs
juice of 2 lemons
1 tablespoon water

Meatballs:

1½ pounds ground beef
½ cup rice
1 egg

¼ cup vegetable oil
1 teaspoon each salt and pepper

Soak 1 cup rice in water to cover for 1 hour (½ cup will be used in meatball mixture). Drain.

Prepare stock by pouring 8 to 10 cups water into large pot. Add celery, carrots and onions, bring to boil, then lower heat; simmer covered.

While stock is simmering, prepare meatballs by combining meatball ingredients in a bowl. Form meat mixture into small balls and add to stock. Cook over medium heat until meatballs are almost tender. Add potatoes and remaining ½ cup rice to stock. Cook until potatoes are tender.

In a small bowl, beat two eggs until foamy; add lemon juice plus 1 tablespoon of water and beat again. Add one cup of stock; stir well. Pour mixture slowly into the stock; continue cooking stock, stirring frequently, until eggs are cooked and stock is slightly thickened. Serve immediately.
Serves 8 to 10.

Per serving (based on 8 servings per recipe): Calories 353 (46% from fat), Carbohydrates 28 g,
Protein 20 g, Total Fat 18 g, Sodium 346 mg, Saturated Fat 5.2 g, Cholesterol 82 mg,
Diabetic Exchanges: starch 1, meat 2, veg 2, fat 1

Souvlakia

2 pounds leg of lamb, cut into 1-inch cubes
salt and pepper, to taste
oregano, fresh, finely chopped, or dried

Marinade:

1 cup olive oil
⅓ cup lemon juice
½ cup dry red wine

2 cloves garlic, chopped
2 large bay leaves

Put lamb cubes in a large stainless steel or glass bowl or deep baking dish; sprinkle with salt, pepper and oregano. Mix marinade ingredients together in small bowl; pour over lamb. Cover with plastic wrap; chill in refrigerator 12 to 24 hours.

Drain lamb cubes; thread on wooden or metal skewers. Grill over hot charcoal or under broiler, turning from time to time, until meat is well seared and browned on the outside and tender, juicy, and pink on the inside. Serve at once.

Per serving (based on 8 servings per recipe): Calories 322 (61% from fat), Carbohydrates 1.02 g, Protein 29 g, Total Fat 21.5 g, Sodium 470 mg, Saturated Fat 4.66 g, Cholesterol 91 mg, Diabetic Exchanges: meat 4

Fried Zucchini

2 medium zucchini
½ teaspoon salt
2 eggs
¼ cup grated Kasseri, Parmesan, or other hard cheese
½ teaspoon dried oregano

2 tablespoons flour
¼ teaspoon pepper
2 tablespoons olive oil
2 tablespoons butter

Scrape, wash and dry zucchini; cut into lengthwise slices. Mix zucchini and salt. Let stand for one hour. Drain well; pat dry with paper towel.

For batter: beat eggs; add cheese, oregano, flour and pepper; mix well.

Heat olive oil and butter over medium heat until foam subsides. Dip zucchini in batter to coat. Fry in hot oil and butter, about 3 minutes on each side, until crisp and golden.

Serves 4.

Per serving: Calories 222 (76% from fat), Carbohydrates 6 g, Protein 7 g, Total Fat 19 g, Sodium 428 mg, Saturated Fat 6.4 g, Cholesterol 114 mg, Diabetic Exchanges: meat 1, veg 1, fat 3

EXCELLENT EGGPLANT

When I lived in the Mediterranean region, while walking to the open-air street markets, I often whiled away the time by choosing adjectives for my favorite vegetables. As I remember there were cooling cucumbers, aristocratic artichokes, caustic cabbages, and elegant eggplants. For the eggplant's appearance is "richness and refinement combined." And certainly when cooked it is "fastidiously tasteful."

The handsome shiny eggplant, grown in several sizes and shapes, often has a dark purple skin, but it can also be white, yellow, red, or even striped. Actually a fruit but widely regarded as a vegetable, the eggplant was once thought to be poisonous and was shunned as a food. However, it has long been treasured in Mediterranean countries, where it is often cooked with garlic, onion, olive oil, fresh and dried herbs, and tomatoes, as well as other vegetables.

Here is the recipe for one of the first foreign culinary specialties I learned to cook. It features two of my favorite foods, eggplant and yogurt, which I was introduced to on my first overseas assignment.

Eggplant-Yogurt Salad

2 medium eggplants, washed, about 1 pound each
2 garlic cloves, crushed
1 medium onion, peeled and finely chopped
¼ cup olive oil, preferable extra-virgin

2 to 3 tablespoons fresh lemon juice
1 cup plain nonfat yogurt
salt and freshly ground pepper to taste
cayenne pepper
chopped fresh dill or parsley

Prick the eggplants with a fork in several places. Put on a baking sheet and place under a heated broiler. Cook, turning occasionally, until the skins become charcoal black and eggplants are soft. (The burning imparts a desirable charcoal flavor to the pulp.) Peel off the skins while still hot. Put the pulp in a bowl and mash thoroughly with a fork or wooden spoon. Pour off any liquid.

Add the garlic, onion, olive oil, and lemon juice, beating after each addition. Stir in the yogurt. Season with salt and pepper. Beat again until light and fluffy. Serve in a mound on a plate, garnished with a sprinkling of cayenne and chopped dill.

Serves 8 to 10.

Per serving (based on 10 servings per recipe): Calories 85 (57% from fat), Carbohydrates 7.3 g, Protein 2.3 g, Total Fat 5.6 g, Sodium 75 mg, Saturated Fat 0.8 g, Cholesterol 0 mg, Diabetic Exchanges: veg 1, fat 1

VALINKA

While I was participating in a conference in Geneva in the mid-1970s, the Ambassador invited me to provide a musical welcome for his Soviet counterpart at a party hosted by the U.S. delegation. He knew that I had played the bagpipes for many years with the Washington Scottish Pipe Band, and had both my pipes and proper Scottish regalia with me in Geneva. As I recall, I piped the distinguished Soviet negotiator aboard the cruise boat we had rented for the evening to the strains of "Scotland the Brave," or some equally prosaic tune. All the while, my disrespectful soul was aching to belt out "When the Saints Go Marching In."

In the mid-1980s, I found myself in Geneva again, at another conference. After my first formal session, I was chatting with the Soviet Deputy Commissioner, who had been a member of their delegation 10 years before.

I introduced myself as the person who played the bagpipes for their Minister at our party on the lake. At that point, my interpreter—one of the State Department's finest—came to a screeching halt. "Bagpipes!?!" It was my shining moment; just by chance I knew the

Russian word. Without blinking any eye, I told him "valinka" and he carried on from there.

That one word is about the only Russian I know, but I'm sure that somewhere in my KGB file there's a comment that I am fluent in Russian even though I pretend not to be. After all, who but a fluent linguist would know an obscure word like "valinka"?

Geneva is also the place where I enjoyed the best Spaghetti Carbonara I have ever tasted in a restaurant. The following is my version; it requires a lot of time-consuming hand preparation—but it tastes so good that it's worth the effort every now and then!

Spaghetti Carbonara (Á la Hotel Royal Geneva)

237 11-inch pieces of thin
    spaghetti (or just the right
    amount for your crew)
2 to 3 pieces bacon
1 skinless and boneless
    chicken breast

4 to 6 slices of flavorful cooked ham
3 to 4 scallions
3 eggs

in amounts to taste:
whipping cream
grated Parmesan cheese

freshly ground black pepper

Cut the chicken, bacon, and ham into approximately ¼-inch squares, keeping then separate. Chop the scallions as fine as possible and set them aside. (Be sure to use a freshly-washed chopping board for each ingredient.)

The following operations require occasional stirring. Fry the bacon in a heavy, 3- to 4-inch deep cast iron pan or skillet, over medium heat. When cooked thoroughly, but not crisp, remove the bacon. Set it aside, but leave the liquid fat in the bottom of the pan. Turn the heat up a notch or two, and add the chicken; cook until nearly done, adding oil if necessary; then, add the ham. Turn down the heat, and boil away the liquid that will appear when the ham begins to cook.

When most of the liquid is gone, put the cast iron pan—containing the cooked chicken and ham—in the oven on warm.

At that point the whole operation can hold for an hour or so, if necessary. The next steps are (1) in a large pot, get water boiling for the spaghetti, (2) break the eggs into a bowl and whisk them lightly, (3) hunt for the already-prepared bacon and scallions, and (4) get the cheese, cream, and pepper grinder ready for the frantic final moments.

Remove pan with chicken and ham from oven. Boil the spaghetti in salted water (we like it al dente). Drain and pour it immediately into the cast iron pan on top of the chicken and ham. Add the raw eggs on top of the spaghetti and mix thoroughly; the heat in the pan should allow the eggs to cook completely (this is why a heavy cast iron pan, which holds heat well, is recommended).

Finally, mix in the bacon and scallions, plenty of Parmesan cheese, and enough cream to give it a pleasing consistency. Top with freshly ground pepper, and serve immediately. The proper accompaniment is a big salad, preferably with lots of capers.

Makes enough to satisfy 4 hungry people.

Per serving (using 16 ounces dry spaghetti, 4 ounces trimmed ham, 3/4 cup of heavy cream, 1/2 cup whole milk Parmesan, and 1/2 teaspoon black pepper): Calories 739 (37% from fat), Carbohydrates 75.9 g, Protein 40 g, Total Fat 30.6 g, Sodium 810 mg, Saturated Fat 15.7 g, Cholesterol 250 mg, Diabetic Exchanges: starch 5, meat 3.5, fat 2

OH, THOSE SWISS TYPEWRITERS!!!

In the mid-1970s, during a conference in Geneva, I was using a foreign built version of an American brand typewriter. The typewriter was nowhere near the quality of the American original, and on a particularly busy day, it was causing me quite a bit of trouble: 1/2 spaces between letters, letters overlapping each other, etc. After about three hours of putting up with this monster, I told my boss that I needed either a different typewriter or a repairman to fix this machine. Each secretary in the delegation had a typewriter, and I was told that no additional typewriters were available. So, I asked the logistics officer to call repair.

About mid-afternoon, the repairman arrived. He spoke no English; I spoke no French. What a beginning! My boss, however, spoke French, so I got him into the act. He explained the problem to the repairman, who then asked me to show him what was happening. Grabbing the *Herald Tribune* newspaper, I started typing from one of the articles. After about two minutes of typing, there was this "No, no, mademoiselle, no, no!" I stopped typing. The repairman conferred with my boss who burst out laughing. I wondered what was the problem. Still laughing, my boss said the repairman told him I was typing much too fast—the typewriter's ball element could not turn that fast—I must slow down considerably. I pointed to the typewriter and asked the repairman to show me how slow I should type. His method was "hunt and peck" at its worst. Now, I began laughing. With all the work to be done that day, there was no way that anything would get out typing at that speed. I asked my boss to tell the repairman that typing at his suggested speed would be the same as asking Mario Andretti to race in the Indianapolis 500 at 50 miles per hour, and expect to win!

Needless to say, in order to get anything at all done, I had to force myself to slow down. Never in my wildest dreams did I ever expect someone to tell me to go slower. I was always expected to get the work out as fast as possible. With the amount of work to be done in our Washington office, "slow" was not in the vocabulary!

Raclette

Everyone knows Swiss fondue. The Swiss have another specialty, raclette, which contrasts to the lengthy time needed for making fondue. All raclette needs is a good heat source and a hunk of cheese.

Raclette is named for the French word "to scrape." The cheese—also called raclette—is a melting cheese, and the best comes from the Valais region. Making the dish raclette is simple: melt a cut piece of cheese—in Switzerland this would be a section of the wheel—scrape off the melted portion onto a heated plate, and return the scraped cheese to the heat source for the next serving.

The heat source can be merely a good bed of coals in the fireplace; place the cheese close to the coals but able to be easily pulled back and scraped. A very hot oven can be used with two or three very thin slices of cheese on a heat-proof plate; heat until runny. To satisfy the gadget-conscious retail trade and restaurant or commercial kitchens, mechanical heating sources have been developed. The end result is always the same; a small pool of melted cheese on individual warmed plates for each diner.

Raclette is eaten by swirling small boiled potatoes, small cocktail onions or cornichons in the cheese. One plateful is never enough; the Swiss tally the amount eaten by stacking the used plates beside each person or writing the number of servings beside each diner. The number of servings consumed indicates a certain "je ne sais quoi" about the diner.

A good white wine, ideally Fendant du Valais, accompanies this dish. Or a good beer.

Failing to find true Swiss raclette, there are alternatives—Gruyere or Appenzeller can be substituted. The French have a raclette too, but the taste differs from the true Swiss version.

Dietitian's note: Because ingredient proportions are indefinite, nutritional values have not been determined.

GLIMPSES OF GENEVA

A friend and I had an evening out in Geneva sans children, shopping (grocery, not couturier), or wifely duties. The concierge assured us it was safe for two unescorted women to be out at night, and we had decided to be truly naughty and indulge in one of those sinful desserts we had seen.

After a leisurely stroll checking our various sidewalk cafes, we finally selected one within sight of the tip of Jet d' Eau, the Swiss fountain in Lake Geneva, an impressive national secret—HOW does it work to spout water that high?

Dessert was magnificent: Large helpings of rich vanilla ice cream bathed with a jigger of bourbon and topped with lots of whipped cream. A cup of good strong coffee on the side. Simple, yet delicious. I have since that time experimented with rum, sour cream, yogurt, and, of course, liqueurs.

· · · · ·

Once after an evening stroll on the mountainside in Wengen, I returned to the hotel and told the concierge I had heard someone's cuckoo clock seeming to strike about 14. "Oh, non, Madam. It was a real, live cuckoo bird."

· · · · ·

Family outings to restaurants and cafes sometimes presented a problem for our children. Menu items were unfamilar, and helpings were often too big. Our nine-year-old son once ordered a ham sandwich. It arrived: An inch-thick slab of ham between two slices of French bread two inches thick—each. The nine-year-old's mouth tried to negotiate a five-inch sandwich (with no mayo, either). It was eaten in sections.

A cafe in Geneva's Ville Cite presented a piece of Gruyere cheese measuring 1x3x5 inches to our three-year-old for lunch. He ate it all.

Melted Cheese in Crust

1 round or oval loaf (about 1 pound) day-old French bread
⅓ cup olive oil (or melted butter)
2 cloves garlic, minced
1 to 1½ pounds Brie, Camembert, or St. Andre cheese

Preheat oven to 350° F.

With a serrated knife, carefully cut around and down through top of bread (do not cut all the way through the bottom crust) to make a shell about ½-inch thick on sides. Slide fingers down alongside cut center of loaf and pull free in a single piece, leaving a ½-inch thick base. Every 1½ inches around the rim of shell, make cuts 1½ inches deep.

Cut the bread pulled out from the center into ½-inch thick slices.

Mix oil and garlic. Brush inside of shell with 3 tablespoons of the garlic oil. Place cheese, with or without rind, in bread shell, trimming to fit. Place filled shell and bread slices in a single layer, in a 10x15-inch, rimmed baking pan. Drizzle remaining oil over bread slices (not over bread shell). Bake in preheated oven until slices are toasted, about 10 to 15 minutes.

Remove bread slices from oven and cool on a wire rack. Continue baking filled shell about 10 more minutes until cheese is melted. Serve immediately.

To serve, place filled shell on a board and surround with toasted bread slices for dipping into melted cheese. When all slices have been eaten, snap off crisp pieces from edge of shell to use as dippers.

Per serving (based on 60 servings per recipe): Calories 60 (56% from fat), Carbohydrates 4 g, Protein 3.5 g, Total Fat 3.7 g, Sodium 126 mg, Saturated Fat 1.7 g, Cholesterol 6.8 mg, Diabetic Exchanges: starch 0.5, meat 0.5, fat 0.5

Vodka Limon

1 bottle inexpensive vodka   12 Tellicherry peppercorns
12 strips of lemon peel

Combine the above ingredients in a bottle. Keep in the refrigerator. Occasionally tip the bottle gently to mix, and enjoy. Serving size—one ounce over ice with a splash of water.

Per 1-fluid ounce serving: Calories 75 (98% from alcohol), Carbohydrates 0.3 g, Protein 0 g, Total Fat 0 g, Sodium 0 mg, Saturated Fat 0 g, Cholesterol 0 mg, Diabetic Exchanges: fat 1.5 (calories from alcohol are counted as fat in the diabetic exchange system)

KARFIOLSUPPE

It was one of those drizzly kind of days in Vienna, in the early fall. My wife and I had just arrived, and this day, with addresses and map in hand, we were out looking for a furnished place to stay. I knew enough German to be able to ask questions, and even understand most of the answers, but you learn a lot when you are house-hunting on your own with no tips or hints to help you along. One prospective landlady bragged that the best air in Vienna was in her part of town. She took one look at us, determined that we were newlyweds, and said she could only rent to us if we agreed to hire a cleaning woman, because Americans don't know how to do the floors.

By 3:00 we were tired, somewhat dejected, and hungry. We soon realized that most restaurants in Vienna closed for a few hours after the midday meal. Remembering that the cafes stayed open and always had something hot for hungry stragglers, we headed towards the nearest one. The cafe was typical, with small, round tables, half curtains made of lace, newspapers and magazines on wooden hangers on the walls available for customers to take to a table and read while nursing a cup of coffee. As usual, the waitress was dressed in black with a small white apron, and high-top shoes with the toes and heels cut out. She was watched over by the headwaiter in black tie, wrapped in a big white apron from chest to knees, complete with a bulging black leather fold-over purse jammed into his belt in the back.

We sat down and were ready to order. A schnitzel? Out of the question; the cook had gone home for the afternoon. Perhaps the Herrshaften would care for a torte? Thank you, no, we would like something hot. Perhaps a soup? We have Karfiolsuppe.

Viennese dialect was not covered when I studied the language, but soup is soup, and it would be hot. The biggest concern for both of us was if it would be some kind of fish soup, maybe Carp? We hoped not. Well, when in Rome, and anyway it would be something to ease our dampened moods. We both ordered Karfiolsuppe.

It came creamy white, sprinkled with a little parsley and looked as if it might be creamed mashed potatoes. It turned out to be cauliflower soup. In German, I knew that vegetable, one of my least favorites, as blumenkohl, but this was Vienna, where most of Eastern Europe once melded into an empire captained by Vienna, and a lot of non-German words had worked into the vocabulary; this was the Hungarian word for the vegetable. If I had known that, I probably would have skipped the soup and ordered the cake. Was it the weather, the mood, the unsuccessful apartment shopping? It was probably the best soup I had ever tasted!

As soon as we could manage it, we added Karfiolsuppe to our culinary repertoire.

Cauliflower Soup

1 quart water
1 head cauliflower, leaves
   and green stem removed
1 medium onion, thinly sliced
2 tablespoons vegetable oil
2 tablespoons all-purpose flour

salt and white pepper to taste
dash bottled hot pepper sauce (optional)
milk, as needed for thinning
1 tablespoon chopped parsley, for garnish

Bring water to boil in a deep pot or kettle. Add cauliflower to boiling water; reduce heat. Simmer, covered, about 10 minutes until tender-crisp. Remove cauliflower from water and break into flowerets; reserve water. In another large pot or a deep skillet, heat oil; add onion slices; sauté onion slices in oil until soft but not browned. Stir in flour; mix well but do not let flour brown. Add the reserved cauliflower cooking water; whisk well to avoid any lumps. Add flowerets. Cover; bring stock to a simmer. Continue to simmer until flowerets are tender.

Remove flowerets from stock with a slotted spoon. Set aside a few flowerets for garnish; put remaining flowerets in blender or food processor fitted with a steel blade. Add some of the simmering liquid; puree until smooth.

Stir puree into stock. Season with salt, white pepper, and hot pepper sauce, if desired. Thin with a little milk if necessary. Serve in individual soup bowls garnished with reserved flowerets and parsley, and accompanied by some good bread and butter.

Per serving (based on 4 servings per recipe): Calories 123 (48% from fat), Carbohydrates 13.5 g, Protein 3.8 g, Total Fat 7.16 g, Sodium 580 mg, Saturated Fat 1 g, Cholesterol 0 mg, Diabetic Exchanges: veg 2, fat 1

DON'T KNOCK THE NOCKERL

Austrians consider Salzburger Nockerl the ultimate finale to a grand dinner, a dessert as elegant as it is tricky to prepare. While serving overseas, I came across the recipe, made some changes, and came up with this delicious, light dessert which I delighted to serve to guests. One day a Viennese friend, who is an excellent cook, came with her children for a visit. I commented that I had recently served Salzburger Nockerl to houseguests. She was quite surprised, asking, "Didn't it fail?" So I took her into my kitchen and whipped up my version for her, using some of the farm-fresh eggs she had just brought. I subsequently repeated the demonstration for other friends.

At a small dinner we gave during a later assignment to Europe, I excused myself from the table after the meal to prepare this same glorious concoction. As I returned with the bubbling, frothy dessert, I could see one guest's eyes widening and he stared as I placed the Salzburger Nockerl on a serving cart between us. He gingerly tasted the dessert, then praised it, explaining that his family owned a fine old restaurant in Austria, and they took great pride in the food they served. The Nockerl I served to him, he said, was as fine as theirs.

Salzburger Nockerl

3 tablespoons unsalted butter	1 teaspoon all-purpose flour
½ cup milk	1 teaspoon grated lemon peel
2 tablespoons granulated sugar	1 tablespoon lemon juice, or to taste
8 egg whites	3 tablespoons orange juice
5 tablespoons powdered sugar, sifted	additional powdered sugar to sift over top
3 egg yolks	

Preheat oven to 450° F.

In a shallow, oval baking dish, place the butter, milk and granulated sugar. Heat in oven until butter melts.

While this is in the oven, beat the egg whites until stiff. Gently fold in the powdered sugar.

Beat the egg yolks; add flour, lemon peel, and juices. Gently fold yolk mixture into the beaten whites. Quickly scoop large mounds of the mixture into the baking dish, avoiding the edges to the extent possible. Bake in preheated oven for 5 minutes until top is golden but the center is soft. Sprinkle with additional powdered sugar and serve AT ONCE.

Oven temperatures and timing are crucial. Be certain everything is ready for serving before starting.

Serves 4.

Per serving: Calories 245 (47% from fat), Carbohydrates 23.6 g, Protein 8.9 g, Total Fat 13 g, Sodium 114 mg, Saturated Fat 7.1 g, Cholesterol 168 mg, Diabetic Exchanges: meat 1, fruit 1.5, fat 2

THE CHEESEBALL CAPER

Sometimes a recipe can be too good. During assignments overseas, I found that foreign dinner guests often asked for those recipes which I knew would only cause confusion and disappointment. American ingredients that I was able bring with me or order from a commissary were not always available in foreign shops and markets. Then there was the problem of U.S. weights and measures for cooking being different from just about everywhere else, and finally, sometimes something got lost—literally—in the translation, as in this story.

My standard contribution to embassy holiday parties was a nut-covered cheeseball—the kind you can buy in any grocery store in the U.S., but which had to be homemade overseas. One year, a foreign associate asked for the recipe so she could serve it at her husband's business party. Her English was far better than my abilities in any foreign language, so I gave her the recipe in English. A few days later I asked her if the cheeseball had been a success and she complained that it was a disaster; surely, she suggested, I had left something out of the recipe. She had known of cooks who did that on purpose in order to protect their cooking secrets. I assured her that was definitely not the case; there must have been another reason for the inedible results. We went over the ingredients and discovered that she had been sure that "pimiento" was the English name for caper, so she had mixed capers into the cheeseball. I imagine the taste was quite unusual!

From then on, I was more careful when giving out my recipes, but even so, it seemed that simple recipes often became quite complicated. A good example is my recipe for a no-bake cheesecake. I have used this simple recipe, given to me by a friend and colleague, many times in many countries. It has never failed to delight our guests, foreign or American, and I have often been asked for the recipe. But, the main ingredient, American style cream cheese, was almost always hard to find overseas. In some countries there were products called creamed cheese or cheese cream, but they had a totally different consistency and flavor. Depending on the place, usually at least one of the other ingredients was totally impossible to find. So, after a while, I learned to give out more than just a recipe I knew would be of no use. I began to include a gift of any hard to find ingredients, and sometimes even added a pie pan or a set of American measuring cups. These extras were always well appreciated. Quite often sharing the recipe led to exchanges of more recipes, and invitations to taste the results. In this way many casual acquaintances became genuine friends.

Here, then, is the cheesecake recipe modified (complicated?) for overseas cooks. And, by the way, if you know of a good substitute for cream cheese, please let me know before my next assignment overseas!

No-Bake Cherry Cheesecake

2 (8 oz.) packages cream cheese (about 454 grams total)
　　(If the local cream cheese is not as thick as American cream cheese:
　　dissolve completely 1 package (about 8 g) unflavored gelatin in ¼ cup
　　(60 ml) water and stir into the beaten cream cheese; otherwise the
　　cake will not set)
½ pint whipping cream, whipped (about 3 dl or 240 ml)
1 cup powdered sugar (about 125 g; known as flour sugar or icing sugar overseas)
1 tablespoon vanilla extract (about 15 ml), or about 3 inches (7 cm) of vanilla
　　bean scraped, then finely crushed (or experiment with vanilla sugar, a
　　staple overseas)
1 (20 oz.) can cherry pie filling (600 g) (or fruit topping for a torte)
1 graham cracker pie crust, purchased, if available, or homemade (see below)

Beat cream cheese until creamy in a large bowl. Slowly stir in vanilla and powdered sugar until well mixed. Fold in whipped cream; mix gently but well. Pour mixture into prepared pie crust; top with cherry pie filling. Refrigerate at least 8 hours before serving.
Makes 10 servings.

Homemade Graham Cracker Crust

1¼ cups graham cracker or local cookies/cracker crumbs (140 g)
¼ cup granulated sugar (50 g)
¼ cup softened butter (50 g)

Preheat oven to 375° F. (190° C.)
In a large bowl combine all ingredients; mix well. Pour into 9-inch (1 liter) pie pan; press firmly against bottom and sides of pan, distributing crumbs evenly. Bake 8 minutes in preheated oven. Cool crust before filling.

Per serving of cake with crust: Calories 460 (51% from fat), Carbohydrates 54 g, Protein 3.5 g, Total Fat 26.6 g, Sodium 355 mg, Saturated Fat 11.2 g, Cholesterol 57 mg, Diabetic Exchanges: starch 1.5, fruit 2, fat 5

DESSERT IN RED

While we were living in Central Europe, we were lucky enough to be part of an international "dining-in" group, similar to a pot luck dinner club. Each month the host couple would prepare a menu, divide it up among the group and send the recipes to each member. The original idea was to try some cuisine new to the group, and expand our culinary horizons. The rule was that the hostess would not cook the main course, but be responsible for the set up and, possibly, dessert. The local tradition of hospitality was hard to overcome, however, and all of our local hostesses insisted on preparing the main course. And, they all chose native menus. However, we learned all about their traditions and had a marvelous time getting to know one another, which, after all, was what it was really all about, wasn't it?

A recurring, and favorite, dessert was this creamy and tart compote.

Red Berry Compote

1 pound red currants
½ pound raspberries
½ pound strawberries
½ pound pitted cherries
   (optional)

⅔ cup sugar
½ cup water
1 tablespoon cornstarch
4 tablespoons water

Wash the red currants, raspberries, and strawberries. Combine in a saucepan with water and sugar; cook over medium heat for 10 minutes. Press through a sieve. Mix the cornstarch with 4 tablespoons water to form a smooth paste, and stir into the fruit mixture. Bring to a boil and cook for 2 to 3 minutes. Add cherries. Pour immediately into a glass bowl or individual glasses, which have been rinsed with cold water. Chill to set. Serve with heavy cream or a vanilla sauce.

Per serving (based on 8 servings per recipe): Calories 142 (4% from fat), Carbohydrates 35.3 g, Protein 1.6 g, Total Fat 0.6 g, Sodium 1.77 mg, Saturated Fat 0.1 g, Cholesterol 0 mg, Diabetic Exchanges: fruit 2.5

SIXTEEN TONS

I should never have eaten a late afternoon snack. I should have known better. We had been invited to the home of a representative from an Eastern European People's Republic. It was our first tour and they wanted to "get to know" us better, in other words, see what kind of people we were, and perhaps nudge us along in the direction of seeing things from their point of view. We were happy to accept the invitation—after all, we would be doing the same thing to them! I expected that we would get a good meal, but I knew that it would be late before we would actually eat, so, I had a snack. I should have known better.

We started off with drinks. I had orange juice, but there was no polite way to refuse a special brandy, "a woman's drink," from their home country. I thought that I had better eat something along with the brandy, so I munched on some cheese and crackers.

Then it was finally time for dinner. We sat down to a scrumptious meal of veal chops.

Only these were prepared in a way I had never eaten before. The veal had been fried along with a coating top and bottom of what appeared to be potato pancakes. The portions were huge and delicious and so heavy that I thought I would not be able to get up out of my chair. Of course, we had the requisite bread, a little salad of grated beets and cabbage, and beer. Our hosts were quite proud of the beer produced near their home town and well recognized around the world. I am not a beer drinker, but I politely forced down my beer. I thought that I could not eat another bite and worried about the dessert that was surely coming, as we returned to the living room.

Now came, not dessert, but goulash soup! I was served first and politely accepted a few ladlesful in my bowl. I accepted only enough to just cover the bottom of the bowl. My husband was not allowed to take such a tiny portion. Our hosts, I might add, took barely a spoonful each. I forced down the soup, which was delicious, but I was so uncomfortable I could not enjoy it. And then, came dessert. A heavy cake with whipped cream. I had to stop after a few bites, despite the protests from our hosts.

My husband had been eating and drinking with gusto all evening, accepting offers of seconds seemingly with glee. By the time we hit dessert, I noticed he had slowed way down. Suddenly, he got up from his chair, excused himself, and rushed off to the bathroom.

As I tried to concentrate on conversing with the hosts in the only language we shared, I heard a splashing, gurgling sound coming from the bathroom. I felt myself turn red with embarrassment as I was sure that my husband's stomach had finally revolted and he had gotten sick. Our hosts carried on as if they didn't notice, and when my husband returned, he looked fine and finished the evening in good spirits.

On the way home I told my husband about my embarrassment and he started to laugh. He hadn't been sick at all. The pipe under the sink that usually connects it to the plumbing in the wall had been missing, and the sink drained into a bucket which had been placed there. The noise I heard was simply water splashing rather loudly into that bucket. We both had a good laugh, and like the proper guest I always was, I didn't get sick until we got home.

Hopefully this tale will not discourage anyone from trying these more simple veal cutlets with international variations, but a better cook than I will have to come up with a way to make them "breaded" with grated potatoes!

Breaded Veal Cutlets

4 boneless veal cutlets or scallopini
flour sprinkled with salt and pepper, for dredging
1 egg, beaten lightly with 1 teaspoon water
1 cup bread crumbs, ready-made or ground at home in a blender or food processor
¼ cup butter or margarine, or mixture of butter and olive oil

Pound the cutlets between wax paper until thin. Dredge on both sides with flour mixture. Dip into the egg and water mixture, then coat with crumbs. (The quality of the crumbs determines the texture of the result. Commercial crumbs are harder, crispier; fresh crumbs have a light texture.) Pat the crumbs into the veal to make sure they stick well. Place the cutlets on a wire rack and let dry at room temperature for at least 20 minutes to help crumbs adhere. Do not refrigerate or the veal will absorb too much fat later while frying.

Heat the butter in a large skillet until hot but not brown; sauté the cutlets about 6 minutes per side, keeping the butter simmering and watching constantly, until golden brown on both sides. Add butter, as needed.

Serves 2 to 4 depending on size of cutlets.

Variations:

1) Viennese style (Wiener Schnitzel): prepare according to basic recipe above; garnish with thin, round slices of lemon topped with an anchovy rolled around a caper.

2) Holstein style: prepare according to basic recipe, top with an egg fried in butter, and a flat anchovy on top.

3) Italian style (Veal Scaloppini): prepare very thin scaloppini according to basic recipe above adding ¼ cup olive oil to the butter before heating. Brown cutlets on both sides; remove from pan. Add ¼ cup beef bouillon and juice of one lemon to the pan; cook over medium heat 1 or 2 minutes to reduce. Return veal to pan; top with thin slices of lemon; cook; covered, 10 to 15 minutes. Several sprigs of fresh parsley can be added for flavor.

Per serving (based on 4 servings per basic recipe, using 6 ounce cutlets): Calories 573 (55% from fat), Carbohydrates 21.3 g, Protein 41.5 g, Total Fat 34.8 g, Sodium 510 mg, Saturated Fat 16 g, Cholesterol 220 mg, Diabetic Exchanges: starch 1.5, meat 5, fat 2

THERE'S MORE THAN BEER IN BAVARIA

This recipe always brings back fond memories of a trip we took during our first overseas tour in 1957. After touring King Ludwig's Neuschwanstein Castle in Bavaria, we stopped for lunch at a quaint restaurant. The highlight of our lunch was a delicious cucumber salad. Very tasty, and unlike any cucumber salad we had ever experienced in our travels. Throughout our tour I made it a point to always order this salad whenever we went to a German restaurant looking for a good meal. Years later while vacationing back in Europe I was in a bookstore and while looking at a German cookbook, to my surprise I found the recipe for this cucumber salad. I modified it slightly to suit our taste and our whole family loves it.

Although the following recipe would serve two people, I usually triple the amounts so we can have leftovers. The longer it sits, the better it gets. Enjoy.

Cucumber Salad

3 large cucumbers
2 tablespoons oil
3 tablespoons fresh lemon juice

1 teaspoon salt
¼ teaspoon pepper
1 tablespoon granulated sugar

Peel cucumbers, cut off ends, and slice thinly. Turn into a bowl or serving dish. Combine remaining ingredients in a small dish; pour over cucumbers. Refrigerate, covered, in refrigerator for at least four hours to develop the flavor.

Per serving (based on 4 servings per recipe): Calories 105 (57% from fat), Carbohydrates 10.5 g, Protein 1.6 g, Total Fat 7.1 g, Sodium 1603 mg, Saturated Fat 1 g, Cholesterol 0 mg, Diabetic Exchanges: veg 1, fat 1.5

GOOD TASTE

In 1951, a group of newly-minted intelligence officers in Frankfurt am Main decided to form a dining/cooking club, which was named the Guter Schmeckers (or, loosely, Fine Tasters). The members, 8 women and 8 men, were all in their salad days, knew little about cooking, but felt that such a club would stimulate them to learn to cook. After each meeting the recipes were typed for inclusion in the Guter Schmecker cookbook. When a member was reassigned elsewhere, a new member of the same gender was invited to join. History does not record how long the club lasted, nor do we at the present time have any of the recipes, but we still remember the 16 charter members and some of us are still in touch with each other.

One of my friends from the original group was assigned to Washington a few years later, and along with some other women, rented a house in Georgetown. When it was time to complete the deal, she met the owners and was greatly impressed by the couple, especially the tall wife. During the conversation with the owners, my friend commented on how well-equipped the kitchen was, mentioning in particular the complete set of pans. The wife explained that she was writing a cookbook. That's how a member of our dining club met Julia Child. I wonder if either guessed at what they had in common—besides an interest in cooking!

German Puffed Apple Pancake

Pancake:

2 tablespoons butter
3 eggs
¾ cup milk

¾ cup all-purpose flour
½ teaspoon salt

Topping:

2 tablespoons butter
1 pound tart apples, cored
  and thinly sliced
3 tablespoons granulated sugar

⅛ teaspoon ground cinnamon
⅛ teaspoon ground nutmeg

Garnishes:

powdered sugar

lemon wedges

Preheat oven to 450° F.

To prepare pancake: melt butter in a heavy 12-inch fry pan in preheated oven. In a blender or food processor with steel blade, blend eggs, milk, flour, and salt until smooth. Pour batter into fry pan; return to oven; bake in preheated oven for 15 minutes. As pancake cooks, it will puff and large bubbles may form; check periodically and pierce any bubbles with a fork or toothpick.

To prepare topping: in a large fry pan over medium-high heat, melt butter. Add apples; sauté briefly. Add sugar and spices, cooking 6 to 8 minutes until apples are tender-crisp.

To serve, remove pancake from oven and spoon topping onto center. Sprinkle with powdered sugar. Cut pancake into wedges and serve at once, garnished with lemon.

Per serving (based on 4 servings per recipe): Calories 356 (42% from fat), Carbohydrates 44.1 g, Protein 8.3 g, Total Fat 16.9 g, Sodium 342 mg, Saturated Fat 9.26 g, Cholesterol 178 mg, Diabetic Exchanges: starch 1, meat 0.5, fruit 1.5, fat 3

HAVE A HEART, BLACKIE

Today is my husband's 50th birthday. It reminds me of our posting in Northern Europe, about 10 years ago. The people there are dog lovers, as anyone who has been there knows. For my husband's birthday, I surprised him with an adorable black Labrador puppy which I was able to purchase from a local farmer.

"Blackie" had been with us only about two weeks when we were preparing to have our first major dinner party. Included in the party were the Chief of Station and a couple of high ranking host country officials and their wives, so I wanted to make the dinner very special. We had been at our new post for about a month. I decided to make a dessert that I had learned to prepare at our previous posting in Scandinavia—heart shaped waffles with raspberry jam and whipped cream.

I spent considerable time making about 20 waffles in my special heart-shaped waffle iron. I placed the whipped cream and the jam in beautiful crystal bowls in the refrigerator, and stacked the waffles high on a plate, loosely covered with waxed paper, on the kitchen table.

Everything was prepared for a lovely dinner, and things went swimmingly, until it was time for dessert. I went to the kitchen to bring out the waffles, but the plate on the table was empty! There was not a crumb to be found. For a few seconds I couldn't think what had happened. Then I saw Blackie, hunched guiltily under the table. She had eaten every one!

With amazing composure I served raspberry jam with whipped cream and a few cookies for dessert that night. I don't think the guests ever knew the difference.

Ten years later, we still have Blackie, who has never repeated her transgression. Here is the recipe:

Scandinavian Heart-Shaped Waffles

5 eggs
¾ cup powdered sugar
1¼ cups all-purpose flour
1 teaspoon ground cardamom
  or ginger

1 cup sour cream
2 oz. unsalted butter, melted
2 tablespoons water

Whisk eggs and sugar together in a small bowl until smooth. With a rubber spatula, fold in half the flour; one at a time, fold in cardamom (or ginger), sour cream, and remaining flour. Lightly stir in butter and water; set batter aside for 10 minutes.

Cook waffles according to according to directions for waffle iron. Serve with raspberry, lingonberry or another tart jam and whipped cream, if desired. Makes about 6 waffles in an ordinary waffle iron or 24 hearts in a heart-shaped waffle iron.

Per serving (6 servings): Calories 397 (45% from fat), Carbohydrates 45 g, Protein 9.7 g, Total Fat 19.8 g, Sodium 68.8 mg, Saturated Fat 11 g, Cholesterol 194 mg, Diabetic Exchanges: starch 2, meat 1, fruit 1, fat 3

KRASNAYA ZVEZDA

During the Cold War, we often invited "East-bloc" officials to our home to give them a glimpse of American life and show off our household conveniences and our varied, plentiful food supply. A typical Thanksgiving feast seemed a good way to display our bounty. Even overseas we were always sure to have the ingredients we needed on hand, bringing pecans or cans of pumpkin pie filling along with us in our household goods shipment, and ordering frozen turkeys through a nearby commissary.

One memorable Thanksgiving dinner for Eastern European guests took place during our first tour abroad. I spent quite a while planning and preparing what I thought was an especially typical American Thanksgiving meal. After serving appetizers, we set out the main course, with all the trimmings, and called our guests' attention to the carving of the turkey. As my husband began to demonstrate both his carving skills and our new electric knife, the most senior guest jumped up and exclaimed that he just had to try out this marvelous modern convenience. With hair flying and elbows waving, he seized the knife and using it like a chainsaw, gleefully chopped up the turkey. Although turkey-in-chunks was not exactly what I had planned to serve, I could see from the smug expression on my husband's face that he was pleased that our guests were so impressed.

Next it was time to serve the side dishes proudly displayed on the buffet table. Among them was one of my favorites, made from uniquely American ingredients—a cranberry and pineapple Jell-O mold. I had searched around for the correct size mold for the recipe, and had practiced making and unmolding it. Now it sat beautifully on a cut-glass platter recently purchased just for this purpose. One of the guests noticed it and announced, "Oh look, how nice, you've made a salad in honor of my country." Sure enough, there on the platter was a gleaming red star! I had unthinkingly made my beautiful, totally American Jell-O mold in the same shape and color as the symbol used by every Communist regime of the time! My husband no longer looked so smug.

Well, the guests seemed to thoroughly enjoy the meal, and several asked for recipes, especially for the "special salad." Over the years, I have come to think of that Jell-O mold as my contribution, if not to intelligence matters, at least to détente, and perhaps even to the downfall of the Communist system. After all, I imagine that at least one of those who left our home with recipe in hand might have stopped to consider that none of them could repeat the recipe in their own home; preparing this red star depended completely on ingredients made in the U.S.A.

Our family Thanksgiving dinners today are not complete without what we have come to call "Red Star Jell-O Mold."

Red Star Jell-O®

1 (6 oz.) package cherry Jell-O®   1 (16 oz.) can whole berry cranberry sauce
  (or other cherry-flavored gelatin) 1 (8 oz.) can crushed pineapple, drained
2½ cups hot water   1 (10 oz.) can mandarin oranges, drained
½ cup pineapple or orange juice   (optional)

Pour Jell-O mix into large bowl. Add water and juice; stir until gelatin is dissolved. In a small bowl mash cranberry sauce with a fork or potato masher; add to dissolved gelatin. Add crushed pineapple; stir. Pour into a 5 or 5½ cup mold. Chill in refrigerator for a minimum of 3 hours until set and firm.

To remove from mold, run a butter knife around the edge to loosen sides of gelatin from mold. Fill sink with hot water as deep as the sides of the mold. Dip mold in hot water for a few seconds. Place serving plate on top of mold; invert, holding plate in place. Tap mold lightly; lift away. Garnish with mandarin oranges, if desired.

Makes eight ½-cup servings.

Per serving: Calories 191 (1% from fat), Carbohydrates 46 g, Protein 1.9 g, Fat 0.1 g, Sodium 74 mg,
Saturated Fat 0 g, Cholesterol 0 mg, Diabetic Exchanges: fruit 3

DANUBE SURPRISE

When my husband was part of an interagency team traveling to many of the U.S. Embassies overseas, I was able to take time off to accompany him on a trip to Central Europe. We particularly enjoyed our stay on the banks of the Danube at a newly renovated hotel that was struggling with the adjustment to Western management. One morning I sat down to a sumptuous breakfast, complete with a chef who stood attentively at a table preparing omelets from everything imaginable and, on that particular morning, one ingredient that proved most surprising.

As I relaxed near the window with my guidebook and leisurely munched on my egg, cheese, and mushroom concoction, I noted a bit more texture than in the previous day's offering. Upon closer examination, I was startled to discover that I had just swallowed a mouthful of egg mixed with fine broken glass. The head waiter who answered my cry of dismay quickly summoned the director of catering, who promptly ran for the manager. In minutes there were three hotel executives peering down at me gesturing frantically and evidently giving me lots of advice in some unknown European tongue as they examined my plate. They then proudly announced that "the problem is solved—it is a champagne glass!" About this time I figured that I would probably be floating in the Danube by sundown.

The hotel staff quickly whisked me out to a limousine and then to a local hospital. My relief at finding prompt medical help was quickly tempered by the observation that, not only did no one speak English, but the facility was already past its prime when the Gabor sisters were born. Well, everyone poked and prodded and appeared relieved that I hadn't expired yet. Finally, they evidently told the hotel manager to take me home, where "we could wait." I was never brave enough to ask, "For what?"

After arriving back at the hotel, I found my room filled with fruit, champagne, and a lovely wooden box containing the most magnificent chocolate torte that I had ever seen. After I recounted the events of the day to my husband, we enjoyed the loot. He said that he knew when he married me that I would do most anything for chocolate, but perhaps there was an easier way.

Although the overly rich torte would probably be better for you in the long run than the glass omelet, I have found a lighter, "healthful" version of the torte that can satisfy your cravings without too much guilt.

Diet Chocolate Torte

For the cake:

½ cup margarine
1½ cups sugar
½ cup liquid egg substitute
1 cup nonfat buttermilk
½ cup water

2 cups all-purpose flour
1 teaspoon baking soda
¼ teaspoon salt
¼ cup unsweetened cocoa
vegetable cooking spray

For the frosting:

¾ cup low-sugar raspberry
   preserves
⅔ cup unsweetened cocoa

¼ cup cornstarch
1 cup skim milk
¼ teaspoon vanilla extract

Optional garnish:

fresh raspberries

fresh mint sprigs

Preheat oven to 350° F.

In a large bowl, beat margarine at medium speed until creamy. Add 1½ cups of sugar; beat until fluffy. Add egg substitute; beat well. In a small bowl, stir together buttermilk and water. In a third bowl, combine flour, baking soda, salt and ¼ cup cocoa.

Alternate adding the flour mixture with adding the buttermilk mixture to the margarine mixture, beginning and ending with the flour mixture; mix well after each addition.

Coat 2 (8-inch) round cake pans with cooking spray; pour batter evenly into pans. Bake in preheated oven for about 20 minutes or until a wooden pick inserted into the center of the cake comes out clean. Remove from oven to wire racks and allow to cool in pans for 10 minutes; remove from pans and cool completely.

Stir raspberry preserves well. Slice each cake layer in half horizontally. Place one layer on a plate and spread with ¼ cup raspberry preserves; place next layer on top of first, and spread with ¼ cup preserves. Repeat with third layer and top with the fourth layer. Cover and chill.

Combine ⅔ cup cocoa, ½ cup sugar, and cornstarch in top of a double boiler. Stir in milk, and bring just to a boil. Reduce heat to low; simmer, stirring constantly with a wire whisk, about 15 minutes or until the mixture is of spreadable consistency. Remove from heat; stir in vanilla. Cover and chill. When well chilled, spread frosting on cake top and sides. To serve, garnish with raspberries and mint sprigs, and cut into thin slices.
Serves 12.

Per serving: Calories 326 (25% from fat), Carbohydrates 57.9 g, Protein 6.3 g, Total Fat 9.4 g, Sodium 296 mg, Saturated Fat 2 g, Cholesterol 1 mg, Diabetic Exchanges: starch 1.5, fruit 2, fat 2

CHEESECAKE BAKE-OFF

Many years ago, I was sent to Eastern Europe by the Marines as one of the first women assigned to Marine Embassy Security Guard duty. Another member of the detachment loved cheesecake and decided to host a cheesecake bake-off. He sent out applications to the entire diplomatic community. I was the A/NCOIC (Non-commissioned Officer in Command) and not allowed to include my cheesecake: the Corporal in charge did not want to have an appearance of collusion. Cream cheese was not a staple item on the local economy, nor did the Embassy commissary carry it in the quantities required for the practice cakes. Many of the participants became extremely creative and frightfully competitive. The Marine hosting the bake-off received many "taste tests" while on duty at Post One, as well as many dinner invitations for "taste tests." On the appointed day, almost 75 entries showed up at the Marine House. Some of the cakes were picture perfect. A professional could not have done better! Other entries included a cake with a large chunk of hard goat cheese baked in it, and a cake made with a package of sour cream and chive dip. Tensions were high, and all participants eagerly awaited the decision of the judging panel, which included the American Ambassador. The prize for first place was a bottle of champagne. A lovely cheesecake made by the wife of a British Embassy employee won first place. The cake was decorated with canned rhubarb and blueberries, since she couldn't find the currants she usually used.

Mary's Family Cheesecake Recipe
(modified for today's low fat living)

Filling:
4 (8 oz.) packages cream cheese [or, 2 (8 oz.) packages cream cheese
    and 2 (8 oz.) packages low or no fat cream cheese], at room temperature
1 (16 oz.) container low- or no-fat ricotta cheese
6 large eggs (or 1½ cups liquid egg substitute)
1¼ cups granulated sugar
1½ teaspoons vanilla extract

Crust:
1 chilled graham cracker crust in 9x10-inch baking pan or 10-inch spring-form pan

Topping:
1 pint lite sour cream (or strained vanilla yogurt)
½ to 1 cup granulated sugar
1 to 2 teaspoons vanilla extract

Preheat oven to 300° F.

Begin with cream cheese at room temperature. Mix filling ingredients in a large bowl: Combine cream and ricotta cheeses and sugar; add eggs one at a time, beating thoroughly after each one. Mix in vanilla. Pour filling into chilled crust. Place in preheated oven with a pan of hot water on the rack below the cake to keep it from cracking. Bake about one hour, rotating the cake several times to ensure even cooking, or until puffed and a wooden pick inserted into center comes out clean. If using a spring-form pan, it will take longer to bake (up to 3 hours). Remove from oven to wire rack. Cool. Chill, covered with plastic wrap, in refrigerator several hours or overnight.

When cake is chilled, prepare the topping. Preheat oven to 450° F. Combine topping ingredients and spread evenly over the chilled cheesecake. Bake in preheated oven about 25 minutes, or until set. Keep an eye on the crust so it does not burn. Cool on wire rack, then chill in refrigerator. Serve plain or topped with currants or other fruit.

Per serving (based on 12 servings per basic recipe): Calories 710 (60% from fat), Carbohydrates 56.1 g, Protein 15.1 g, Total Fat 48.3 g, Sodium 459 mg, Saturated Fat 26.8 g, Cholesterol 213 mg, Diabetic Exchanges: starch 1, meat 2, fruit 2, fat 8

WHO KNOWS THE WAY?

An assignment to a hard-core Communist country always came with certain assumptions—the house would be "bugged," we would be followed, and the restaurants would be unexciting. That last assumption was certainly true during one of our tours of duty in a Communist capital city. So it was with great excitement that the American community greeted the news that a restaurant with an exotic foreign menu had opened on the outskirts of town. A group of us quickly decided that we would visit the restaurant as soon as possible. The easiest way to get reservations to anything worth going to was through a local employee at the Embassy. If she liked you, she would make the necessary arrangements, and presumably inform the local security service of your plans. But we didn't care who knew where we were going as long as we had the chance to try something new, so someone whom the local employee liked asked her to get reservations for us all.

When the night finally arrived, we all gathered with great anticipation at the home of the one person who had more than a vague idea about how to get to the restaurant. We filled up three cars and set off, convoy style, for our evening's treat.

Now, in this particular country, at that particular time, it was possible to buy a locally made (and therefore, more easily serviced) car with special coupons purchased with Western currency. There was a choice between two models: big or compact. Most Americans preferred the compact. The only other choice was the color—if you wanted a certain color you could wait for the prescribed day that the color was available and go to buy the car carrying along your boxful of hard currency coupons. We had chosen the compact, and had opted for the rarely seen dark blue, even though it meant a longer wait. Within a few months, our car became a trend setter as quite a few Americans began to buy dark blue.

On the night of our restaurant excursion, every car in our convoy was the same dark blue compact model. It must have made it easy for the people following us to keep us in sight. It certainly made it easy for us to notice several large light-colored cars trailing along after us as we left the city traffic behind on our way out to the far suburbs. After a while, our lead driver pulled over to announce that we had gone as far as he had figured, but the restaurant was not anywhere in sight. We drove around a bit and wound up in a more populated area. The first driver stopped to ask directions from a traffic policeman.

Now, in this particular country, at that particular time, no policeman with any sense of pride would admit to a foreigner, especially an American, that he did not know how to get somewhere. So, the policeman gave a few directions, and off we went, all of those dark blue compacts, down a road, around some turns and straight into a dead end. One by one, the dark blue compacts turned around, and with our car somehow now in the lead, headed back to the policeman. We noticed he was conversing with the driver of a light-colored car, which moved away as we approached.

When my husband rolled down his window, the policeman proudly proclaimed, "Now, I know which way you should go," and he gave us new directions. Apparently our "tails" had had enough of us driving around aimlessly and had given the policeman the correct directions. And just to be sure, another light-colored car pulled out from behind us, and took its place slightly ahead of the line—and we followed it directly to the restaurant.

I cannot remember what exotic food we ate that night, or even if it was good. But I do remember that we had a great time. In order not to embarrass them, and possibly wind up with slashed tires, we had all pretended not to notice the people in the light-colored cars sitting in the parking lot when we came in, but we stayed at the restaurant long enough for our meal and some dancing, and long enough, we hoped, for our "guides" to relax and perhaps even enjoy something to eat, before we ALL headed for home.

Exotic Swordfish in Marinade

1½ pounds swordfish steaks or fillets

Marinade:

½ cup light soy sauce	½ cup orange juice
4 tablespoons catsup	2 tablespoons lemon juice
¼ cup chopped parsley	¼ teaspoon black pepper
4 cloves chopped garlic	¼ teaspoon dried oregano

In a large bowl, mix marinade ingredients together; add swordfish; cover. Marinate in refrigerator at least one hour, or for best results, overnight.

Bake fish in marinade, covered, in preheated 350° F. oven for 25 to 30 minutes or until done, but not dry.

Or cook on the grill, basting often with the marinade.

Per serving (based on 4 servings per recipe): Calories 263 (24% from fat), Carbohydrates 12.5 g, Protein 36 g, Total Fat 7 g, Sodium 2395 mg, Saturated Fat 1.9 g, Cholesterol 66 mg, Diabetic Exchanges: starch 0.5, lean meat 4

CRAZY LEGS

It was a warm summer day. We were in Moscow when it was still the capital of the U.S.S.R. My husband had the day off, so we decided to take a walk and enjoy the pleasant weather. It was the first time in our assignment that it was warm enough to wear shorts, and I put on a favorite summer outfit for the occasion. My husband decided that he would also dress for the weather, and put on a casual shirt and a pair of Bermuda shorts.

As we walked along the always busy sidewalks in our neighborhood just across the river from the Kremlin, we noticed people looking at us and smiling. Must be that everyone is enjoying the sunshine, today, we thought. We rounded a corner and walked past a woman sweeping the entranceway to a building. She looked up at us and shouted out, "Crazy! You must be crazy!"

We hurried down the street, wondering what her problem was, and then continued our stroll passing alongside of a small candy factory. From one of the windows on the second floor we heard giggling and glanced up in time to see a woman turn from the window and hear her call to her coworkers. Soon several more women appeared at the window, all laughing and pointing at the sight!

We hurried home so my husband could change into long pants. He never wore shorts on the streets of Moscow again! Of course, when winter came, we created the same sort of uproar when we each wore earmuffs—but that's another story.

No matter what the weather, we always enjoyed tasting Russian dishes. Once we spent an evening with a Russian family in our home at another post. They wanted to serve us a typical meal but wished to prepare it in our large and modern kitchen. I had a hands-on lesson that evening in making pilmeny, a kind of Russian ravioli. As a remembrance, our guest cooks presented us with a pilmeny maker. This kitchen tool, with a pistol grip and a round, serrated cutting end is used to cut and decoratively seal the pilmeny. Even if you are not lucky enough to have a "pilmeny gun," you can still make and enjoy this special dish.

Siberian Pilmeny

¾ pound lean, boneless beef
¾ pound lean, boneless lamb
1 onion, cut into chunks
salt and pepper to taste

3 to 4 cups all-purpose flour
3 eggs, beaten
¼ to ½ cup water
5 quarts boiling water

In a food grinder, grind beef and lamb together with onion and salt and pepper. Form meat mixture into balls, using about ½ tablespoon of mixture for each ball. Set aside in refrigerator.

In a medium bowl mix together flour and eggs, adding a little water until a soft dough forms. Knead quickly until smooth and elastic. Divide dough into two portions. Cover one portion with a damp cloth and place other portion on a floured board. Roll out dough to scant ⅛-inch thick. Cut circles of about 3-inch diameter with a cookie cutter, jar lid or juice glass. Place 1 ball of meat in the center of each circle. Fold dough over to enclose meat, wet edges of dough slightly and gently press with a fork to both seal and decorate. The two bottom corners can be brought together and sealed to form a ring. Work quickly to keep dough from drying out. Repeat procedure with remaining portion of dough.

To cook pilmeny, bring water to boil in a large pot. Drop pilmeny into boiling water. (Drop in only as many as will cover surface of water in one layer. Keep uncooked pilmeny covered with damp cloth until ready to cook.) Reduce heat to keep water between a simmer and a boil. Cook, uncovered, until pilmeny rise to surface and dough is tender, about 8 to 10 minutes. Taste to be sure dough and meat are thoroughly cooked. Remove pilmeny from water with slotted spoon and place in a large bowl. Set aside. Add fresh water, if necessary, to pot of boiling water and repeat as above until all pilmeny are cooked. Drain bowl of cooked pilmeny before serving.

Serve in individual bowls dressed with white vinegar and a little vegetable oil, or mixed with generous portion of sour cream or butter.
Makes about 60 pilmeny.

Variations: 1. Cook pilmeny in beef or chicken stock; serve in bowls of soup.
2. Fry drained pilmeny in butter until golden; serve with sour cream or butter.
Uncooked pilmeny may be frozen in plastic food storage bags in small amounts.
Cook without thawing; increase cooking time.

Per serving (two pilmeny each): Calories 97 (23% from fat), Carbohydrates 11.5 g, Protein 6.3 g, Total Fat 2.5 g, Sodium 89 mg, Saturated Fat 0.9 g, Cholesterol 31 mg, Diabetic Exchanges: starch 0.5, lean meat 1.0

MOSCOW SOJOURN

We served in Moscow at a time when relations between the U.S. and the U.S.S.R. were at an all-time low. We were there for the Afghanistan invasion and the Olympic boycott. All of us in the Embassy felt the constrictive nature of the society, and we had constant surveillance. One of the highlights of our routine would be the excitement generated throughout the Embassy when, on a rare occasion, the hard-currency grocery store got in a shipment of something exotic, like bananas or oranges. We could never plan our menus and then go shopping, but only the reverse—go shopping and then plan our meals around whatever was available. What we could always count on were onions, beets, and the ubiquitous CABBAGE.

One dreary, dark winter day we came up with the idea of holding a Cabbage Cook-Off contest. The whole Embassy got in the spirit of the project, and we had many entries, ranging from cabbage daiquiris to dessert cabbage cakes. Many recipes were a one-time never-to-be-repeated experiment, but we did publish a cookbook, entitled "The 1st Annual Moscow Ground Hog Day Cabbage Cook-Off Cookbook." (There never was a 2nd Annual!) The two winning entries were both stir-fry, which, in my opinion, don't count because everything tastes good when stir-fried! It was more of a challenge to come up with something tasty either raw or baked. These two recipes won 2nd and 3rd prizes in the salad category:

Apple and Cabbage Salad

¼ head green cabbage, chopped

2 red apples, cut into wedges

2 carrots, peeled and diced

1 cucumber, diced

¼ cup chopped onion

¼ cup raisins (optional)

Dressing:

⅓ cup vegetable oil

2 tablespoons vinegar

2 teaspoons dill weed

½ teaspoon garlic salt

2 tablespoons mayonnaise

In a large serving bowl, toss vegetables together. In a cruet or screw-top jar, mix dressing ingredients together thoroughly. Pour over salad and toss.
Serves 6.

Per serving: Calories 216 (63% from fat), Carbohydrates 19.3 g, Protein 1.6 g, Total Fat 16.1 g, Sodium 132 mg, Saturated Fat 2.2 g, Cholesterol 3 mg, Diabetic Exchanges: fruit 1, veg 1, fat 3

Cole Slaw Soufflé

(an elegant side-dish that is simple to make)

1 (8 oz.) can crushed pineapple	3 egg whites
1 (3 oz.) package orange-flavored gelatin	1 cup shredded carrot
	½ cup each raisins and walnuts
¾ cup boiling water	1 cup finely chopped green cabbage
¾ cup mayonnaise	

Fold 22-inch piece of aluminum foil in half lengthwise, and tape it firmly around 1-quart soufflé dish to form a 3-inch collar above the rim of the dish.

Drain pineapple, reserving liquid. Dissolve gelatin in boiling water; add reserved liquid. Beat in mayonnaise until smooth. Pour into loaf pan (a metal pan works best); freeze about 20 minutes, until firm 1 inch from edge, but still soft in the center.

In large bowl beat egg whites until they form soft peaks. Fold in partially frozen gelatin mixture. Fold in pineapple and remaining four ingredients. Pour into prepared soufflé dish. Chill about 1 hour until set. Remove foil before serving.

Per serving (based on 8 servings per recipe): Calories 299 (61% from fat), Carbohydrates 25.7 g, Protein 4.8 g, Total Fat 21 g, Sodium 174 mg, Saturated Fat 2.8 g, Cholesterol 12 mg, Diabetic Exchanges: starch 0.5, meat, 0.5, fruit 1, fat 3.5

RAINCHECK

I watched from a kiosk across the street. A few cars passed, their foglights turning the rain puddles into yellow smears, but the sidewalks were empty. It was a working class neighborhood, and people went to bed early, particularly on a cold March night in a drizzle that stung the eyes and soaked the sturdiest shoes. I could see a few heads in the window of the restaurant, drinking red wine in a thick gray cloud of cigarette smoke. I wanted to be inside the restaurant eating country paté on a thick baguette, a pot au feu or cassoulet, a house Burgundy the color of Indian rubies...where the hell was he?

Ah, but he was on time. A small Asian hunched inside a cheap windbreaker, walking down the street from the direction of the Metro station. He turned into the restaurant. I waited five more minutes. A woman and her dog came from the opposite direction. A man in shirtsleeves ran out to his doorway. It looked clear. No surveillance. Good. I crossed the street and entered the restaurant.

He was at a table by the back wall, still wearing his wet jacket. He smiled when he saw me. He was smoking a cheap bleu but hadn't ordered a drink. He couldn't afford it. We shook hands. His hand was like ice, almost lifeless, but the face was eager, expectant. We talked about the weather and family. How were his common-law wife and three children? Fine, but there was no heat, no running water in the two rooms they called home. Coffee? I asked. Tea, please, he countered. We sipped our hot drinks and smiled at one another. I pointed to the menu and the bored waiter.

The food could wait, he said, but please, it was important to him. He had to know the answer. Did we find him a job, the job that would give him what his alien status could not: a chance to earn a salary, to be the breadwinner in the family, to earn his neighbors' respect? A steady job was all he wanted in return for his help against the target. Paying him as an agent wasn't the same thing, didn't I understand?

I did, but I couldn't tell him the truth. That Washington thought he was of poor moral character. Sure, they'd said, we have an obligation to defectors, we did more than enough for him ten years ago, and even recognize his certain potential now. But how could we condone the use of a man who had tried suicide, who had slashed his wrists during his desperate search for identity, who wanted to die because he had lost his name, his country, his self-respect?

No, all I could say was I couldn't help him with a job. We stared at one another for the longest minute of my life. Thank you, he said. He carefully put out his cigarette. He glanced down at the tea cup and then pushed it away. He stood and wished me a good evening. He went out of the restaurant door without looking back. Out into the black rain.

I sat over my coffee. The waiter came back to the table, a questioning glance toward the doorway. Monsieur, he asked, would you like to order now? The check, please, I replied, pointing to the drinks. Then I, too, walked out into that black rain.

IN MEMORY OF

He had been a spy half his life. He had been many other things, too. A young war hero who had ridden his horse at full gallop right into the machine guns of the German lines; a lawyer whose scandalous love affair with the wife of a nobleman forced him into exile; a military attaché sent to jail as a war criminal; a journalist; a diplomat; a teacher. He spoke four languages, all of them fluently. He was a collector of rare books, a student of history, a raconteur, a novelist, and a poet. He hobnobbed with European royalty and its literati. He cut quite a figure in any circle.

He also was quite a cook. He taught cooking, wrote cook books, and created culinary treasures in his kitchen for small dinner parties that would do justice to a table at Maxim's. He would have loved this cookbook project. He would have swarmed all over it, filled its pages with recipes, dozens of dishes to delight the eye and the taste. And behind each dish, there would have been a story—or two.

He was also a spy. He worked for CIA for many years, in many places. He was a man of giant charm and wit, captivating in any social setting, disarming in his elicitation efforts, clever in his manipulations. He spotted, he developed, he recruited. A passionate anti-Communist, he found that no obstacle in working against hard target objectives. He could also be a rascal, a cheat. He was once caught fabricating his reports. He also got his wrist slapped on more than one occasion for padding his expense accounts.

Those of us who worked with him, who met him at car pick-up sites or on subway platforms, or who sat at his table, we who cannot name him or ourselves, remember him with great admiration and affection. He was one of a kind, a character you would expect to meet only in the pages of a Graham Greene novel.

I learned of his passing years after the fact. That happens in this business. Spies come and go. Each agent turnover is a new beginning or a final ending—you might send an unsigned Christmas card once a year, but even that's frowned upon. I often wonder if anyone from our end of it attended his funeral. Kind words and vivid memories of his many accomplishments may have been spoken by relatives and friends, I suppose, but nothing said, not even whispered, of the secret chapters of his life.

If you know of his grave or pass that way, you might want to drop a white carnation on it. From me.

The Middle East

- - - - - - -

A Conversation with Julia Child

I certainly would try to learn the language just as soon as possible. Now I think that's essential, because you won't have any fun unless you can go out and do your own shopping and chew the fat and so forth. And, I think, try to live off the land as much as possible. And meet many people . . . .

. . . I had had French all of my life, all my life, and when I got over there I could neither understand nor speak a word. It was a pity. I went to the Berlitz every day. Luckily, when I got into the Cordon Bleu school there was no English spoken, and I also got in with some French art historians who didn't speak any English, so I really learned by doing, but I was an example of the dreadfully inadequate way that foreign language had been taught in this country before the U.S. Army "Spoken Language" system was developed . . . So I really feel proud that I learned French just by being there, and being drowned in it.

- - - - - - -

SOMETIMES YOU MUST MAKE DO

In spending nine straight years in Muslim countries, where pork and pork products are taboo, I had to find something to substitute for our morning bacon. One of the cheapest cuts of meat I could find to buy was whole tenderloin. I fixed it every way possible, but my husband especially relished steak and eggs for breakfast. Imagine his disappointment when we returned to the States for an assignment, and discovered that 2 pounds of bacon cost as much as our whole tenderloin had overseas. That was the last he saw of either of his favorite breakfasts for a while!

The editors recommend trying one of the following meatless breakfast specialties suggested by two colleagues.

Overnight French Toast

1 pound egg bread,
  brioche or white bread
12 large eggs
1 tablespoon vanilla extract
3 tablespoons granulated sugar

2 tablespoons grated orange peel
½ teaspoon grated nutmeg
1¼ cups half-and-half or light cream
½ cup butter

Slice bread into 1-inch slices and spread in a single layer in one or two deep baking dishes or pans. Beat eggs in large bowl until well blended. Add vanilla, sugar, orange peel and nutmeg; stir in half-and-half. Pour batter over bread, turning slices to coat both sides. Cover and refrigerate overnight.

To serve, preheat oven to 150° F. Remove bread from refrigerator. Melt butter in a large skillet or griddle. Fry bread slices until golden brown on both sides. Keep fried slices warm in oven until all are ready to serve. Serve dusted with powdered sugar or topped with syrup or jam.

Per serving (based on 12 servings per recipe): Calories 297 (55% from fat), Carbohydrates 23 g, Protein 10 g, Total Fat 17.9 g, Sodium 332 mg, Saturated Fat 8.9 g, Cholesterol 239 mg, Diabetic Exchanges: starch 1, meat 1, fat 3

Cinnamon Stack Biscuits

3 tablespoons granulated sugar
2 cups all-purpose flour
1 tablespoon baking powder
½ teaspoon cream of tartar
½ teaspoon salt
½ cup butter, margarine, or
  vegetable shortening

scant ⅔ cup milk
¼ cup butter, melted
¼ cup granulated sugar
1 tablespoon ground cinnamon

Preheat oven to 425° F. Grease regular size (for 12 muffins) muffin pan.

Sift flour, 3 tablespoons sugar, baking powder, cream of tartar, and salt into a large bowl. With pastry blender or 2 knives cut shortening into dry mixture, until it resembles fine meal. Add milk; mix until dry ingredients moistened. Knead briefly to make a soft dough. Turn out onto lightly floured board; roll into a 10x16-inch rectangle. Brush with melted butter. Combine cinnamon and ¼ cup sugar in a small bowl; sprinkle onto dough. Cut dough lengthwise into 2-inch strips. Stack strips. Cut into 12 pieces and place cut side down into prepared muffin pan. Bake in preheated oven for 12 to 15 minutes until golden. Dust with powdered sugar, if desired.

Variation: For an interesting texture, use ⅓ cup sour cream and ⅓ cup milk in place of ⅔ cup milk.

Per serving (based on 12 servings per recipe): Calories 224 (52% from fat), Carbohydrates 24.7 g, Protein 2.7 g, Total Fat 13 g, Sodium 257 mg, Diabetic Exchanges: starch 1, fruit 0.5, fat 2.5

ACROSS THE STREET

During most of my posting in the Middle East, I lived in a small compound in a quiet residential neighborhood. Walking home from a local market one day, I met one of my local neighbors from across the street. He was just coming home from work. He greeted me, introduced himself, and invited me to drop by for tea.

Private houses in that capital city were, with few exceptions, surrounded by high walls and gates, so this was my first real look at one of the larger ones. It needed to be large, as it housed an extended family of over 40 people. Moreover, I was told, the family patriarch was a prince (the royal family numbers in the low thousands) who administered a town just outside the city, and he hosted a majlis, a sort of town meeting, about once a month. That explained the days when I would come home from work to find 40 white Toyota pickups parked along the street and, as often as not, blocking my driveway.

Tea was in a sitting room adjoining the courtyard in front of the house, where I found a group of young men reclining on cushions, sipping very sweet tea or Arabic coffee from small cups, watching TV or VCR tapes, and talking. Everyone was introduced as Cousin So-and-So.

The coffee was prepared and served by an African servant, whom my host explained was a former slave from Nigeria. The government had legally banned slavery only in 1970, but many ex-slaves had chosen to stay rather than return to poverty in their own lands. I expect that the legal change meant little to them. In parts of the Middle East there is no clear linguistic or cultural distinction between servants and slaves.

I was invited back the following week for dinner, which was served in the courtyard. The main dish was a kabsa, a huge circular platter mounded with rice and topped with meat (usually lamb, although in this case it was chicken). Various cooked vegetables and sauces ring the central mound. The procedure is to sit cross-legged around the platter and eat with the right hand (no utensils); using the left hand is acceptable so long as it doesn't touch a communal dish. You tear off chunks of meat, roll them into little balls with the rice and other edibles, and pop them into your mouth. For drink there was water, or laban—similar to buttermilk, and a bit rich for my tastes.

An uncle of the younger men joined us for dinner and engaged me in conversation in Arabic. I welcomed the change, since my host spoke excellent English and I hadn't been getting much practice. He told me he was looking for a wife (four is the legal limit; I didn't ask if he had any already), and he wanted an American girl. He specified that she had to be Moslem, able to speak Arabic, and to cook. I explained, truthfully, that I didn't know anyone suitable. He didn't seem convinced, but let the matter drop.

Cardamom Coffee

1 liter (about 32 oz.) water   1 teaspoon ground cardamom
6 tablespoons ground coffee

Heat coffee and water which has been stirred together in a coffee pot, over low heat until reduced to a bitter coffee essence. Add cardamom. Pour into small cups; serve with dates.

Per 3-fluid ounce serving: Calories 3, Carbohydrates 0 g, Protein 0 g, Total Fat 0 g, Caffeine 89 mg, Saturated Fat 0 g, Cholesterol 0 mg, Diabetic Exchanges: negligible

Dietitian's note: Sodium content will vary with the water source.

DOWN HOME DINNER IN THE DESERT

My love of cooking goes back much further than my association with Foreign Service agencies, but I never realized how much both would completely change my life. I joined the Department of State as an Administrative Officer in 1988. During my background investigation interview, I was asked about my extracurricular activities. At the time I was balancing graduate school with caring for my invalid father and I explained that I had no extra hours to spend on additional activities. The interviewer must have heard about my culinary interests, however, because he finally exclaimed, "All I've heard from anyone I have spoken with about you is that you are a great cook!" He joked that my cooking skills were greatly needed at some of our embassies.

As it turned out, I didn't get to put those skills to much use during my first junior officer tour where my cooking was limited to baking cakes for Marine balls, or front office parties. For my second tour, I lobbied hard for a position in the Middle East just after the war. Since everyone was eating MREs and T'Rations, I like to think the rumor of my culinary abilities held some influence in my getting the job.

I arrived at my new post at night, amidst oil fields and driving heat. The next morning, anxious to get started, I walked onto the compound, and noticed an attractive man among the trailers that served as offices. I tried to pay attention to the various people I was meeting, including my bosses and Foreign Service National employees, but this guy kept popping up around the compound. When I finally asked who he was, I was told his name and that "He's one of THEM."

Intrigued, I maneuvered to be around whenever he was in the area of my office. I watched out the window to see when he went for lunch and then rushed to the snack bar, pretending to be there at the same time just by chance. The lunch menu always featured the same beef tips and rice, but at one lunch the cook had obviously been too liberal with the salt shaker. The Dead Sea could not have tasted this salty. Everyone was complaining. I casually mentioned that I liked to cook and could probably do better. I had earlier discovered that my lunch companion was from the South and had been raised in a family environment similar to my own, so I asked him if he liked chicken fried steak and cream gravy. When he said yes, I promptly invited him to my house for a true Southern dinner.

The hard part became finding all the ingredients—this was, after all, a war-torn Middle Eastern country. I was able to find okra only after searching through several local markets. I also found corn on the cob and green beans at about ten dollars a pound, and the beef was at least fifteen. When the ingredients were finally gathered, I set about painstakingly preparing the Lucullan feast.

Shortly after my guest arrived, I went into the kitchen to put the finishing touches on the meal. Nervous about making the right impression, I inadvertently placed a glass pan of homemade yeast biscuits on a burner that I thought was off. Within a few minutes, a sharp explosion ripped though the kitchen. The pan had burst, sending shards of glass into all of my carefully prepared food.

We worked together to pick out all the glass and at last sat down to eat. After the first few bites, I knew I had him.

Not too long after that evening, I resigned my State Department position and became an Agency spouse. I still enjoy cooking—safely—for my husband and two children, as well as for his office. Chicken fried steak is still a family favorite.

Chicken Fried Steak with Cream Gravy

4 tablespoons all-purpose flour
1 teaspoon salt
1 teaspoon black pepper
⅛ teaspoon cayenne pepper
⅛ teaspoon garlic powder

4 tenderloin steaks (¼ pound each),
    pounded flat
1 cup milk
½ cup cooking oil

Combine flour and spices in a shallow dish. Dredge each steak in flour mixture; dip in milk. Rest steaks on a platter. Reserve any remaining flour mixture and milk.

Heat oil in a large skillet (may use an electric skillet heated to 350° F.). Brown steaks in hot oil, turning once, about 5 to 7 minutes on each side. Remove from oil and drain on paper towels.

To prepare gravy: Pour off all but one tablespoon of oil from skillet. Add additional salt and black pepper and two to three tablespoons of the leftover dredging flour mixture, adding more flour if necessary. Stir the flour into the oil over medium heat until the flour is thoroughly incorporated. Gradually whisk in the leftover milk until the gravy thickens and there are no lumps. At this point, if you wish a thinner gravy, add more milk. Adjust seasonings to taste. Serve the

steak with mashed potatoes, and the gravy on the side.
Makes 4 servings.

Per serving: Calories 599 (78% from fat), Carbohydrates 9.25 g, Protein 23.5 g, Total Fat 51.8 g, Sodium 612 mg, Saturated Fat 14 g, Cholesterol 83 mg, Diabetic Exchanges: starch 0.5, meat 3, fat 7.5

LOVELY LUMPIA

Lumpia, a world-renowned delicacy from the Philippines, is a staple food in my house today, but it has not always been so. I was introduced to lumpia by one of the best lumpia makers in the world. That was back in 1986 in the Middle East. So, what is the connection between a Philippine food and the Middle East? Well . . . that's where I met the remarkable cook—my wife. And therein lies the romantic tale of love and lumpia.

At the time I was assigned to the U.S. Embassy in a Middle Eastern capital, my wife-to-be was working as a contract registered nurse in a hospital in Beirut, Lebanon. When war broke out and it became a dangerous place to live, she got concerned and wanted to find work in a safer city. She had a friend who had a friend at our Embassy in Beirut, and this friend knew me. Eventually, my wife found a job in a hospital in the city where I was living, and when the time came for her to travel there, I was asked to meet her at the airport and take her safely to the hospital where she would live. Of course, I had never met her before, and she knew nothing about me, but that fateful first meeting at the airport eventually led to my tasting my first lumpia—and, of course, marital bliss! To this day, lumpia and love are staples in our house; all because there was a war in Lebanon.

Philippine Lumpia

2 pounds lean ground beef
1 tablespoon vegetable oil
1 clove garlic, chopped finely
1 medium yellow onion, chopped
1 cup beef broth or bouillon
2 cups fresh green beans, washed and trimmed
4 medium carrots, diced in small squares
1 teaspoon monosodium glutamate
¼ teaspoon black pepper

1 teaspoon Mrs. Dash® seasoning, original flavor*
1 (15 oz.) can sweet yellow corn, drained
2 stalks celery, thinly sliced diagonally
2 large white potatoes, diced in small squares
1 (8 oz.) can water chestnuts, sliced diagonally
2 cups green cabbage, sliced into diagonal strips
2 packages lumpia wrappers, 100 count
2 egg whites (slightly beaten)
vegetable oil for deep-frying

Heat oil in a large pot. Sauté beef in hot oil, breaking apart with a fork, until barely browned; add garlic and onions; sauté until liquid in pot is gone, but do not overcook beef. Add beef broth; cook until almost boiling. Add beans, carrots and seasonings; bring to boil; cook for 5 minutes; add corn, celery, potatoes, and water chestnuts. Cook just until the vegetables are snap tender-crisp. Do not overcook. Add cabbage and cook until cabbage is wilted. Remove from heat; drain and cool.

Using lumpia wrappers, put heaping tablespoon of cooled meat-vegetable mixture in center of each wrapper, in a long and narrow cylindrical shape. Wrap one at a time like spring rolls: fold one long side of wrapper over filling, then fold over each of the two short ends; finally, fold over remaining long side, sealing this side closed with egg white.

In a large, deep frying pan or deep-fryer, deep-fry several filled lumpia at a time, in very hot oil, until the wrappers are golden brown.

Author's note: Use lumpia wrappers from the Philippines for best results. They are very thin and should be handled gently when wrapping. Thick wrappers do not give the same results.

*Mrs. Dash® is a salt-free seasoning blend of herbs and spices which can be found in supermarkets. If unavailable, substitute any combination of onion powder, dried parsley, ground coriander, ground cumin, garlic powder, dry mustard, and/or cayenne pepper.

Per serving (2 lumpias each): Calories 106 (24% from fat), Carbohydrates 14.4 g, Protein 5.9 g, Total Fat 2.8 g, Sodium 186 mg, Saturated Fat 1 g, Cholesterol 14 mg, Diabetic Exchanges: starch 1, meat 0.5

FLOUR IN MOTION

After several overseas tours, many in the "boonies," my wife quickly learned to cope with adjusting various recipes she was using with whatever was available in the local market that particular day. After returning home from a rather trying morning at the market, she unloaded her purchases from her string bag and was about to transfer some newly bought flour into her sealed flour can when the flour moved...in fact, it was really moving. Seems the trick is to sift the flour and discard all the "things that move," or never buy flour ever again.

That experience led to the following recipe for your own "fresh" version of pre-made baking mix. It can be kept on hand and used in recipes that call for Bisquick® or other biscuit/baking mix.

Baking Mix

Be sure to measure accurately:

9 cups sifted all-purpose flour
⅓ cup baking powder
1 cup plus 2 tablespoons
   non-fat dry milk powder

4 teaspoons salt
1¼ cups vegetable shortening

Sift flour, baking powder, milk powder, and salt into a large mixing bowl. Cut shortening into dry ingredients until mixture resembles coarse cornmeal.

Store in tightly covered container, in cool dry place, up to 6 weeks.

Substitution: 1½ cups lard can be substituted for shortening; mix made with lard must be stored in refrigerator.

Per 1 cup (based on 12 cups of mix per basic recipe): Calories 604 (46% from fat), Carbohydrates 70.6 g, Protein 11.1 g, Total Fat 30.8 g, Sodium 1226 mg, Saturated Fat 7.6 g, Cholesterol 1 mg, Diabetic Exchanges: starch 5, fat 6

ALI BABA AND THE 40 COURSES

My first experience in a private home in the Middle East became an experiment to see just how much I could eat without exploding. We were attached to the Embassy in the capital city, and had immediately embarked on an education in the fine art of carpet-buying. Our carpet dealer had invited us to his home for a traditional dinner.

What I didn't know was that dish after dish would be brought out—one at a time. There was a salad, a dish of yogurt, mint, cucumbers, walnuts, and raisins, and then what I thought was the main dish, a khoresh, or stew, served on a bed of rice. It was delicious and I had a large portion. Then came a pilaf, a rice dish with chicken or lamb cooked in one pot. I did less justice to this marvelous dish.

I almost fainted when the houseboy brought yet another khoresh with its accompanying white rice. In addition, there were several vegetable and other side dishes. To my great consternation, the last was the most delicious. It was at this point that I really began to think that I was about to insult our hosts by not eating any more! Luckily, the next course turned out to be dessert.

As a postscript to this story, in the years following, we were to enjoy many meals with our friends, but never again did each dish come separately. Only buffets from then on!

Khoresh E Bademjan (Lamb Stew)

2 pounds lean lamb, cut into small cubes	4 cups boiling water
	½ teaspoon ground cinnamon
2 cups water	1 teaspoon ground turmeric
4 tablespoons oil, divided	6 small eggplants
1½ pounds tomatoes, sliced	3 large onions, chopped

In a large pot, boil lamb cubes in 2 cups of water and 2 tablespoons of oil until water is absorbed and meat has browned. Add tomatoes; again, cook until liquid is absorbed, and tomatoes are browned. Add 4 cups of boiling water, salt, cinnamon and turmeric. Reduce heat; cook slowly, covered, over low heat.

Peel eggplants and cut into strips. In a skillet fry eggplant in remaining 2 tablespoons oil. Add to meat mixture. Reserve oil. Simmer meat mixture one hour. Fry onions in reserved oil until well browned; add to meat. Continue to cook mixture slowly until all ingredients are tender, and sauce is reduced to gravy consistency. Serve on rice.

Per serving (based on 8 servings per recipe): Calories 346 (35% from fat), Carbohydrates 30.5 g, Protein 27.7 g Total Fat 14 g, Sodium 211 mg, Saturated Fat 3.3 g, Cholesterol 77 mg, Diabetic Exchanges: meat 2, veg 6, fat 1

Chelo Rice

2½ cups rice (Basmati or
   other long grain rice)
1½ tablespoons salt
2 quarts water

2 tablespoons salt
½ cup melted butter
2 tablespoons water

Wash rice well. In a large bowl soak rice in cold water to which 1½ tablespoons of salt have been added. Use enough water to cover the rice. Soak 1 to 2 hours or longer. Pour off the soaking water and discard. In a large pot boil 2 quarts water to which 2 tablespoons of salt have been added. Add rice to boiling water and cook for 10 to 15 minutes. Stir once or twice to prevent sticking. Pour rice and water into strainer and rinse with lukewarm water.

Pour ⅓ of the melted butter into the bottom of the pot in which you cooked the rice. Add 2 tablespoons of water. Add the rice, a spoonful at a time, to the pot, distributing evenly. Allow it to mound into the shape of a cone. Pour the rest of the melted butter over the rice, distributing it evenly.

Cover the pot with paper towels and place the lid on top. Or, wrap the lid in a dishcloth and place it on the pot. Cook on medium heat for 10 to 15 minutes. Reduce heat and cook for 25 to 35 minutes on lowest heat.

If the rice is cooked at the proper temperature, a crisp, golden crust much prized by Middle Eastern chefs will form on the bottom. Put the pot in a sink filled with a few inches of cold water for a few minutes before serving. This makes it easy to remove the crust, and, later, to wash the pot.

Dietitian's note: This recipe cannot be accurately analyzed for nutritional values due to the soaking/cooking process; however, it can be noted that it is high in fat and sodium. Cholesterol is relatively low (maximum of 35 mg per serving).

AULD LANG SYNE

The best New Year's Party we ever gave was in the Middle East. Our cohosts were a local doctor and his Italian wife. She and I did all the cooking for about 75 people.

Almost everything that could have gone wrong, did. We hired a bartender and a waiter, but the bartender could not mix drinks, so our two hosts ended up in the kitchen mixing drinks. One of our two kitchen helpers cut her hand on a broken glass and had to be taken to the hospital. The man we had hired to take coats got them all mixed up.

But for some reason, it did not matter. We danced to records in the hallway, enjoyed a belly dancer with her 5-or 6-piece band, champagne at midnight, and best of all, we had someone else do the cleaning up. Almost 30 years later, our cohosts still hear from their friends that that party was the best ever.

Kabab E Barg (Lamb Kabob)

2½ pounds lean boneless lamb,
   or ground lamb
1 medium onion, minced
½ cup plain yogurt or
   2 tablespoons fresh lemon juice

1 teaspoon salt
½ teaspoon pepper
ground sumac** for garnish (optional)

Cut lamb into strips ½ inch wide and 2 inches long. Combine remaining ingredients in a mixing bowl. Add lamb and coat well with marinade. Cover bowl and marinate 2 hours, or up to 2 days in the refrigerator. Thread strips onto skewers (if using ground lamb, form into patties or cylinders). Grill over hot charcoal about 12 minutes, or until done, turning frequently. Or, set skewers on broiler pan; broil 4 inches from preheated broiler until browned and just cooked through. Garnish with ground sumac**, if desired.

Serve with hot rice which has been flavored with butter and egg yolk. Good accompanied by quartered raw onions and grilled whole tomatoes.

**Editors' note: Ground sumac is a spice, not to be confused with the plant known as poison sumac. Purchase from a Middle Eastern specialty market; do not use a plant from your yard!

Per serving (based on 6 servings per recipe): Calories 326 (43% from fat), Carbohydrates 3.1 g, Protein 41.5 g, Total Fat 15.1 g, Sodium 470 mg, Saturated Fat 5.9 g, Cholesterol 133 mg, Diabetic Exchanges: lean meat 6

MID-EAST MUDDLE

Many years ago (1958) my wife and I had just arrived in the Middle East, where we were to spend three years. It was our first day there and I had gone to the office, leaving my wife and children at home. We had a chauffeur, Reza, as required at post there. My wife did not know the local language, but did have a dictionary. She was planning dinner and asked Reza to go to the market to get meat. Reza had worked for an American family before, so my wife communicated with him in English, of which he knew a little. My wife decided she wanted beef liver for dinner, and using a combination of English with a few local words from the dictionary thrown in, she sent Reza to the bazaar to buy half a kilo of liver. A little while later he came back all excited. He said the butchers wouldn't sell it to him, and they told him he was crazy. I had just arrived home from the office as this was going on and asked what was the matter? My wife told me she had ordered half a kilo of liver which Reza was unable to buy. After consulting with Reza, I started to laugh. I explained to my wife that instead of "half," Reza had understood her to say the native word meaning "eight"! She had ordered eight kilos (about 17 pounds) of liver for the five of us: two adults, two children, and a 6-month-old-baby! We all laughed and Reza went back to the butcher. He soon returned with a half kilo of liver and said he and the butchers had a good laugh over the situation.

We learned you have to be careful in using two languages in another country. To this day my wife has never forgotten the word for half!

Beef Liver with Onions and Peppers

1 pound beef (or calves') liver	2 cups beef broth or bouillon
¼ cup all-purpose flour	4 tablespoons vegetable oil
½ teaspoon salt	1 large green pepper
¼ teaspoon pepper	1 large red pepper
2 large onions	1 tablespoon Worcestershire sauce

Cut liver into 2-inch strips. Combine flour, salt, and pepper on wax paper; coat liver pieces with flour mixture; set aside. Peel onions and cut into rings; halve and seed peppers and cut into large pieces. Heat oil in a large skillet; sauté pepper pieces and onion rings until both are soft, but peppers are still bright; remove with a slotted spoon and set aside.

In the oil remaining in the skillet, cook liver quickly, a few pieces at a time, until it loses red color and begins to brown; remove with a slotted spoon and set aside. Add beef broth and Worcestershire sauce to the skillet and stir together. Heat until mixture bubbles, stirring constantly. Return onions, peppers and liver to skillet. Heat slowly 2 minutes or until heated through. Serve with rice. Makes 6 servings.

Per serving: Calories 255 (49% from fat), Carbohydrates 15.2 g, Protein 17.3 g, Total Fat 13.9 g, Sodium 528 mg, Saturated Fat 2.8 g, Cholesterol 270 mg, Diabetic Exchanges: starch 0.5, meat 2, veg 1, fat 1

HASTY EXIT

I was one of the last Agency officers to serve in a base located on the coast of Libya. We had arrived there shortly after Captain Moamar Quadaffi seized power from the country's reigning monarch in a bloodless coup. In the process, Quadaffi nationalized Libya's oil operations and prohibited all things "western," which included liquor. Our base town was hot, dusty, and politically inhospitable, and the new regime's policy changes made it even worse.

Eventually it was decided to close our small office. The Libyans gave us 10 days to pack our official and personal effects and depart. I had to devote all my time to closing out the office, while my wife had to attend to the myriad details of shipping out our personal effects at the same time looking after a small child and a baby. This was not a pleasant experience for a woman in that male-dominated society.

We managed to get everything done within the 10 day deadline. We and other office families were convoyed to the airport to catch a flight to Tripoli and an onward flight to London. At the airport we were treated to a good dose of harassment. Every bit of our luggage was meticulously inspected, accompanied by questions of "what is this?" and "what is the purpose of that?" Our passports were carefully and s-l-o-w-l-y perused at the immigration desk. After running this gauntlet, we noted that flight announcements were made in Arabic only, since the use of English was forbidden by official policy. We identified our flight by looking for people with boarding passes the same color as ours.

When our plane left the ground, we breathed a collective sigh of relief that the ordeal was over—at least, so we thought. Upon our arrival in Tripoli, we were herded into a shed-like structure which was identified as the transit area. Again, we were required to go through a detailed customs and document check, along with the verbal harangue that accompanied our confusion over questions posed to us only in Arabic. The 90-plus degree heat did not help to keep tempers in check. After what seemed to be an endless wait, we were directed out to a chained-off holding area on the hot tarmac, to await our final departure. About five hundred yards away, a British aircraft stood waiting for us to board. The added delay on the tarmac was the final straw—we were drenched in sweat and our nerves were on extreme edge. Being under constant surveillance by armed and quite grim looking security guards added to the tension.

As we stood in the oppressive heat, a group of about a dozen English oil workers nudged their way up to the departure gate. I was struck by their nervous mannerisms; they kept looking around suspiciously as if they expected something was going to happen. I looked at them; then I looked at the armed guards and suddenly a very troubling thought entered my agitated mind. "My God," I thought. "Did we go through all this abuse just to be massacred here on the tarmac?" I pointed out to my wife how nervously the oil workers were acting and suggested that it might be a good idea to keep close to them in case something did happen.

Time passed slowly. The oil men shuffled closer to the chained gate with their small totebags. They looked even more anxious than before. I grabbed my daughter's hand, my briefcase, and my son's diaper bag. My wife was holding our infant son and a bulky carry-on bag. Suddenly the unsmiling Libyan guards dropped the chain from the gate and stood aside, still holding their AK-47 weapons. The oil workers bolted through the gate at a full run towards the aircraft. I yelled at my wife to start running, and away we went after the Englishmen. As we sped across the tarmac, I glanced behind us and saw that all the other passengers were now running as well. It was a frightening sight. I felt sure that something tragic was about to happen. Still, we all kept running as fast as we could. The Englishmen, unhampered by bulky carry-on articles, were well out in front. My family and I could not keep up the pace and quickly fell behind. When we finally reached the aircraft, everyone was out of breath and soaked with perspiration.

A line had formed at the rear entrance to the aircraft. The oil workers were all at the head of the line. We were so winded we could not speak. Amazingly, nothing had happened. Curiosity got the best of me, and after catching my breath, I walked up to the front of the line and confronted the Englishmen who had started the stampede for the plane. "Why did you all take off running like that?" I asked. "Nothing happened and surely we will all have seats on the plane; why the rush?"

"Mate," came the serious reply. "Libya doesn't sell any beer or whiskey in their bloody country; the blokes here and I haven't had a drink in six months, and this plane only has enough booze for the first four rows! We had to make sure we were first in line!"

I stared at them in disbelief, and then started chuckling. This had been the only humor I had known in over 10 days, and it was a welcome relief.

Upon our arrival in London later that evening, the oil workers in the first four rows of the plane were roaring drunk, while a small group of Americans quietly reflected on our last 10 days in Libya.

Sweet Onion Rings in Beer Batter

1½ cups all-purpose flour,
   divided
1 (12 oz.) can of beer
pinch of salt

2 cups corn oil
1 pound Vidalia or other sweet onions, cut
   into ½-inch thick rings

Make batter by mixing together 1 cup flour, beer, and salt in a bowl. Cover bowl with plastic wrap and let it sit at room temperature for 2 hours.

Arrange several layers of paper towels on a platter and set aside.

In a deep skillet or frying pan, heat the oil to medium. Working with a few rings at a time, dredge onion rings in remaining ½ cup flour; dip in batter; and put them immediately into the hot oil. Fry rings about 30 seconds, until they turn a rich golden brown. Using tongs, carefully remove the fried rings from the skillet and drain them on the paper towels on prepared platter. Cover the cooked rings with more paper towels to keep warm. After all rings are cooked, remove them to a clean platter and serve immediately.

Serves 8.

Per serving: Calories 203 (49% from fat), Carbohydrates 22.8 g, Protein 3.1 g, Total Fat 11.2 g, Sodium 28.8 mg, Saturated Fat 1.5 g, Cholesterol 0 mg, Diabetic Exchanges: starch 1, veg 1, fat 2

BUT HOW DO YOU TELL YOUR CHILDREN?

Growing up in our service has given our four children many unforgettable experiences. They have very special memories of their father saving a small dog from an attack by a Tibetan mastiff and ending up himself trapped with the attacker behind a high fence. They still talk about having to trek higher and higher up the snowy Himalayas because the lower camps were fully occupied by a Japanese climbing group. They remember a night in northern Thailand when the dragon tried to swallow the moon, and all the villagers had to light firecrackers to save the moon. Some of them remember an afternoon in Paris when they met the Vice President of the United States, Richard M. Nixon, and then walked quietly down the Champs Elysees to the Arc de Triomphe in the midst of thousands of Parisiens honoring the memory of Charles de Gaulle.

Three of the four were born overseas separated by 16 and 18 months. The fourth is three years younger than his closest sibling. As the children grew older they began to realize that there was something different about their father's position in the community. By the time our eldest was in the early teens, that position was such that we could share our true affiliation. My husband did not realize that a family tradition was being born when he took our eldest son out to lunch to share "the secret." The special lunch was repeated the following year with the next child and the year after. Then there should have been a lapse of lunches, but the three older ones argued convincingly that the youngest was very mature and ready to handle the responsibility of the secret. I do wish I had been there at the end of the lunch, after the secret had been divulged and explained, to hear the shocked response of our youngest, "Do you mean we're Russian!?!"

Grown-Up Knife and Fork Soup

½ pound sweet and hot
   sausage, quartered
½ cup water, divided
2 tablespoons olive oil
4 white potatoes, thinly sliced
1 red pepper, sliced into
   thin strips
1 green pepper, sliced into
   thin strips

1 small red or yellow onion,
   chopped
3 to 4 cloves garlic
1 teaspoon dried oregano
½ teaspoon dried rosemary
¾ cup tomato paste
4 cups beef or chicken broth
salt and pepper, to taste

Optional toppings:
grated Parmesan cheese, croutons, minced scallions

In a large covered skillet, over low heat, simmer sausages in ¼ cup water for 4 minutes. Uncover; discard water; continue cooking until sausages are browned. Remove sausages; set aside. Pour off fat.

Add oil to skillet; raise heat. Add potatoes, peppers, onions, garlic, oregano, and rosemary; sauté 5 minutes. Stir in tomato paste, remaining ¼ cup water, broth, and reserved sausages. Cover; cook 10 minutes over medium heat until all ingredients are tender. Season with salt and pepper. Serve in bowls. Top with desired amounts of cheese, scallions, and croutons.

Per serving (based on 8 servings per recipe): Calories 233 (49% from fat), Carbohydrates 21 g, Protein 9.5 g, Total Fat 12.9 g, Sodium 1089 mg, Saturated Fat 3.7 g, Cholesterol 24 mg, Diabetic Exchanges: starch 1, meat 1, veg 0.5, fat 2

DUCK AND COVER

Cover can be an ongoing problem for most of us who have to live with it, but for those of us who have children, the decision of when, if, and how to tell them about working for the Agency is usually particularly troublesome. However, in our case, the tables were turned on us when our seven-year-old son told me where we worked.

That year my husband had the misfortune of breaking his knee and having to wear a straight leg cast for six weeks. It then fell to me, of course, to drive him to and from work every day. Since we lived near the office at the time, the drive itself was not the problem. The problem was that sign in front of the building announcing to the world that this was the CIA. At that time, the two younger children, aged seven and eight, had heard only our cover story and did not know that their father and I worked for the Agency. He and I drove to work together in the morning after the children left for school, but since I worked part-time and came home at 3:00, I had to go back to pick up Dad at 5:30 or so. Normally, one of the older two children was at home and could watch the younger two for the 30 or so minutes that I had to be gone. But, as luck would have it, one day I was forced to take the seven year old along. So, crossing my fingers and hoping he wouldn't notice the sign, we set out.

Imagine my shock, when after a couple of minutes, he popped out with, "You work at the CIA, don't you?" Frankly, I didn't know quite what to say, but quickly decided that denial probably wouldn't work in this case and so I said that I did; and before I could explain further, he went on to say, "And Dad works there, too, doesn't he?" At that point, I was really nonplused and could only stare at him. Finally I said, "Yes, he does, too" and tried to explain why we couldn't talk about it and that it was important not to tell anyone else. He seemed to take it all in and to understand and nothing much more was said. About a week or so later I picked him up at school one afternoon and asked the usual, "How was school?" and "What did you do?" It was then that I knew he'd be O.K. with this "cover stuff." He told me that he'd had to write a story in class that day about what work his parents did. Only thing was, he couldn't remember where I was supposedly working, so he just said I worked in a bank and was that O.K.?

My Friend Pat's Famous Torte

(famous in our house for birthdays and special occasions for over 20 years)

1. Prepare cinnamon meringue shell
(plan ahead to allow time for shell to cool completely after it is baked):

½ cup granulated sugar   ¼ teaspoon salt
¼ teaspoon cinnamon   ½ teaspoon white vinegar
2 egg whites

Preheat oven to 275° F.

Cover a cookie sheet with brown paper (a clean, cut up grocery bag is perfect). Draw an 8-inch circle in the center; set aside.

In a small bowl combine sugar and cinnamon; set aside. In a large bowl, beat egg whites with salt and vinegar until soft peaks form. Gradually beat in sugar-cinnamon mixture, beating until very stiff and all the sugar is completely incorporated. Pour mixture onto center of paper-covered cookie sheet; spread within the circle. Form sides of shell by mounding edges about 1¼ inches high. (Good luck! Mine never did look as good as Pat's.) Bake in preheated oven for one hour. Turn off oven and let meringue dry in the oven with the door closed for at least two hours. Remove from oven; peel off paper. Allow shell to cool completely before filling (it may be chilled in refrigerator overnight).

2. Prepare filling:

1 (6 oz.) package chocolate   ¼ cup granulated sugar
   chips (see note below)   ¼ teaspoon cinnamon
2 egg yolks, beaten, or   1 cup heavy cream
   ½ cup liquid egg substitute
¼ cup water

Optional garnish:
whipped cream   chopped nuts
chocolate shavings

Carefully melt chocolate chips in microwave or on stove according to package directions (do not overcook); stir. In cooled meringue shell, spread enough melted chocolate to cover bottom; set aside.

To remaining chocolate, add egg yolks and water; blend thoroughly. Chill chocolate-yolk mixture until thick, about 15 minutes, checking often.

In a small bowl, combine sugar, cinnamon, and cream; whip until stiff. Spread half of the whipped cream over the chocolate in the shell. Fold remaining half of whipped cream into the chilled, thickened chocolate mixture. Spread over whipped cream layer in shell. Chill in refrigerator several hours. To serve,

garnish with dollop of whipped cream and sprinkle with shaved chocolate or chopped nuts.
Makes 6 to 8 servings.

Author's note: Although the recipe calls for a 6 oz. package of chocolate chips, I always buy a larger package and melt about 8 oz. to assure there will be enough melted chocolate to evenly cover the bottom of the meringue shell.

Per serving (based on 8 servings per recipe): Calories 296 (53% from fat), Carbohydrates 33.4 g, Protein 3.1 g, Total Fat 18.6 g, Sodium 96 mg, Saturated Fat 11 g, Cholesterol 94 mg, Diabetic Exchanges: starch 1, fruit 1, fat 3.5

STARSTRUCK

When I first came to work at the Agency, I was assigned to an office that did name traces of Soviets and Eastern Europeans. Travel to the U.S. for tourism from that region was rare in those days, and we routinely received visa photos of all Soviet Bloc types who applied for U.S. visas. Among these photos were some of individuals of no intelligence interest but who had visited the U.S. One of these last was Mikhail Barishnykov, and every now and then we (young female employees) would get out his picture and drool over it.

Anyway, everyone in this office was quite young (who with any sense or experience would want to do this job?) I think we were later replaced by a computer. Many of us lived in tiny apartments and could barely cook. But, as was typical of this age group, we all liked to have a good time and we would alternate having parties at each others' residence. No one would ever offer to cook a meal, but we would always have chips and dips. Someone came up with a couple of easy-to-make dips, and these were the only recipes any of us knew. Whenever there was a party, one of us would volunteer to make one of "our" dips.

To this day, I still pull out these two recipes for easy, fool-proof appetizers that always get a lot of raves.

Shrimp Cheese Dip

2 (8 oz.) packages cream cheese   1 (4 oz.) can shrimp, drained
1 (5 oz.) jar Kraft® Old
   English Cheese Spread

Preheat oven to 350° F.

Let cream cheese soften. With electric beater, in a medium bowl, beat together all ingredients. Bake in preheated oven for 40 minutes until top is slightly brown and bubbly. Serve with crackers.

Per 1-ounce serving: Calories 85 (77% from fat), Carbohydrates 1.2 g, Protein 3.7 g, Total fat 7.3 g, Sodium 117 mg, Saturated fat 4.5 g, Cholesterol 32 mg, Diabetic Exchanges: lean meat 0.5, fat 1

Dried Beef Dip

1 (8 oz.) package cream cheese
1 (2 oz.) jar dried beef

½ pint sour cream
1 medium green bell pepper, chopped

Preheat oven to 350° F.

Let cream cheese soften. Dice dried beef. In a small bowl, beat together all ingredients. Bake in preheated oven for 15 minutes until heated through and cream cheese is melted. Serve with crackers.

Per 1-ounce serving: Calories 71 (82% from fat), Carbohydrates 1.1 g, Protein 2.2 g, Total fat 6.5 g, Sodium 151 mg, Saturated fat 4 g, Cholesterol 19 mg, Diabetic Exchanges: meat 0.3, fat 1

CARRYING CHILI TO NEW CASTLE

Following is a chili recipe that I have given out at state chili cooking contests. I have been participating in them since 1981 . . . have won some, have lost some. The events are great fun (up to 100 cooking teams—we insult one another's cooking), with proceeds from the admission fee going to local charities. This recipe has served me well, and I have used it when I was overseas with whichever meat choice was available (beef, buffalo, fowl, etc.).

My in-laws are citizens of Bolivia, South America. It was a treat for them, when I cooked this dish while visiting them in La Paz (13,000 ft. up in the mountains), using not only materials from local vendors, but also from the "gringo grocery," an American-style grocery patronized by the American community there.

At first glance this must seem like "carrying coals to New Castle," but chili is a uniquely American food, not available locally overseas. There are several chili societies (Chili Appreciation Society, International Chili Society) that sponsor chili cook-offs worldwide for homesick Americans needing their "dose of red."

Chili Barato (Cheap Chili)

3 pounds lean ground beef
1 pound steak (cut into ½-inch cubes), rustled beef, or any road kill
2 tablespoons bacon grease or other fat
2 large white onions, coarsely chopped
6 cloves garlic, minced
3 to 4 jalapeno peppers, cleaned and chopped
4 tablespoons chili powder
1 tablespoon paprika
1 tablespoon black pepper
½ tablespoon dried oregano, preferably Mexican
1 teaspoon salt
2 (or more, see recipe) (12 oz.) cans of beer, preferably Mexican
1 (16 oz.) can of tomato sauce

In a large kettle, brown meat in heated grease or fat, mixing with a fork. Add onions, garlic, and peppers; cook 5 minutes. Stir in spices. Add 1 can of beer to the pot (the rest goes to the cook); add tomato sauce. Bring mixture to a boil, reduce heat and simmer uncovered 2½ hours. If mixture gets too thick, add more beer to the pot (and to the cook). One half hour before serving, taste and adjust seasonings.

Per serving (based on 12 servings per recipe): Calories 333 (46% from fat), Carbohydrates 8.9 g, Protein 32.2 g, Total Fat 17.1 g, Sodium 562 mg, Saturated Fat 6.8 g, Cholesterol 64 mg, Diabetic Exchanges: lean meat 4.5, veg 1, fat 1

SWEDISH MEATBALLS GO HAWAIIAN

Growing up in a northern Minnesota mining town, I encountered early in life wonderful foods from around the world, because many of the local mining families were first-generation Americans from many European countries. My mother was given a recipe for meatballs by a Swedish-American friend. The recipe became a family favorite.

As I traveled abroad on assignment, the original "old favorite" recipe was modified by the availability of its ingredients—or lack thereof—in the underdeveloped countries in which we lived. Ground beef (or "mince" as people of the British Empire called it) was usually available, in frozen form in the Embassy-supported commissary (canned foods and frozen meats), and fresh in the "modern" shops on the local economy of a few more developed countries. In "hardship posts" one had to be careful that extraneous flies and other bits and pieces had not been included. Spices could be brought in shipments of household goods or sent from home by helpful friends.

The recipe has traveled well, reflecting new ways of entertainment as well as new friends. For a hearty family meal in a cold climate, the meatballs can be large and served cooked in cream. For a cocktail party, tiny meatballs can be cooked in barbecue sauce and served on picks from a flaming chafing dish, adding eye-appeal and flavor to a party table.

A Hawaiian friend provided the barbecue sauce recipe. This was tasty and it reduced the calories and fat of the original recipe's whole cream. Also, the fresh cream could be unsafe to eat and was easily curdled by unskilled hands.

In Asia, I discovered the joys of Kikkoman® soy sauce, used by local families from gallon jugs. Even the smallest open-front shops displayed huge pottery jars of soy sauce, painted with big black symbols identifying the manufacturer. There were various brands, but Americans generally preferred the mildness of Kikkoman®. When we returned from Asia, I had to travel to Washington's "China Town" to buy this brand, but now it is available in many grocery stores across the country.

Asia also introduced browned sesame seeds as an ingredient to the sauce or sprinkled over the meatballs just before serving.

A chafing dish, I found, was a cooking utensil that was familiar to household helpers in the Far East and Africa, where cooking was done for the most part over small charcoal fires. Fresh ginger, I discovered in Asia, is a very different spice from the dried ginger with which I was familiar. And its exotic white flowers can perfume a home wherever in the world they are.

Sweden, Hawaii, the Far East, and developing countries of Africa—my family recipe now reflects them all.

Chafing Dish Meatballs

2 pounds ground round steak
1 pound ground pork
2 eggs, beaten
1 cup mashed potatoes
1 cup dry bread crumbs
½ cup water
sesame seeds (optional)

1 teaspoon brown sugar
1½ teaspoons salt
½ teaspoon black pepper
½ teaspoon each ground ginger, nutmeg,
   cloves, and allspice
1 cup milk or ½ cup evaporated milk plus
   ½ cup water

Combine ingredients in a large bowl. Form 1½-inch balls and roll in flour. Brown evenly in a small amount of heated fat or oil in a large skillet. Cover, lower heat, and simmer slowly 35 to 45 minutes until meat is tender. Or, bake in covered dish for 50 minutes in preheated 325° F. oven.

Pour cooked meatballs and any sauce into chafing dish. Sprinkle with sesame seeds, if desired. Serve warm.

Variations:
1. Smaller, bite-size meatballs may be formed, if desired, and prepared as above reducing cooking time to avoid overcooking. Use toothpicks to serve.
2. For Swedish style, after browning, simmer meatballs in 1 pint cream. Omit sesame seeds; serve with noodles.
3. For Hawaiian style hors d'oeuvres, simmer in Hawaiian Barbecue Sauce (see recipe below).

Per serving (based on 8 servings per recipe): Calories 446 (51% from fat), Carbohydrates 16.8 g, Protein 36.6 g, Total Fat 25 g, Sodium 715 mg, Saturated Fat 9.7 g, Cholesterol 167 mg, Diabetic Exchanges: bread 1, meat 5

Hawaiian Barbecue Sauce

1 tablespoon brown sugar
1 tablespoon mustard
1 tablespoon cornstarch
6 tablespoons soy sauce*

1 tablespoon bourbon
3 cloves garlic, crushed
1 small joint ginger root, peeled and crushed
lemon juice or catsup (optional)

Mix brown sugar, mustard, cornstarch. Add soy sauce, bourbon, garlic, and ginger; heat through. Add browned meatballs and simmer in sauce. As meat is cooking, water can be added to keep sauce from getting too strong. Lemon juice can also be added. Tomato catsup will add a different flavor.

This recipe can be successfully doubled, tripled, or quadrupled.

Additional uses: This sauce can also be used to marinate beef, pork or chicken and as a basting sauce when grilling, broiling or baking the meat. Add water and thicken with cornstarch for gravy.

*If genuine Chinese brands are used, add water and small amount of sugar, to taste.

Per serving (based on 8 servings per recipe): Calories 28 (13% from fat), Carbohydrates 4.2 g, Protein 1.1 g, Total Fat 0.4 g, Sodium 772 mg, Saturated Fat 0 g, Cholesterol 0 mg, Diabetic Exchanges: negligible **197**

A GIFT

Some years ago in a university setting, I had a neighbor from another country who was particularly anxious about having people she did not know in her home. One evening, she nervously asked me to stop by her house in about an hour. Against her better judgment, this widow had invited someone to her house instead of to her office to discuss a class she taught. She wanted to know someone could be there for her in case she needed help.

I arrived at 7:35, as requested, "to borrow some sugar." All was well, the woman and visitor were chatting comfortably, and I left with my cup of sugar.

The next day the woman knocked at my door with a beautifully tied white bakery box as a thank-you. Inside, nestled in pleated cups, were six beautiful baklava. She had made them herself, and they were the best I have ever eaten. She later showed me every step of their production, and I have been sharing them, and the recipe, with friends ever since.

Baklava

3½ cups walnuts
  (approx. 1⅓ pounds)
1 tablespoon ground cinnamon
1 teaspoon ground cloves

¾ pounds unsalted butter
1 pound phyllo dough (approx. 24 sheets)
1⅓ pounds honey (about 1⅓ cups)

Preheat oven to 350° F.

Chop walnuts very fine. Add cinnamon and cloves; mix with walnuts in large bowl. Set aside.

Melt butter and brush 15 x 10-inch pan with butter. Place in the pan eight sheets of pastry, each brushed with butter. Fold ends of pastry as needed to make it fit the pan, alternating sides so as to avoid a buildup on one side or another. Sprinkle a scant ½ cup of the walnut mixture on the 8th sheet and add remaining sheets, continuing to sprinkle walnuts on the 8th to 16th sheets or until all nut mixture is used. End with a final eight layers of pastry, brushing each layer with butter.

Trim edges with knife; make 5 lengthwise cuts to form 6 rows, then cut diagonally to make diamonds. Bake for 45 to 55 minutes or until lightly browned. Remove from oven and pour honey over hot baklava. Allow to stand 12 to 24 hours before serving to allow honey to soak in. Freezes well, and will keep in refrigerator a month. Serve each piece in fluted papers (muffins cups or smaller). Makes 60 pieces.

Per serving: Calories 138 (62 % from fat), Carbohydrates 11.6 g, Protein 1.6 g, Total Fat 9.4 g, Sodium 39 mg, Saturated Fat 9.4 g, Cholesterol 12 mg, Diabetic Exchanges: fruit 1, fat 2

SCANDINAVIAN SECRET POTION

There are few mystery stories or spy novels, from Agatha Christie to Charles McCarry and Tom Clancy, which don't contain reference to some secret potion, injection, or nefarious concoction.

While my late husband Doug's 25-year career with the Agency seldom strayed beyond throw-weight and verification (Arms Control was his corner of the world), our annual Christmas Glögg Open House may well have been accused of having the same effect on our guests.

Our Glögg Open House originated in 1968 as a result of my Scandinavian heritage (Swedish and Norwegian) and concern for the many of our friends for whom the holidays away from home were, at best, gloomy. My recipe is the result of all those years of tasting and trying.

Over the years the tales surrounding glögg have mounted as fast as the snows of the winter of '96. The one which probably most clearly reflects the need to adapt and cope as the situation presents itself involves a flight we made to a family Christmas in Minnesota.

Of 26 years of glögg gatherings, only one has ever been cancelled because of weather, and that year we had 22 inches of snow in about 12 hours. With 5 gallons of glögg the question was WHAT TO DO?? The only natural thing was . . . to take it with us to Minnesota!! Of course there was one small problem . . . how does one transport this sacred cargo?? On an airplane . . . how else??!! After several call transfers, long silences on the other end, and questions about the content of our "home brew," we finally found a supervisor who assured us that we were certainly welcome. HOWEVER, the bottles had to stay corked and we would not be allowed to sample it with our roasted peanuts.

All's well that ends well and no bottles broke and the glögg didn't freeze, despite the 30 degrees below zero temp . . . you aren't surprised???

Two final ingredients . . . snow and lots of hot coffee!!

George's Glorious Glögg

2 quarts dry red wine	10 to 15 whole cloves
2 quarts muscatel (use port if muscatel unavailable)	2 to 3 pieces fresh ginger (ground, if need be)
1 pint sweet vermouth	4 sticks cinnamon
2 tablespoons Angostura bitters	½ to ¾ cup Aquavit (more or less)
2 cups raisins	½ to ¾ cup granulated sugar (less is better for my taste)
orange peelings from one orange	1 cup sliced or whole almonds
2 to 3 tablespoons ground cardamom	

Combine first 10 ingredients in a large enameled or stainless steel pot. Cover and let stand for at least 12 hours until flavors are blended.

Shortly before serving, add Aquavit and sugar and bring to ALMOST boiling over medium-high heat. Add almonds.

Can be kept on low temperature on the stove while continuing to refill the punch bowl.
Serves 20 to 25 (multiples are easy).

Per 4-fl. oz. (plus solids) serving (based on 25 servings per recipe): Calories 374 (71% from alcohol), Carbohydrates 21.3 g, Protein 1.6 g, Total Fat 2.2 g, Sodium 10 mg, Saturated Fat 0.2 g, Cholesterol 0 mg, Diabetic Exchanges: fruit 1.5, fat 6 (calories from alcohol are counted as fat in the diabetic exchange system)

ONE IS ENOUGH

Grocery shopping in a foreign country with a foreign language can create amusing situations, but I have no excuse—my story took place here at home.

I invited a few friends over for an informal supper and decided to serve spaghetti with meat sauce. I had all of the ingredients on hand, except for one item. I went to the grocery store and proceeded to the butcher section. I pressed the buzzer for the butcher to appear. I asked him if I could have one pork chop.

He said, "Only one?"

"Yes," I replied. "I only need one pork chop because I am only having about eight people for supper."

"Madam," he said, "I hope this one pork chop goes far!" He walked away laughing before I could tell him that I only use the pork chop to add flavor to the tomato sauce.

Quick Meat Sauce for Pasta

1 pound lean ground meat or turkey
1 pork chop, cut up
1½ cups chopped onion
6 cloves garlic, crushed or minced
4 (15 oz.) cans tomato sauce
2 oz. tomato paste (⅓ of a 6 oz. can) (freeze remainder for later use)
¼ cup dry red wine

4 teaspoons dried oregano leaves, crushed
2 teaspoons dried basil leaves, crushed
2 teaspoons dried parsley
¼ teaspoon ground black pepper
1 teaspoon granulated sugar
16 oz. dry pasta, cooked and drained

In a large saucepan or deep skillet, brown meat and pork, stirring with a fork, until red color disappears. Drain off all but about 2 tablespoons accumulated fat. Add onion and garlic; sauté until tender. Stir in remaining ingredients, except pasta. Bring to a boil. Reduce heat and simmer, uncovered, 30 minutes. Serve over hot pasta.
Makes 8 servings.

Per serving: Calories 426 (19 % from fat), Carbohydrates 64.4 g, Protein 21.8 g, Total Fat 9.3 g, Sodium 1047 mg, Saturated Fat 3 g, Cholesterol 38 mg, Diabetic Exchanges: starch 3, meat 1.5, veg 0.5, fat 1

BASIC FRIED DUMPLINGS INTERNATIONAL

I have often been pleasantly surprised to find delicious fried dumplings on the menu in many different parts of the world. Below I have tried to explain in the simplest of terms how to make four very different fillings for fried dumplings using wonton wrappers. You make the filling, stuff the wrapper and deep-fry for a few minutes. Voilá! Several international delicacies.

To defrost frozen round or square wonton wrappers, let sit at room temperature an hour or so in warm weather or briefly defrost in the top of a steamer. The wrappers to be used should be kept under a damp towel so they will not dry out; the remaining wrappers, if not completely defrosted, can be refrozen. Specific proportions of ingredients are not given in these recipes.

Remember, in each instance, when the filling is placed inside the wrapper, the edge of the wrapper should have a little water rubbed on it with your finger and be crimped slightly with the prongs of a fork to keep the filling from running out.

Brazilian Pasteis

Round wonton wrappers   Mozzarella, Jack or Swiss cheese,
                                                                       cut in ½ inch squares or smaller

Place cheese in the wrapper, seal, and fry.

Bulaunee Gandana or Afghan-inspired Scallion Dumplings

Square wonton wrappers   Finely chopped scallion,
                                                                       fried in a little butter with salt and pepper

Fill wrappers with cooked, drained scallions, seal and fry. Serve with a mint yogurt side dish as appetizer.

Chinese Wonton

Square wonton wrappers
Ground pork or beef, salt and pepper, monosodium glutamate, and garlic powder fried in vegetable oil

Fill wrappers with drained meat mixture, seal and fry.
Serve with Szechwan dipping sauce (recipe follows) as appetizer.

Samosas (from Africa, India)

Round wonton wrappers
Finely chopped onion or scallions, garlic, ginger, ground lamb, salt, hot chili, garam masala, chopped fresh coriander, lemon juice, and turmeric fried in vegetable oil

Fill wrappers with drained filling mixture, seal, and fry.
Serve with chutney or yogurt sauce.

The same deep-frying technique is used for all of the above.

Pour vegetable oil to about ½ inch deep in a wok or deep pan. Turn on the exhaust fan (safflower or peanut oil does not smell as much as corn oil does). Heat the oil to medium hot. (Test the temperature of the oil by dropping a small piece of wonton wrapper into the oil. The temperature is correct when bubbles form on the wrapper and it sizzles lightly in the oil.) Slowly add the filled wrappers and cook 2 to 4 minutes until crispy and just slightly bronze on the outside. Remove from the oil and place on paper towels or a cake cooling rack over newspaper to drain. Place on serving platter and serve.

Several of the different dumplings can be served together, such as the cheese pasteis and the scallion dumplings with yogurt. The samosas take the most time to prepare.

Editors' note: For additional international dumpling variations, and for wrapping techniques, see recipes for Appetizer Empanadas, Philippine Lumpia, and Siberian Pilmeny.

Dietitian's note: Because ingredients and proportions vary, nutritional values for the dumplings have not been determined.

Szechwan Dipping Sauce

Chinese wonton taste delicious when accompanied by this sauce. The proportions are not exact to accommodate individual tastes. The sauce keeps for several days.

equal amounts minced garlic
  and minced scallions
2 portions soy sauce

1 portion white vinegar
¼ portion sesame oil (or chili
  oil if preferred)

Combine all ingredients and hold at room temperature.

It is traditional to give each guest a very small bowl filled with about 2 tablespoons of sauce to enhance the flavor of the wonton.

Per 2-tablespoon serving of Dipping Sauce (using sesame oil, and 1/2 teaspoon per serving each garlic and scallions): Calories 36 (52% from fat), Carbohydrates 3.1 g, Protein 1.3 g, Total Fat 2.1 g, Sodium 1266 mg, Saturated Fat 0.1 g, Cholesterol 0 mg, Diabetic Exchanges: fat 0.5

A NEW ADVENTURE

Being overseas can be the most exciting and fulfilling time of your life. While new sights and sounds can be very rewarding and stimulating for adults, they can be awfully scary for children. I have always tried to help my children adjust to their new surroundings by preparing them ahead of time with books, brochures, and videos which deal with some aspect of the new city. Getting them involved in planning things that they would like to see and do after arrival and allowing them to pick out special items for their new room has helped them look forward to their new home. I would also suggest finding out ahead of time if there are any children with whom they could become pen pals before arrival. Knowing about their new home and having a new friend waiting when they get there can make a new place a little less scary.

Here are two recipes for home-made molding dough. Although not designed for eating, both doughs are nontoxic—just in case!

Play Dough #1

1 cup flour
½ cup salt
1 cup water

2 teaspoons cream of tartar
food coloring (optional)

Mix all ingredients and cook on low fire, stirring occasionally until dough forms a ball. Cool and store in resealable plastic bags.

Play Dough #2

1¼ cups powdered sugar
¼ cup milk

1 cup corn syrup
1 cup peanut butter

Mix well until a proper consistency for molding.

LAND OF THE FREE

Our five-year-old daughter, born in Europe, had spent very little of her young life in the United States. We had returned to live in Virginia when she was ten months old, but by the time she was two, we were assigned to Southern Europe. Two and a half years later we moved to Asia, so she really had very little first-hand knowledge of the U.S.

Carefully watched and closely supervised, she knew a world limited first to nursery school, fenced yards, or holding Mommy's hand when out among the population. In Asia, nannies and walled compounds were part of life, her daily routine even more strictly circumscribed to protect against disease, unsavory characters, and even wild dogs.

We returned to the States on home leave during the summer she turned five. We were staying at my sister's home in Connecticut. On our first afternoon there, my daughter came running indoors, shocked and bewildered. "Mommy! Mommy! Johnny (her young cousin) rode his bike outside our compound!" She was completely overwhelmed and frightened.

I explained carefully, "That's O.K., Honey. You can go out of the compound, too. You can go up the block and down the block as far as the corner, as long as you don't go into the road or cross the street."

She could hardly believe her good fortune.

"We're in the United States, now," I continued. "It's O.K. to go anywhere you want on this block." She was overjoyed, and quickly ran to join her cousin.

That night at bedtime, I tucked her in and listened to her say her prayers. Her words will remain with me always. Concluding her long list of those to be blessed, she signed off, "And thank You, God, for America!"

Hamburger Pie

Biscuit crust for 9-inch pie pan (recipe follows)	salt and pepper, to taste
1 pound lean ground beef	2 tablespoons all-purpose flour
1 medium onion, minced	1 cup cottage cheese
1 clove garlic, minced	2 eggs, beaten
thyme or oregano, to taste	

Preheat oven to 375° F.

Prepare biscuit crust according to recipe below. Do not bake. Set aside.

In a large skillet over medium-high heat, brown beef, breaking apart with a fork; push to the side and add onions and garlic; sauté until onions and garlic are tender. Remove from heat; stir in flour, thyme or oregano, salt and pepper.

Fill crust with meat mixture; set aside.

Combine cottage cheese and eggs in a small bowl; season with salt and pepper. Spoon over meat filling. Bake in preheated oven for 15 to 20 minutes until crust is golden and knife inserted into center comes out clean.

Serves 6.

Substitution: Sprinkle 1 cup of shredded cheddar cheese, or other favorite cheese, over top before baking instead of cottage cheese and eggs.

Biscuit Crust

1 cup all-purpose flour

2 teaspoons baking powder

¼ teaspoon salt

4 tablespoons butter or margarine

⅓ cup milk

Sift flour, baking powder, and salt into a large bowl. With a pastry blender or 2 knives cut butter or margarine into dry ingredients until mixture is crumbly and resembles cornmeal. Gradually stir in milk; mix until dough forms and pulls away from sides of bowl.

Turn out onto lightly floured board; roll out into a circle ¼-inch thick. Ease dough into 9-inch pie pan, pressing to eliminate air bubbles. Trim excess around edges. Flute edges, if desired.

Per serving (of pie and crust, based on 8 servings per recipe): Calories 292 (50% from fat), Carbohydrates 17.6 g, Protein 18.6 g, Total Fat 16 g, Sodium 671 mg, Saturated Fat 7.8 g, Cholesterol 105 mg, Diabetic Exchanges: starch 1, meat 2.5, fat 1

Just for fun

Cobra Soup

1 cobra (medium size)
1 whole head garlic,
    coarsely chopped
1 teaspoon salt

2 dashes bottled hot pepper sauce
1 teaspoon monosodium glutamate (MSG)

Catch a cobra. Cut off the head of the cobra and remove the skin and internal organs. Chop the body into 2-inch pieces. Put pieces in a large pot, with ½ gallon water and boil for 45 minutes. Add remaining ingredients, and boil for 30 more minutes. Serve hot.

DAWA

(a legendary cure for ancient ailments)

8 tots vodka
8 ounces lime juice

4 teaspoons honey

Rub the rim of four old-fashioned glasses with a lime quarter and dip the rims into a saucer of sugar. Mix, in a separate clean vessel, the above ingredients and stir well with your magic Dawa stick. Caution, do not add ice, as it will congeal the honey and be difficult to stir. When thoroughly mixed, add ice to the glasses and pour in the finished Dawa. Be forewarned that Dawa has been known to hurt your head, and sometimes the cure is worse than the disease.

Elephant Stew

1 elephant
200 gallons brown gravy
30 rabbits

1½ gallons bottled hot pepper sauce
salt and pepper to taste

Cut elephant into bite-sized pieces; cover with gravy and cook over fire at 465° F. for 4 weeks. This serves 3,800 people. If more are expected, add rabbits. However, this should be done only if necessary, as people don't like finding hare in their stew.

Stuffed Camel

150 eggs, boiled
40 kilos (88 pounds) tomatoes
20 chickens, roasted

4 lambs
1 medium camel
salt and seasonings to taste

Stuff eggs into tomatoes.
Stuff tomatoes into chickens.
Stuff chickens into lambs.
Stuff lambs into camel.
Roast until tender.
Adjust seasonings.
Serves 150 people.

Helpful Hints

Tips for the Cook, Tips for the Overseas Cook,
Tips from a Conversation with Julia Child,
Measurements, Yields, and Substitutions

Tips For The Cook

- **Keep homemade bread crumbs** on hand by storing bread about to go stale and heels of bread loaves in a plastic bag in the freezer. Cut up large pieces before freezing. When needed, process frozen bread in food processor or blender.
- **When baking bread,** put a small dish of water in the oven to keep the crust from getting too hard.
- **To freshen stale Italian or French bread,** hold loaf under running water for 2 to 3 seconds; wrap in foil; heat in 200° F. oven for 15 minutes. To freshen other types of bread, place bread in clean paper bag, just moisten the outside of bag; heat in 350° F. oven about 5 minutes. Serve refreshed bread immediately.
- **To soften hardened brown sugar,** place sugar in small bowl with 1 slice of bread or an apple wedge; cover bowl with plastic wrap; microwave on high for 35 seconds.
- **To peel a tomato easily,** first plunge it into boiling water for 30 seconds, then into cold water until it is cool enough to handle; the skin will readily slide off.
- **To grate cheese easily,** first chill the cheese.
- **To melt chocolate chips easily,** microwave 1 cup of chips, uncovered, on high for 1 minute; stir; continue cooking on high, checking and stirring every 10 seconds, until melted.
- **To dry fresh herbs,** arrange the herbs between two white paper towels; microwave on high for 1 to 1½ minutes or until herbs are dry and begin to crumble; adjust time according to amount and type of herb, and keep a record of times for future referral.
- **To avoid lumps when adding flour to hot liquid,** allow a little bit of the liquid to cool, then blend the flour into the cooled liquid (or blend into cool water instead) to form a thin paste; then stir paste slowly into the hot liquid.
- **To prepare pasta in advance of serving,** undercook it very slightly, drain, then rinse in cool water. Place pasta in a bowl with fresh cold water to cover; refrigerate until serving time. When ready to serve, drain, place in fresh bowl and add boiling salted water to cover; let stand until pasta is hot. Drain, place pasta in serving bowl, and serve.
- **To help sauce adhere to cooked pasta,** do not rinse the pasta. Do rinse if serving pasta cold in a salad.
- **When planning to serve pasta,** keep in mind that the guests should wait for the pasta; the pasta should never wait for the guests.
- **When cooking cauliflower,** add some milk to the water to keep the cauliflower white and looking fresh.
- **When boiling potatoes,** add a few drops of lemon juice to the water to whiten the potatoes.
- **When cooking with vinegar,** do not use an aluminum pot; otherwise the food may take on a metallic taste.
- **After handling raw onion,** use fresh lemon juice to remove scent from hands.
- **When cooking cabbage,** place a small cup of vinegar near the pot to absorb the odor.

- **To retain freshness,** store ground coffee in refrigerator or freezer.
- **To help sour cream last longer,** store in refrigerator upside-down to prevent air from getting into carton.
- **To slice meat into thin strips easily,** first partially freeze it.
- **To assure meat is nicely browned rather than steamed:** allow meat to stand a bit after removing from refrigerator to take off the chill; remove excess moisture by blotting meat with paper towels; heat pan over medium-high heat so that meat will brown quickly; and brown only enough meat at one time as fits in the pan without crowding.
- **For baking,** if the recipe calls for two 9-inch round cake layer pans and none are available, two 8-inch square pans or one 13 x 9 x 2-inch pan may be used instead. Reduce baking time when using glass baking dishes.

Tips For The Overseas Cook

- **Baking at High Altitudes:** It is probably best to obtain high-altitude recipes for the country to which one is assigned. But if none are available, this list can be used to modify an old family sea-level recipe. When two amounts are given, try the smaller adjustment first. If a cake still needs to be improved, use the larger adjustment next time. Experiment at family meals first!
    reduce baking powder— for each teaspoon in a recipe, decrease ¼ teaspoon
    reduce sugar—for each cup in a recipe, decrease 2 to 3 tablespoons
    increase liquid—for each cup in a recipe, add 3 to 4 tablespoons
- **Using meat of uncertain origin:** Tapeworm can be transmitted through meat insufficiently cooked. Always thoroughly cook meat. Thorough cooking at high altitudes is difficult; for example, grilled meat which is "done" in the lower altitudes of the U.S. may be unsafe at higher elevations. Freezing meat before use will destroy the possibility of transmitting tapeworm.
- **When using a cookbook which has been translated into English:** Be sure to check whether the recipes use British or American measurements; it can make a difference with liquids. A British cup, for example, holds 10 fl. oz., while an American cup holds 8 fl. oz. Also be aware of British or European ingredient names: single cream is light cream and double cream is heavy cream; minced meat is ground meat; icing sugar is confectioner's or powdered sugar, caster sugar is granulated sugar; biscuits are cookies; Maryland cookies are chocolate chip cookies; and corn flour means cornstarch.

Tips From A Conversation with Julia Child

What would you advise a young person going overseas for the first time to take for the kitchen?

A heavy 10" nonstick frying pan, sharp knives with a sharpener . . . you could get along with one 10" and one 6" and one small one, and a good pair of shears. And I'd take a wire whisk, sort of a medium size, and I guess you'd have to have one saucepan, probably. I'd have a fairly heavy stainless saucepan, about 2½ quarts. That's not very big, but at least you'd have something.

What about herbs or spices that you think are essential for most dishes, or is there such a thing?

No, I don't think so. It would be nice to have pepper in a pepper grinder.

Are there any favorite appliances that you would take or recommend?

I think a hand-held mixer would be very convenient . . . I would certainly take a food processor . . . But then, you don't know what the electricity is going to be like.

Which cookbook would you take?

Well, I would take the *French Larousse Gastronomique*; I think that's a marvelous book. But I probably might take the old *Joy of Cooking*. Of course, I would have to take one of mine; I'd take *The Way to Cook*.

Thank you very much for your time.

I'm sorry I didn't interview all of you as to where you were.

Weights and Measures
with approximate metric equivalents

¼ tsp. = 1.25 ml

½ tsp. = 2.5 ml

1 tsp. = 1/3 Tbs. = 5 ml

1 Tbs. = 3 tsp. = 15 ml

⅛ cup = 2 Tbs. = 1 fl. oz. = 30 ml

¼ cup = 4 Tbs. = 2 fl. oz. = 60 ml

⅓ cup = 5⅓ Tbs. = 5 Tbs. + 1 tsp. = 80 ml

½ cup = 8 Tbs. = 4 fl. oz. = 120 ml

⅔ cup = 10⅔ Tbs. = 10 Tbs. + 2 tsp. = 160 ml

¾ cup = 12 Tbs. = 6 fl. oz. = 180 ml

1 cup = 16 Tbs. = ½ pint = 8 fl. oz. = 240 ml = 2.4 dl

1 pint = 2 cups = 16 fl. oz. = 480 ml

1 quart = 2 pints = 4 cups = 32 fl. oz. = 960 ml = 9.5 dl

2 quarts = 4 pints = 8 cups = 64 fl. oz. = 1/2 gallon = 1.89 liters

1 gallon = 4 quarts = 8 pints = 16 cups = 128 fl. oz. = 3.79 liters

1 milliliter (ml) = .03 fluid ounces (fl. oz.)

1 deciliter (dl) = 100 ml = about 1/2 cup

½ liter = 5 dl = 500 ml = about 1 pint

1 liter = 10 dl = 1000 ml = about 4½ cups = 1.1 quarts = .3 gallons

1 jigger = 1½ fl. oz. = 3 Tbs.

weight:

1 oz. = 28 gram (g)

8 oz. = ½ lb. = 227 g = .23 kilogram

1 lb. = 16 oz. = 454 g = .45 kilogram

10 g = 1 decagram (dkg) = .4 oz.

1 kilogram = 1000 g = 100 dkg = 2.2 lbs.

Oven temperatures:

very slow = 250-275° F. or 120-135° C.

slow = 300-325° F. or 150-165° C.

moderate = 350-375° F. or 175-190° C.

hot = 400-425° F. or 200-220° C.

very hot = 450-475° F. or 230-245° C.

extremely hot = 500-525° F. or 260-275° C.

To test oven temperature when thermometer is unavailable:
Sprinkle all-purpose flour into a shallow pan; place pan in heated oven.
At 300-325° F. flour should be light brown in 5 minutes.
At 350-375° F. flour should be medium brown in 5 minutes.
At 400-425° F. flour should be very dark brown in 5 minutes.
At 450-475° F. flour should be very dark brown in 3 minutes.

200° F. = 93° C.	325° F. = 163° C.	450° F. = 232° C.
225° F. = 107° C.	350° F. = 177° C.	475° F. = 246° C.
250° F. = 121° C.	375° F. = 191° C.	500° F. = 260° C.
275° F. = 135° C.	400° F. = 204° C.	
300° F. = 149° C.	425° F. = 218° C.	

QUICK AND EASY APPROXIMATE METRIC CONVERSIONS:

To convert **teaspoons to milliliters,** multiply number of teaspoons by 5.

To convert **tablespoons to milliliters,** multiply number of tablespoons by 15.

To convert **fluid ounces to milliliters,** multiply number of fluid ounces by 30.

To convert **cups to liters,** multiply number of cups by .24.

To convert **quarts to liters,** multiply number of quarts by .95.

To convert **gallons to liters,** multiply number of gallons by 3.8.

To convert **ounces to grams,** multiply number of ounces by 28.

To convert **pounds to kilos,** multiply number of pounds by .45.

To convert **Fahrenheit to Celsius,** subtract 32 from degrees F, multiply by 5, divide by 9.

To convert **milliliters to teaspoons,** divide number of milliliters by 5.

To convert **milliliters to tablespoons,** divide number of milliliters by 15.

To convert **milliliters to fluid ounces,** divide number of milliliters by 30.

To convert **liters to cups,** divide number of liters by .24.

To convert **liters to quarts,** multiply number of liters by 1.06.

To convert **liters to gallons,** multiply number of liters by .26.

To convert **grams to ounces,** multiply number of grams by .035.

To convert **kilos to pounds,** multiply number of kilos by 2.2.

To convert **Celsius to Fahrenheit,** multiply degrees C by 9, divide by 5, add 32.

How Much Does It Make?

Approximate Ingredient Yields

1 lb. butter = 4 sticks = 2 cups
1 stick butter = 4 oz. = 8 Tbs. = ½ cup
1 lb. cheese = 4 cups grated = 2⅔ cups cubed
1 lb. cottage cheese = 2 cups
1 cup whipping cream = ½ pt = 2 cups whipped
1 lb. All-purpose flour = 4 cups unsifted
1 lb. cake flour = 4½ cups unsifted
1 lb. cornstarch = 3 cups
1 (¼ oz.) pkg. active dry yeast = 2¼ tsp.
1 lb. granulated sugar = 2 cups
1 lb. powdered sugar = 4 cups sifted
1 lb. brown sugar = 2¼ cups firmly packed
1 oz. chocolate = 1 square
1 slice bread = ½ cup soft bread crumbs = ¼ cup dry bread crumbs
1 cup dried beans = 2¼ cups cooked
1 lb. rice = 2 cups = 6 cups cooked
1 cup uncooked rice = 3 cups cooked
8 oz. uncooked macaroni = 4 cups cooked
8 oz. uncooked spaghetti = 3½ - 4 cups cooked
8 oz. uncooked noodles = 4 - 5 cups cooked
4 oz. nuts = ¾ cup chopped
1 lb. coffee = 5 cups ground
1 lb. cranberries = 4 cups
1 lb. currants = 3 cups
1 lb. raisins = 3 cups = 4 cups cooked
1 lb. apples = 2 - 3 medium
1 lb. peaches = 4 medium
1 medium lemon = 2 - 3 Tbs. lemon juice
5 - 6 medium lemons = 1 cup (8 oz.) juice
1 medium lemon = 1 Tbs. grated peel
1 medium orange = 3 - 4 Tbs. orange juice
1 medium orange = 2 Tbs. grated peel
1 medium carrot = ½ cup chopped or sliced
1 medium celery rib = ½ cup chopped or sliced
2 - 3 ears corn = 1 cup kernels
1 medium tomato = ½ cup chopped
1 medium garlic clove = ½ tsp. finely chopped
2 medium green onions = 1 cup chopped

1 large onion = 1 cup chopped
1 lb. cabbage = 4 cups shredded
1 lb. potatoes = 3 medium
1 lb. mushrooms = 12 - 15 large, 25 - 30 medium or 36 - 45 small = 5 cups sliced
2½ to 3 lbs. chicken = 2½ cups cooked and diced
1 lb. boneless meat yields 4 servings
1 lb. leg of lamb with bone-in yields 1 serving
1 lb. whole fish yields 1 - 2 servings
1 lb. fish fillet or fish steak yields 2 - 3 servings
1 lb. shrimp (in shell) yields 2 - 3 servings
1 lb. cut up chicken yields 1 - 2 servings
1 lb. skinless boneless chicken breast yields 3 - 4 servings
1 lb. whole turkey yields 2 servings

What To Use Instead?

Suggestions for Ingredient Substitutions

1 cup whole milk = 4 Tbs. nonfat dry milk powder + 2 tsp. butter
+ 1 cup water
1 cup skim milk = 4 Tbs. nonfat dry milk powder + 1 cup water
1 cup light cream (half-and-half) = 1 Tbs. melted butter + enough milk to make
1 cup
1 cup whipping cream = ⅔ cup evaporated milk chilled then whipped
= 1 cup nonfat dry milk powder whipped with
1 cup ice water
1 cup sour cream for cooking = 3 Tbs. butter + ⅞ cup buttermilk or yogurt
1 Tbs. cornstarch for thickening = 2 Tbs. flour = 2 tsp. arrowroot
1 cup corn syrup = 1 cup sugar + ¼ cup additional liquid same as
used in recipe
1 Tbs. flour for thickening = ½ Tbs. cornstarch
1 cup sifted cake flour for baking = ⅞ cup all-purpose flour (texture will be coarser)
= 1 cup all-purpose flour less 2 Tbs.
1 cup all-purpose flour for baking = 1 cup + 2 Tbs. cake flour
1 cup self-rising flour = 1 cup all-purpose flour + 1¼ tsp. baking
powder + ⅛ tsp. salt
1 cup packed brown sugar = 1 cup granulated sugar + 2 Tbs. molasses
1 tsp. baking powder = ½ tsp. cream of tartar + 1/4 tsp. baking soda
1 (¼ oz.) pkg. active dry yeast = 1 (.6 oz.) cake fresh = 2¼ tsp. active dry yeast

1 square (1 oz.) unsweetened chocolate = 3 Tbs. unsweetened cocoa + 1 Tbs. butter or margarine

1 square (1 oz.) unsweetened chocolate = 3 Tbs. carob powder + 2 Tbs. water

6 oz. semisweet chocolate chips = 6 squares semisweet chocolate

6 oz. melted semisweet chocolate chips = 6 Tbs. unsweetened cocoa + ¼ cup granulated sugar + ¼ cup shortening

1 cup bread crumbs = ¾ cup cracker crumbs

1 cup graham crackers = 14 square crackers

2 cups tomato sauce = 6 oz. can tomato paste + ½ cup water

juice of 1 lemon

= 3 Tbs. lemon juice concentrate

6 oz. can mushrooms = 1/2 lb. fresh mushrooms

1 tsp. Worcestershire sauce = 1 Tbs. soy sauce + dash bottled hot pepper sauce

¼ cup soy sauce = 3 Tbs. Worcestershire sauce + 1 Tbs. water

½ cup wine for marinade = ¼ cup vinegar + 1 Tbs. granulated sugar + ¼ cup water

1 cup dry white wine for cooking = 1 cup dry vermouth

1 chopped onion = 1 tsp. onion powder

= 1 Tbs. dried minced onion

1 clove garlic = ½ tsp. garlic powder

= 1 tsp. garlic salt (reduce salt in recipe by ½ tsp.)

1 Tbs. prepared mustard = ½ tsp. dry mustard + 2 tsp. vinegar

1 Tbs. fresh ginger = 1 tsp. ginger powder

= 1 Tbs. candied ginger (wash off sugar)

1 tsp. allspice = ½ tsp. cinnamon + ⅛ tsp. ground cloves

for quick substitution:
1 Tbs. fresh herbs = 1 tsp. dried herbs
fresh herbs can be substituted 2 to 1 for dried herbs
dried herbs can be substituted ½ to 1 for fresh herbs

for healthier, lower fat and/or cholesterol cooking, instead of:
fat, when baking, try applesauce (substitute 1 to 1)
whole milk try skim milk
whipped cream try commercial whipped topping
oil-packed tuna try water-packed tuna
fried bacon try grilled Canadian bacon
1 whole egg try 2 egg whites or ¼ cup liquid egg substitute

Geographic Index

Acknowledgements
Bisquick® is a registered product of General Mills, Inc. (Betty Crocker)

Jell-O® is a registered product of Kraft General Foods, Inc.

Kikkoman Soy Sauce® is a registered product of Kikkoman Foods, Inc.

Minute Tapioca® is a product of Kraft General Foods, Inc.

Mrs. Dash® is a registered product of Alberto-Culver USA, Inc.

Ritz® Crackers is a registered product of Nabisco, Inc.

General Index

Story Index